W9-AKV-195

Alaska Gold Trails

The Pioneers

With
Jim Madonna

Volume III

**Life in Alaska's Frontier
as Told by the Pioneers Who Blazed the Trails**

Cover Photo:
Tim Sander with the author's 1964 Cessna 206 at a remote airstrip located high in Alaska's Brooks Range.

ISBN: 1-891733-18-4

Published by A.P. Publishing
Fairbanks, Alaska

Dedicated To
Tim Sander

Acknowledgement

The thought of hosting a mining-related, radio talk show became a reality in 1987, because of the faith of Michael Dresser, Bill Walley and Frank DeLong, of KFAR radio, who urged me to consider developing such a show. Without the faith of these three people I would not have had the first-hand opportunity to interview and pay tribute to the many pioneers that appeared as my guests. In addition, one should also recognize the contribution of the many sponsors, who, because of their interest in preserving Alaska history, willingly supported the program.

From the beginning the listening audience grew and urged me to consider assembling the interviews into a book. It was through this public influence that I began to consider the literary presentation of the interviews. My wife, Leah, was enthusiastic and interested in the project and pursuaded me to take on the challenge. She taped every show and worked with me on guest selection. My long time friend Sharon Kessey was also enthusiastic regarding the preparaton of a book from the interviews and as a result spent long hours transcribing the tapes, then critically reading and editing the Alaska Gold Trails Series. From the beginning, and throughout the years of the project, these people have been there at the appropriate time, to provide support and guidance. I cannot thank them enough.

Once initiated, the Alaska Gold Trails radio show opened many new doors for making new friends. Many of these new friends joined my old friends in contributing to the success of the program and ultimately the books. Roger McPherson's contribution of Tony Galardi's presentation of the Iditarod gold rush is a priceless contribution to Volume I. Similarly, Bill Suess's captivating presentation of Leon Tromley's prospecting adventures in the Melozi district of Alaska was a fascinating addition to Volume II. In addition, gratitude and distinction must be given the 60-plus pioneers who so willingly took the time to provide the interviews that made the Alaska Gold Trails series of books possible. I am forever indebted to these people.

Finally, I would like to express my gratitude to my family and friends, who provided moral support and interest in the project and patiently waited through the long period that presenting the achievements of these Alaskan pioneers deserved.

Table of Contents

Figure I: Alaska Communities

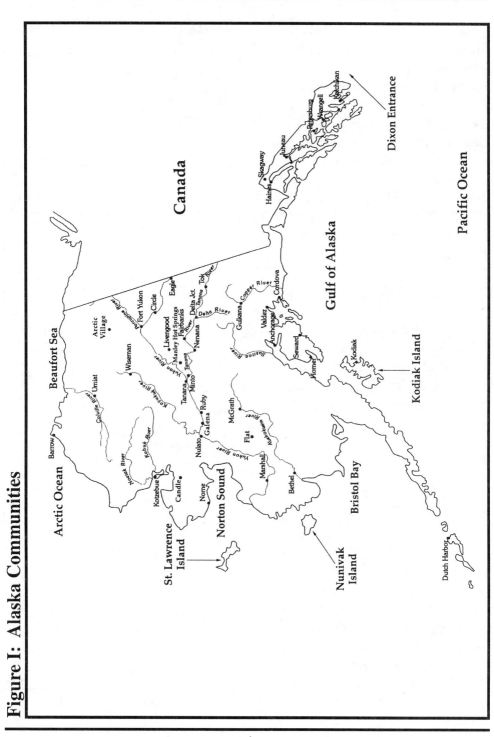

Figure II: Route of the Alaska Highway

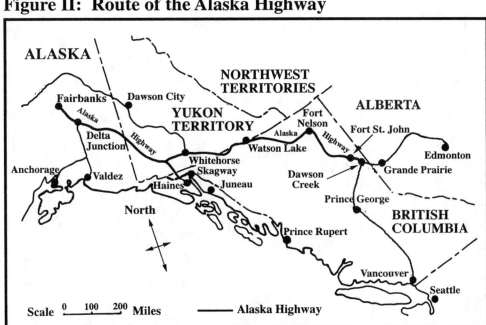

Figure III: 1949 Fairbanks, Alaska City Map

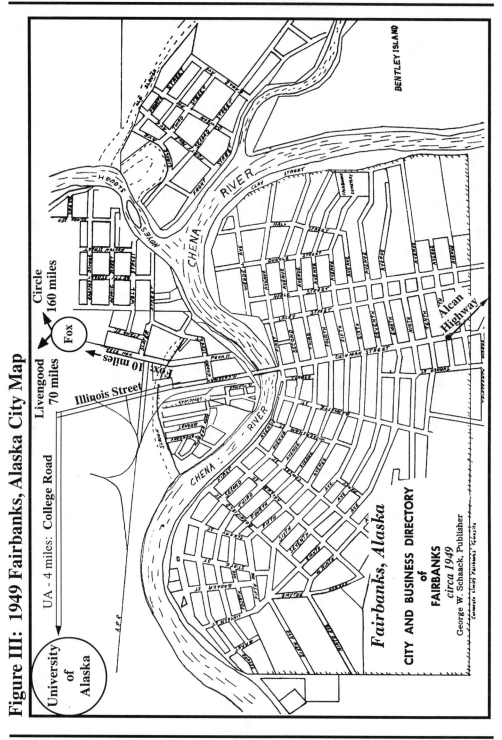

Part I

Introduction and Previews

Introduction and Previews

There are always challenges we dream of facing in our lives, but for some reason, known only to us personally, we never quite get around to them. Time alone dictates that we cannot be or do all things in this short time we have on Earth. Fortunately, those of us interested in the rugged outdoor adventure associated with Alaska's vast wilderness can live some of our dreams through the lives and experiences of the early frontiersmen and settling pioneers. As you read these accounts of their colorful frontier lives and the obstacles they faced during the time they blazed the trail into the country, perhaps one of their experiences will stir your restless spirit, and spark an unresistable challenge that forces you to take the first step down the trail to that one last big frontier adventure—the fulfillment of your destiny.

Ed Ashby: Ed tells the story of how he came to Alaska: My cousin and I decided the best way to get to Alaska from Seattle would be to buy a little boat and run it up. So in the spring of 1938 we went down on Lake Union and found this little 24-foot boat for $125. It had an old 1926 Dodge motor in it—four-cylinder. So we worked with that and got it going right, and we built a little deck on the back of the boat and a little pilot house, and then we got some supplies and took off. We had one key chart showing the route from Seattle to Ketchikan. We had a few stops. It took us 29 days to make that trip. We got lost, we ran low on grub, and we gave out on gas. We picked up a little bit of food on the way, catching fish, and we'd shoot crows—shot several crows and ate them. We'd put a line out at night, and in the morning, invariably, we'd have a nice fish on. We ran into a good clam bed; that was on Vancouver Island, I think. We stocked up on those. And my cousin got one deer, and of course, we weren't supposed to do that, but we were pretty hungry at the time. Then we ran low on gas just as we got across Dixon's Entrance, and we ran ashore at a little lighthouse called May Island Lighthouse, and they said they had a little gas there that was for that purpose, and so they gave us five gallons of gas, and that got us into Ketchikan.

Jim Bell: Jim Bell describes his memorable experiences in 1967, when he first came to Fairbanks in the military: It was pretty fascinating to come to a completely brand new territory, as it was, and then be subjected to first an earthquake and then a couple of weeks later—I think actually that earthquake was in June or July, and then in August—it was August 14th I think or 11th that the flood came, and I was out at the base. It really was memorable because the hospital was slightly higher than most of the surrounding buildings so a lot of canoes and rowboats were actually rowing up to the hospital and depositing sick children and pregnant women, and helicopters were flying in to the one high spot and landing patients, and then we'd do this cross-hand-carry business where we'd carry people into the hospital through chest-deep water. People say, "Oh, that's impossible," but it wasn't. It actually happened and it was fascinating. The elevators gave out in the hospital, and the maternity wards were on the fourth floor, and we had to carry a lot of ladies. Every lady within 300 miles was delivering at that time, of course. It must have been due to the stress factor or something.

Bob Cowgill: Bob came to Alaska in 1949. When asked what kind of work he did when he arrived, he replied: Well, I was a salesman, Jim. When I came to Alaska I joined an outfit called the Covey Brokerage Company. We had a fine line of grocery items, as well as the Alaska Distributors Company line. I traveled widely through the bush communities by single engine aircraft, selling groceries. I did that for about three years, finally tiring of it, however. Well, actually, one morning about 2 o'clock, when I was in a place for business purposes in Kodiak, I got a phone call offering me a job in Fairbanks, and I quit my job of traveling—it was just getting too much for me; I was gone all the time, and collections being what they were at that time, it was a beastly job—and I quit and came into the retail liquor field in Fairbanks. I had a brief stint as the general manager of Jimmy Ing's liquor operations. He had five, I think, at the time, and he put his efforts to other things. I did that for about three months, and then he and I had some differences because we lived by different codes. He was one of the most astute businessmen that I have ever been associated with. He came out of Illinois. I think he came out of Joliet, but he had a criminal background, and we didn't see eye-to-eye on many things. As I said, I stayed three months, and then Alaska Distributors, who was our principle supplier, decided to open up a warehouse in Fairbanks, and they asked me to be their manager, which I did until my retirement in 1978. Jimmy Ing was into a couple of capers that made the newspaper. For example, his Morrison-Knutsen payroll check caper. He imported a couple of his ex-associates from Joliet, and they cooked up a thing, having stolen some Morrison-Knutsen payroll checks, had them made out to fictitious characters, and set up a five or six man team, apparently, to merchandise them around the retail stores of Anchorage and Fairbanks, and on the highway too. One team came up the highway. One person was caught, convicted and sentenced. However, there was not enough evidence to really put Jimmy away. He slipped out of that one.

Janet Cowgill: When asked about her first real job, Janet replied: I left Harrigat, Tennessee, where I was raised, and went to Detroit. My brother lived there then. I worked on the B-29 wing. I was "Rosie the Riveter" except they called me "Honey-Chile" all the time 'cause I called everybody Honey.

Bob Hamilton: When asked how he would determine where the best areas to go prospecting were and how to survive, he replied: There are various offices and libraries where you can search through the literature, and then also it could be helpful talking to the old-timers. We're starting to run out of old-timers, but I found that they are not only interesting but very informative to talk to. A lot of the old-timers have been out in various places in the bush country and they can provide a lot of information. Not necessarily where to find the precise spot to go dig a hole, but about how to exist in the country and how to get through the country and how to do what you needed to do—what you needed to take and all that sort of thing.

Jerry Hassel: When asked if he had any life-threatening experiences, he stated: None as far as mining's concerned, but the closest one I had was back about 1955. I had an airplane. I also had a partner in this airplane. We had a service station down here on Wendell and Noble, and quite often we'd get in the airplane and fly up to Chena Hot Springs and take a bath afterward. You know, it only took an hour—less than an hour—to fly up there. And we'd fly up, take a bath and then come back. This partner didn't have a pilot's license, but I did. Well, this one time, I thought I'd let him do the flying. I sat back and went to sleep. Well, he took off, and I don't know how long we'd been up in the air—more than an hour—and I woke up and says, "Where are we?" He says, "Well, I'm not too sure." So, if you ever tried to look at a map after you've been sleeping up in the air, and try to figure out where you're at, you know you've got problems. You feel so alone. So I said, "Well, all we can do is start following one of these rivers down. After quite a while—it seemed like quite a while—I looked and I says, "Jacques, I think these rivers are getting smaller." Sure enough, we were going up the river. So, we turned around and went down, and we saw a little landing strip down below. We landed on it, and a fellow walked up to the side of the strip, and we asked, "Where are we?" He says, "You're at No Grub Creek." What a relief, this is up the Salcha River. We says, "All right, now we know where we are."

Phil Holdsworth: When asked about one of his most memorable experiences during his mining career, Phil replied: Well, okay, at this one mine where I worked, the jig-back tram that used to carry the ore from the mine down the hill to the mill was an old ramshackle deal. It was noisy and always in need of repair. Anyway, I put in a new one. Not only did it have Timken roller bearings, everything was nice and quiet and it had good brakes. I laid it out so that the bumper log down at the lower end dumped the ore into the ore bin at the mill. The bucket went down that far before it was stopped, so it dumped. There are just two buckets on this tram—just one bucket each way. A jig-back tram is the only way you could do it, because you had no power on it. The only real control was the brake. The full bucket traveled by gravity down to the mill bin. As it approached, brakes were applied until it hit the bumper log at the end. The bumper log would kick a latch on the bucket, allowing it to swivel and then forcing it to dump. The first time we started running that thing, I was at the upper end, near the mine portal. The elderly fellow who had been operating the old tram, Ole, was hard of hearing. I think he was 65 years old. He could tell by the vibration on that old tram when it was going full speed and when it was slowing down. In both cases, he could see the bucket coming up the other side if the weather was clear. So I was up there, and we sent about four or five bucket loads of ore down this new tram. Each bucket could carry about 800 pounds of ore. I watched them going and how Ole operated it and so on. It got up to 60 miles an hour in the middle of that span and only took two-and-a-half minutes to run the full bucket to the mill. It really surprised him; he couldn't hear that thing running it was so smooth, but he could see the buckets. After we ran several of those down, I climbed on top of the ore in the next bucket and started to ride down. Just about that time, a fog bank rolled in and Ole couldn't see the bucket after it got the first 100 feet down that cable, and I couldn't see any more either; I was in the fog. I began to wonder whether they could see the bucket coming up the other side. Anyway, he had cut her loose, and boy that bucket was traveling about 60 miles an hour in the middle of that span, then of course it began to slow down. It was such a smooth-running system, that the operator really had to put the brakes on to slow it down and get it stopped. I finally came out of the fog, and here I could see I was almost down to the bumper log at the end and Ole was not applying any brakes to the cable. Keep in mind that the bumper log spanned across the top of the ore bin and below, and in front of that was a fifteen-foot-long, five-foot-wide deck, which butted up against the ore bin outer wall. On the other side of the ore bin was the wall of the mill building. We were rapidly approaching that bumper log, and Ole was still not putting any brakes on. I saw what was about to happen, so as I saw this bumper log looming up, I just automatically swung my feet over the side. As I told you, I had a lot of good experience on timing, dropping parcels to the wife out at the homestead from a small, single-engine aircraft; I would open the door and drop it right into her hands almost. So, I just automatically swung my feet over the side and timed it and left that thing before it reached the deck. I landed on the approach of that 15-foot deck and threw myself flat on the wood surface, then began to slide. There was a four-by-four support timber standing up there and my left shoulder struck that and snapped it off. I didn't even know it. I continued sliding the distance and ended up with my scalp plastered against the wall on the other side. It took a chunk of the scalp. Meanwhile, the bucket hit that bumper-log and it stretched the cable to the point where the bucket on the upper end went clear by the operator and sailed clear up into the excavation. But more than that, when that bucket hit the bumper-log it sent that 800 pounds of rock flying and it tore the side right out of the mill building. Of course, the bucket came off the cable. The guy who was standing along side of Ole up there at the controls said, "Ole, Phil must be hurt." Ole said, "Phil isn't hurt, he's dead." He was sure he'd killed me.

Bob Jacobs: When asked if he ever had some extraordinary airplane problems during his flying time up on the Seward Peninsula, Bob replied: Well, in those days, airplanes weren't as reliable as they are today. For example, most of the airplanes that we were flying in those days had radial engines in them, and a lot of the airplanes that were operating up here at that time didn't have any kind of cowlings on them. And these big radial engines had these cylinders sticking out in the cold air, and a lot of times when it was cold, like it is here now, you'd have a temperature inversion, and maybe you'd take off from a place in Alaska where the temperatures were warm enough to operate this particular airplane OK, but you'd be going into an area where maybe the temperature was 40 or 50 degrees below zero, or colder, and the top of this cold air would usually be somewhere between 1000 feet and 3000 feet, and the airplanes, the majority of them, carried a thermometer out on one of the wing struts there, and you could look out there and see the temperature change real quick, when you drop down into that cold air. And a lot of times those old engines would freeze up, and the engine would quit. And so, you'd better be in a position where you could land someplace without too much trouble. Of course, we would put the airplanes on skis along about this time of the year, maybe a little later, depending on how much snow we had, and of course that gave us a little more flexibility regarding landing spots.

Neville Jacobs: Neville tells us the story of what happened during her walrus hunt on Diomede Island: This trip went on and on. Some fellow had crossed from Little Diomede Island to Big Diomede Island, which is Russian territory. As a result, on our way back we were detained and queried by the OSI and the FBI. Finally we left Diomede and made our way back to Cape Prince of Wales, and a storm came in at our heels, and we were holed up at Cape Prince of Wales for a week. Finally this raging high wind went down a little bit—we were staying in the schoolhouse, about 20 of us, from this little 35-foot boat, and the wind went down. Then there came the drone of an airplane, and Sammy Mogg jumped up, and he ran over to the window and he said, "There comes Bob Jacobs, there comes Bob Jacobs. Only Bob Jacobs can fly in this weather." So we all looked over, and everybody rushed down to the beach and they pulled the boats off the beach, and the dogs, and the barrels, and cleared the beach, so the airplane could come in and land. By this time quite a bit of time had gone by. So I scribbled a postcard to my parents at Nome, to let them know I was alive. I rushed down to the airplane, and I said to the pilot, "Here is a postcard, but I don't have a stamp. Would you please mail it for me?" And he was handing out bags of mail, and he looked down, and my parka hood went back and I had yellow hair that cascaded forward around my face, and he nearly fell out of the airplane. And that's the man I married.

Ray Lester: Ray tells us his adventure as a young boy during his father's and uncle's year in Alaska's bush: We were about 80 river miles north of Bettles, on the Alatna River. I really don't know why they chose the Alatna. It's something that I know my dad and uncle must have talked about for some time. They just wanted to spend a winter out there in the woods, so to speak. There was no cabin or anything there. It was early '60s. In fact, there was just my dad, my uncle and myself to begin with. I was only about six years old at the time. The three of us continued on our way and settled in an area about 80 miles or so north, near a village I believe was Allakaket, and proceeded to build a cabin. I was about five or six at the time. I did what I could to help build the cabin. We ended up with a one-room cabin that was big enough for eight people. It was a very crude log cabin. As far as I can remember, we had a cookstove, and a kind of barrel-type stove for heat. Heat really wasn't a major problem. During that year my dad and uncle did some prospecting in the spring and summer and they trapped martin and wolf throughout the winter. They also hunted—all I can remember is living off moose and caribou. We also ate a lot of fish. I can remember one instance when we went fishing one morning in a creek near our cabin. During the day we had a lot of rain, and there's a log over one creek where we would always cross. On the way back, the creek had flooded. Lo-and-behold, I slipped and fell in. Keep in mind now, I was just a little boy. Luckily the jacket I was wearing somehow had gotten stuck in some of the branches of the fallen tree that we had used. At that point, my dad went down underwater looking for me. I can't remember how much time actually elapsed. I was submerged and tangled in the branches, that's about the last I remember. I will say that if it wasn't for my dad looking for me and grabbing me out of there, you might not have a guest today.

Leah Madonna: When asked about the problem with the extraction of gold from gravels with a high clay content, Leah replied: Well, that's a little out of my line of expertise. I do know that clay is a problem in many areas of Alaska, and of course, miners do have many systems that they are using in placer mining today, from high pressure washing through trommels to concentrating tables and wheels. Some people run half-inch material through desliming cyclones before running it through jig systems. It is especially important for those large rocks to be very thoroughly cleaned, because clay clings to those rocks and small gold or platinum particles cling to, or are picked up by, the clay as the clay-coated rocks roll through the sluice and are deposited in the tailings.

John Miscovich: John describes events surrounding the Otter Dredging Company's three-and-a-half-foot bucket-line dredge: Well, that was a wooden-hull construction, shipped to Flat from Nome, where it had gone in on a property that failed, and there was a promoter, by the name of George Riley, who shipped it into Flat and took over the claims on Flat that the drift miners had.

And by the way, George Riley was shot at Flat by a crew member that he had. The fellow that shot him was hung in Fairbanks here behind the old wooden courthouse that they had, and that was a good lesson for promoters, of course. It was a tragedy, but it was certainly one that stopped promoting. After he was shot in 1918 the dredge went into limbo.

Maurice Oswald: Maurice describes one of his hunting trips: I probably had my strangest bear encounter when I wasn't surveying. Lew Dickens and I used to fly down to Pilot Point to hunt ducks and geese every fall. We used to pick and clean our birds as we got them. At that time, we could have a three-day limit. We could bring back a three-day limit in possession. I don't remember what that was, but it was around 20 geese. We had been there for several days, and had gotten our limits of geese, and were on the verge of getting our limits in ducks. We had them all picked and cleaned, and we would hang them from the struts of the float plane to drain and cool out. One morning we got up, and we didn't have any birds left on our airplane. There was a sand dune right up in back of our camp. We crawled up there, and looked out in the dunes, and here were nine brown bear. It was three mothers with twins, and the cubs were probably two-year-old twins. They were not small bear by any means, but they'd come in that night when we were sleeping and cleaned out our birds, just wiped us out. We were fortunate that they didn't damage the plane.

Tim Sander: When asked what the worst thing he ever did before he went to the seminary to begin his training as a monk, Tim responded: Well, I set fire to the grass and trees on that hill where we lived. I lit a match, and it went up in flames—I mean it burnt all the vegetation all the way up the hill. I was coming home from school—I was walking home from where the bus left us off. I was cold, and I thought, "Hey, I'll have some fun here and get warm." I lit the match, touched it to the grass, and it took off. Burnt the whole damn hill down— I mean it burnt all the dry grass and trees off that hill. I didn't get into any trouble because nobody knows to this day that I did it. **Jim:** Well they do now!

Mary Shields: Mary came to Alaska in 1965. When asked to tell us about her experience in the Iditarod dog race she stated: Well, I had heard about this Iditarod Trail the year before. I'd never gone very far before with my dogs. In Christmas of '73—'74, John and I went on a trip by dog sled from Fairbanks over to Tanana to visit some friends. We really liked getting out and seeing new country. I heard of this race that was "a thousand miles of broken trail." A thousand miles of broken trail sounded real inviting. So I called up Anchorage and signed up for the race. The voice on the other end of the phone sounded real suspicious. I don't think they believed I would really show up at the starting line. I only owned six dogs. I had to buy a couple more, because I needed eight to start the race. So I rounded up two more and arrived there with my eight dogs, and off we went. The starting line was certainly the scariest part; just having all those people hollering and cheering. Neither my dogs nor I had been in front of a big crowd like that. So that was pretty scary. I remember the first four or five miles or ten miles goes through downtown Anchorage or suburbs of Anchorage. I remember a bunch of people standing along a fence there, and some fellow hollered at me in kind of a real nasty voice. He said, "You better turn around now, you're never going to make it all the way to Nome." I don't know who he was, but I sure thank him for that encouragement. Boy, if there were ever moments when I wondered what I was doing out there, I just remembered what he said. I knew I was going to make it all the way to Nome. It took me 28 days to get there, and I finished 21st or 22nd out of 49 teams.

Tom Snapp: Tom is a well known newspaper man in Fairbanks. He relates his most interesting story: Well, I think the most interesting story is the one that's been put out while I was with the News-Miner. It was a Kentucky tourist, William Waters, who was lost in the wilderness up in Charlie River country. He was a retired railroad worker and he had come to Alaska and he liked to fish very much. He'd fished a lot in Canada, and he went up to Circle City and he parked his car there at Circle, and he started fishing and he disappeared. And he was turned in. No one had seen him. His car was sitting there such a long time, and the police made an investigation. They got bloodhounds. They thought he had gone out in the water and drowned. I was covering the police beat then, and I had talked to some News-Miner pressmen who had been up there at the very time that he had disappeared, and they believed that he had wandered off further and hadn't drowned at this place where they had been searching, because they had found a lean-to where there was an empty Lucky Strike cigarette package, and it was the brand that he smoked. Anyway, this man was lost. He started out for the foothills and it took him three days to get there, and in the meantime he ran out of water and started drinking out of chuckholes. Then he reached Birch Creek and he started going down; he'd read in a book that if you got lost you should go south. So he was following Birch Creek south, which went for several hundred miles with hardly anything on it, real twisty, and as the summer wore off, as it became fall, the temperature became colder, and the only thing he was eating was rosehips and berries, and they began to disappear and it began to get cold, and finally he gave up. I think he had something like 17 matches, and he would build a fire and then he would try to take pieces of the fire and build a fire a little further down. Finally, he ran out of matches, it began to get cold, and he picked out a sort of decayed log, lay down, and decided that his time had come. Luckily some moose hunters from Fairbanks—Ray Casola, who had won the Yukon 800 and Millie Webb were up there moose hunting. Ray and Millie went by in a motorboat and that gave him a lot of hope. He got down to the riverbank, through a lot of tall vegetation, and when they came back down the river, why he tried to wave and attract their attention. But it was right at dusk and they didn't see him and went by. So then he went back disgusted, thinking he had missed his only chance of being rescued. And the next day they came by again, and that time, even though he was very weak and had trenchmouth and whatnot, he was able to wave them down, and they came by and got him and they brought him into the hot springs resort. They gave him beer and some things to eat, which they probably shouldn't have, him having trenchmouth. Then they gave him a hot bath, in water so hot he could hardly stand it. Then they put him to bed and put nine yarn blankets on him. And the next day they brought him into St. Joseph's Hospital in Fairbanks, and they couldn't find a thermometer that would measure his temperature—I mean his body was below 92. He made medical history because he had adapted to the cold, and he lost over half his weight—he looked like someone who had come out of a concentration camp. Well now the reason that is the most amazing story that I covered is that I talked to him when he first came in, in the morning, and I asked him, "These sisters won't let me come back unless you tell them that I'm to come back every night." So he did, he told them that I was to come back every night. So then, of course, other reporters tried to get in and they had no permission, but I did. So from there on for, oh four or five weeks I came every night. The most amazing thing to me about this story was—you know you can go out to your garden every day and you can see vegetables and things have grown a little—similarly, in this case, this man's appearance changed from day to day for about 10 days, and I took pictures of him. His recovery was the most amazing thing I'd ever seen and reported on.

Sandy Stillion: Sandy relates some of her experiences when she arrived in North Pole, in the early 1950s: I was pretty much thrilled with the remoteness of it all. We had to use an old pitcher pump to pump water into the house. One of my oldest memories of living out there was trying to get that doggone powdered milk to mix up, to get the lumps out of it. We sort of grew up with powdered milk, canned milk and very little fruit. To this day I can't get enough fruit, because in those days fruit was a seasonal thing. It came in just certain times of year and you only got so much of it, and that was it.

Oden Stranberg: Oden describes what led him to become interested in the Alaska mining industry: My father was wrapping up his mining engineering degree at the University of Alaska, and he moved our family up to Fairbanks in mid-year 1957. In the summer periods we spent the time out in a Kuskokwim mining camp. When he finished up his degree and moved back to the Anchorage area, I continued working in the mining camps, and in 1959 started school in the mining engineering curriculum at the University of Alaska.

Mary Lou Teel: Mary Lou tells of her mining activity following staking her claim on Deadwood Creek: I started out collecting some flour gold, until Simon, a geologist, came down the creek and told me, "Gee, I think maybe if you start digging over in this section here you might do a little bit better." Well, his advice was great, because I got my first two real nice nuggets out of there the fall of '69, and then another real good one in 1970. And those three I still have, 'cause I had them made up into a ring. And I did quite well just by my little pick and shovel, because I had very little overhead. I would leave here Friday night, after work; take my 357 pistol, my German shepherd, and my tent, and that's how I lived up there.

Helen Warner: When asked how she met her husband, Henry, she replied: Actually, they would teach classes from the University of California at Davis or University of California at Berkeley, right on the lab premises (where she worked in Livermore, California). Henry and I happened to have registered for a course in radio chemistry and nuclear physics. Henry was the principle research technician for Chemistry, so he worked over in Building 312, I believe, or some wonderful designation, and I was over in Headquarters for Radio Chemistry. We sat next to each other in the class. It was wonderful. We were arguing about valence, which deals with positive and negative charges? It was romantic. Now this is indeed how we happened to get started—we were discussing whether chlorine had only one valence, or whether perhaps it could behave with two different valences. That led to a longer discussion, which ultimately led to a gold mine in Alaska.

Swede Wasvick: Swede gave us his story of one of his most hair-raising experiences living in Southeastern Alaska: It was in the summertime and we were fishing down towards Portland Canal. We had just delivered some fish, and we were on our way home when we ran into some engine trouble coming up along the coast. We couldn't get it going and we drifted onto a breaker. Of course, it smashed the boat up to where she sunk. So we all had to take to a skiff. We had life jackets on, jumped into a skiff and was going ashore. The sea was running pretty heavy and it swamped our skiff. There were three of us on the rig and we were all in the water, and we swam ashore while the water batted us about. We got up on the beach, no shoes on, walking along on the barnacles and one thing and another. Finally, a cannery tender came from down towards Tree Point. As luck would have it they were in close enough where they saw us on the beach. We were standing there waving our shirts and one thing and another, and they picked us up and took us to Ketchikan.

Nedra Waterman: Nedra describes her adventures during her first mining adventure with her new husband, Wes Waterman: We met a lot of good folks. It was a different way of life for me. Vancouver, Washington, where I was born, was a very small town, but I had not lived with an outdoor privy and no running water and lights, and such. We got out to Falls Creek where we landed, after we were married. He had built a wannigan, but he hadn't brought enough lumber for an outhouse. So he had a board and he measured it between two trees. Well, he measured it for his legs, not mine. And I was pregnant, and I had quite a summer with the outhouse, pretty near fell in a couple of times.

Wes Waterman: Wes relates one of his many "believe it or not" stories: Now this happened when I lived back in Talkeetna. There was a young fellow that came up from Anchorage. He went to work there at the same section as the gandy dancer crew, and he was up working on the railroad. This one friend of ours, Fos, had a nice wife, and this young guy got to playing around with her, and he got to braggin' about it. Oh, he could go to bed with her anytime, and he was going to take her away and marry her here in a little bit, and everything he was going to do. Well, ol' Fos, he didn't quite go for that, so he decided he was going to put a stop to it. They were working up on the railroad about a mile-and-a-half or two miles out of town, maybe a little further. Fos took his .30-30, walked up to where they were working, and he was talking to the guys. They asked him what he was doing. He said he was goin' to take care of some business. He pulled up his .30-30 and put three bullets right through this guy's breadbasket. He said, "Well, that'll end that." He gave the crew his .30-30 and they loaded the guy up, and of course, brought him back to town. Well, they sent poor Fos into town. They got to checking around and it seemed like the other guy was a deserter out of the Army and he was wanted here and there for crimes. Pretty soon they almost gave Fos a medal for getting rid of him. Where else but in Alaska, in the early days, can you put .30-30 slugs through a guy's belly and almost get a medal?

Jack Williams: Jack talks about his high school days and how he defied the rules of separate dorms for girls and boys: Well, in my senior year, we did have, well you might call it a regular escape pipeline, where we had a system set up to get girls out of one certain window on the second floor of the dormitory. Of course, in the wintertime it was too cold, but in the fall and in the spring we did that pretty successfully. Until we got caught.

Part II

The
Pioneers

Ed Ashby
with
Jim Madonna
June 15, 1989

Jim: Good afternoon ladies and gentlemen. Today our guest is Ed Ashby. Welcome to Alaska Gold Trails, Ed.

Ed: Well, thank you Jim.

Jim: Ed, give us some background. Where and when were you born and tell us a little bit about were you were raised.

Ed: Well, I was born a few years ago, in 1919, in South Carolina, and I was born and raised on a small farm. We raised tobacco, cotton, corn and potatoes. And I went to high school there. I got the notion of coming to Alaska two years before I finished high school. I was in Washington visiting a cousin and we were listening to the radio when they made the announcement of Will Rogers' and Wiley Post's accident in Barrow. We got to talking about Alaska, and we decided we'd like to come to Alaska when we finished high school. So I went back to South Carolina, my cousin stayed in Washington, and we corresponded back and forth for two years, making plans to come to Alaska. Two weeks after I finished high school, I left South Carolina and went to Washington and met my cousin. We decided the best way to get to Alaska would be to join the Merchant Marines. So we went to Baltimore and joined the Merchant Marines, and we went down, looked around for a ship, and finally we found a banana boat, going to Cuba. So we signed on that banana boat as deckhands and went down to Cuba, got a load of bananas, and spiders.

Jim: Spiders? What did you do on the boat? What was your job?

Ed: Well, I was a deckhand, my cousin was too, and we scrubbed the decks and painted, and then we'd take shifts in the bow as lookouts, and then we'd take shifts on the helm, at times. And we'd work four hours on and eight hours off. This one trip was all we made on that banana boat. It took a couple weeks. And then we got off, and we thought we'd get a ride immediately to Alaska, but it didn't work out that way. We got separated, and I made a couple of trips to Europe and to France and Germany, and my cousin made a couple trips to the West Coast. Finally, I got a boat going to the West Coast—an oil tanker. My cousin was in dry dock in Seattle. So, I worked around, went through the canal, and finally I caught up with him in Seattle.

Jim: Did you get to Seattle on that oil tanker, or where did it go?

Ed: Well, that's a little story, there. I went as far as Portland, and there was no letter from my cousin, so I went back to San Pedro on this oil tanker, and there was a letter from my cousin waiting for me.

Jim: Is that San Pedro in southern California?

Ed: Yes. That's outside of San Diego. So I got off the boat there, and I decided to get a freight train coming north, to meet my cousin in Seattle. So, the tracks had been washed out; there'd been a lot of rain and floods down there. This was in the spring of '38. So I didn't make too good a time on the first train, so I got off in San Luis Obispo.

Jim: You didn't make very good time, did you?

Ed: Before San Luis Obispo, but then I caught a ride on the highway and went to San Luis Obispo and decided to catch another freight. That was the wrong thing to do.

Jim: Why?

Ed: Well, the railroad dick got me at the railroad station, and he decided that I'd better take a bus on, and not catch the freight train. So he took and put me on a bus. I had to pay for the ticket, of course, and I went on the bus as far as Portland, and then I got off and I got on the highway and hitchhiked another ride and got on into Seattle.

Jim: And you met your cousin?

Ed: Yes. That's when I met up with him.

Jim: And then how did you come to Alaska?

Ed: Well, we decided the best way to get to Alaska from Seattle would be to buy a little boat and run it up. So we went down on Lake Union and found this little 24-foot boat for $125. It had an old 1926 Dodge motor in it, four-cylinder. So we worked with that and got it going right, and we built a little deck on the back of the boat and a little pilot house, and then we got some supplies and took off. We had one key chart showing the route from Seattle to Ketchikan.

Jim: What time of year was it that you took off?

Ed: This was the spring of 1938.

Jim: You had a 24-foot boat with a little cabin, you had grub, you had fuel, and you and your cousin were ready. Tell us about your adventure, Ed. Where were you heading first?

Ed: Well, we were heading for Ketchikan.

Jim: Was that non-stop, or did you have stops planned along the way?

Ed: Oh, we had a few stops. It took us 29 days to make that trip.

Jim: It wasn't a real quick trip, then. Where did you stop along the way?

Ed: Well, I couldn't pinpoint the places we did stop, because of this chart. But anyway, we got lost. We ran low on grub, and we gave out on gas, but we finally made it.

Jim: You ran low on grub.

Ed: Well, we sorta picked up a little bit of food on the way, catching fish, and we'd shoot crows—shot several crows and ate them.

Jim: How'd you catch the fish?

Ed: Well, we'd put a line out at night, and in the morning, invariably, we'd have a nice fish on. And we ran into a good clam bed—that was on Vancouver Island, I think. We stocked up on those.

Jim: You hunted and you fished, and as a result lived on crows, fish and clams?

Ed: Well, my cousin got one deer, and, of course, we weren't supposed to do that, but we were pretty hungry at the time.

Jim: Did you have any other problems?

Ed: We ran low on gas just as we got across Dixon's Entrance, and we ran ashore at a little lighthouse called May Island Lighthouse, and they said they had a little gas there that was for that purpose, and so they gave us five gallons, and that got us into Ketchikan.

Jim: OK, that was probably what, around the end of May?

Ed: I would say it was in May, sometime.

Jim: So you got into Ketchikan. You were lucky, weren't you?

Ed: We were real lucky. We had some narrow escapes. Oh, one real narrow escape was when we were crossing Queen Charlotte Sound. My cousin was asleep, and I was steering the boat, and I saw a commotion up ahead, and I kept watching it, and I thought we'd get a little closer to it and see what was going on, and I saw this log. All of a sudden it started going around in circles. And pretty soon it got smaller and smaller circles, and then all of a sudden the log—it was a log bigger than the boat - it just turned up and went right straight down. And I figured that we better get out of there.

Jim: A whirlpool.

Ed: It was a whirlpool. I'd heard about 'em, but I never had seen one, and I was uncomfortably close to that. And going across Dixon's Entrance, why we ran into a blow, and we were having a little trouble with water getting in the gas, and we almost got swamped at that point, but we made it.

Jim: By golly the trip sounds like a real adventure. You were out for an adventure, anyway, weren't you—young and spirited.

Ed: Well, two kids that didn't know all that much about boats or anything. We did real well to get to Ketchikan.

Jim: What did you do when you arrived at Ketchikan?

Ed: Well, we looked the place over a little bit, and the first job I got there was helping to unload a fish packer. An old salt there, an old captain, Jim Leeds was his name, he talked me into going over to the west coast of Prince of Wales Island. So, my cousin and I took our little boat and ran it around the north end of the island and down to Craig, and I stayed in Craig for four seasons, and during that time I took the little boat that we had fishing the first year, and I didn't do all that much, but I paid expenses. But finally I had to go to work for a cannery. And they put me out on a floating fish trap. I think they're outlawed now, but these traps were anchored off of the points down there off the island, where the fish run, and they caught a lot of fish in those traps. And we'd stay out there for the full season. There were two of us on the trap. And we had quite a time just floating out there. You had to sit the storms out and everything, right on those traps.

Jim: Was that an exciting job, or was it boring? Tell us about it.

Ed: Well, it was interesting. The fish would come in and they would get caught. The nets would funnel them into areas where they would be held until the boats came to take them to the cannery.

Jim: Did you use your own boat, that little $125 job you had?

Ed: Yeah, I trolled with it, for a while, that first year.

Jim: And did you do the same thing all four years?

Ed: No. I went seining, purse seining, one year, and then I worked in the traps for two years. So, I enjoyed all of that, but I didn't make any big money that way.

Jim: Was Craig a village or a cannery, or what was Craig at that time?

Ed: Well, there were a couple of canneries there. And it had a population of about half native and half imports. It was a nice little town. I guess we had about 350, 400 people there. The mail boat would come in twice a week and that would be about our only contact, except a plane—a float plane. Bob Ellis would fly in there every once in a while, bringing passengers, and he'd bring some mail too.

Jim: He was out of Ketchikan?

Ed: He was flying out of Ketchikan at that time.

Jim: He still flies out of Ketchikan, or at least his business is still called Ellis Flying, out of Ketchikan.

Ed: Yes. I think that's a big service now. I think he started out with that one little float plane.

Jim: Well, what happened following that period of time when you were in Craig? You say you fished for four years? Then what did you do, Ed?

Ed: Well, in the winter I did different things. One winter I went trapping for a little while. Didn't know anything about trapping, but it was fun.

Jim: What kind of trapping? Special kind of animal or fur?

Ed: Well, I caught one mink and one otter. This was a land otter, not a sea otter. But it was fun.

Jim: That was the extent of your trapping career?

Ed: Well, yeah, I didn't trap too long.

Jim: Where did you go from there?

Ed: Well, when the war came along, in '41, that was my last year up there. I went outside and I got involved with airplane mechanics' school, and then I went in the service. And when I got out, I had to stick around for a while. But in 1947 I was all ready to come back to Alaska. So I got ahold of an old Army ambulance, and I rigged it up for the trip. Then I took off and came back to Alaska. I came to Fairbanks at that time. I arrived in May of 1947.

Jim: Did you fix the Army ambulance some special way to travel over the rough Alaskan highway?

Ed: Well, I tried to get some pretty good tires that would take the trip, and I had all the things I needed for the trip, in the truck, so I could be self-sufficient.

Jim: My Dad made it up to Alaska in a military ambulance, about that same period of time; I believe it was 1946—47. And the testimony was that they lost a lot of tires along the way. Of course, I guess he didn't start out with very good tires to begin with. Did you have any experiences like that, Ed?

Ed: Well, I didn't have any trouble with tires, but I did break a rear spring, and the Canadians were very helpful in getting me going again.

Jim: That was the only troubling event you had on the whole trip to Alaska, in your ambulance? One broken spring?

Ed: Yes. That was the only real trouble that we had.

Jim: You got by easy, didn't you?

Ed: Oh yes.

Jim: At what time of year did you arrive in Fairbanks?

Ed: We got into Fairbanks on the third of May 1947.

Jim: What was Fairbanks like, in those days?

Ed: Well, it was a little bit rough, at that time. There was very little pavement for the streets, and there was one narrow bridge crossing the Chena. So you had to be real careful going across there, especially when you were meeting a bus.

Jim: Did you meet a bus, Ed?

Ed: Well, as a general rule, the buses would come right down straddling the middle. You either had to back out, or wait for them if you saw them coming.

Jim: I see. And what kind of activity went on in town? Was it a frontier atmosphere, or was it anything like it is today?

Ed: Well, it was beginning to become civilized. It was a sort of a frontier atmosphere, because it was way out in the wilderness?

Jim: You bet it was. What excited you, what drew you to Fairbanks? I know that you heard about the plane crash up at Barrow, with Will Rogers and Wiley Post, and that aroused your interest, but what really brought you to Alaska? Because it was a frontier?

Ed: Well, the reason I came to Fairbanks was first because there was no road into Southeastern, and I wanted to drive, and I'd always wanted to come to the Interior, to see what Fairbanks was like and to take a look at the gold industry.

Jim: Oh, I see. So it was about the lure of gold. They were mining a lot of gold here at that time, weren't they?

Ed: Well, at that time gold was pretty slow. The FE Company was working then—big companies working—but I think most of the small outfits were closed down.

Jim: Was that because of the war effort and they hadn't reopened yet?

Ed: Yes, then they began to open up.

Jim: Did they start opening up during your time here?

Ed: Well, the price of gold was still pretty low at that time. So people hesitated to go into gold mining.

Jim: What kind of work did you do, when you came into the Fairbanks area?

Ed: Well, there was quite a bit of work going on at Ladd Field. So I got a job out there. I was working in the shop as a mechanic. And I was giving a lot of thought to taking advantage of the veterans' benefits for school. Finally I made up my mind to go back to school. So I went back to South Carolina and went to the University of South Carolina and did my freshman work. Then I transferred to the University of Alaska, here at Fairbanks.

Jim: Did you get a degree?

Ed: I got a bachelor's degree.

Jim: What was your major?

Ed: Well, I majored in biological science, and I had a double minor—history and anthropology.

Jim: Oh, I see. And who was the president of the University of Alaska at that time?

Ed: Well, Dr. Moore, Harris Moore, was the president when I finished, in '53.

Jim: Was Bunnell the president when you started?

Ed: Yes.

Jim: And did you ever apply the education that you received at the University of Alaska?

Ed: Well, only once—this was quite a number of years later. I was in South Carolina and I took a job with the South Carolina Vocational Rehabilitation Department. And it was because of my education that I got that job.

Jim: I see. So it played a role in obtaining employment. How long were you there at the one job that you obtained?

Ed: I was there two-and-a-half years.

Jim: Let's step back. Once you finished your degree at the University of Alaska, did you stay in Fairbanks?

Ed: Yes. I was here quite a few years. I went into construction. I bought a little front-end loader tractor and I dug a lot of basements for homes around Fairbanks.

Jim: How long were you in business?

Ed: Well, I don't remember exactly, but I think eight or ten years. But I specialized in digging basements under houses that were already built. I dug some basements before houses were built, but most of them I dug after the houses were built. People found out they had to have a basement to keep the house warm.

Jim: That must have been an art, to build a basement after the house had been positioned.

Ed: Well, at times it gets kind of scary. But if you're careful, you don't get hurt or hurt anybody else.

Jim: Where did you go from there, Ed?

Ed: Well, circumstances were such that I had to go back to South Carolina and this is where I got that other job at South Carolina Vocational Rehabilitation Department.

Jim: How long did you stay there?

Ed: I was out, actually, over a period of about 10 years. But I held on to my cabin here. I had a little cabin in College that I lived in for a long time.

Jim: And what year was it when you came back to Alaska?

Ed: I came back in 1974.

Jim: And moved back into your little cabin? Was it still there?

Ed: It was burned down at that time.

Jim: Oh-oh. Somebody else got there.

Ed: Yes. Somebody moved in and they lived in it a while, and finally it was burned down. So I had to rebuild it. I saved some of the walls, but everything else was gone. I rebuilt it right on the same spot.

Jim: Oh, good. And is it still there now?

Ed: No. That spot is underneath where the present post office is.

Jim: That's over there on Geist Road.

Ed: Yes. Real convenient to the University.

Jim: Tell us a little bit about what you did after you rebuilt your cabin. What adventures did you take on next?

Ed: Well, Jim, I've always been a freelancer at heart. And people ask me what I free-lance, and I say, "Anything that comes along." And at times I would take jobs and work for a season or a month, or however long. But I always had it in mind that I wanted to give my try at gold mining. So I eventually decided to go over to the Seward Peninsula on a mining venture.

Jim: Sounds exciting. We have a call here, Ed. Let's see what they have to say. Hi, welcome to Alaska Gold Trails. You're on the air with Ed Ashby.

Caller: Yeah, ask Ed if he remembers what we used to call that area down there where he had his house.

Ed: Other than Geist Road, I can't remember. I'm not sure what you're talking about.

Caller: Then you don't remember it being called Vulture Flats?

Ed: Oh, yeah, I heard of Vulture Flats.

Caller: That's where the vultures stayed that lived off the University.

Ed: Yeah, I never did call it that.

Jim: Is there some story behind this voice?

Caller: Well, it was the vultures that lived off the University. They still live there. Ask him if he's still got that old Dodge ambulance.

Ed: No, it got away from me.

Caller: I was gonna call and tell you I had a lot of parts for one of them.

Ed: Well, that'd be good to have, but I'm sorry, the old ambulance got away from me. And that's a long story.

21

Caller: I'll check in with you later.

Jim: OK, thanks for the call, my friend. Ed, tell us about that exciting mining experience you had on the Seward Peninsula.

Ed: Well, I must say that it was a little mistake I made, but it was an experience, and I had to fly everything over to Kotzebue and then fly everything from Kotzebue over to Cameron. And I didn't know very much about gold mining, and I shouldn't have been in an operation like this. But anyway, I took everything, including the kitchen sink out there with me, and I got involved in several little activities over there. One was pumping a pond out. And I pumped this pond out. There were thousands of gallons of water there. It took several days to pump it out. And then I had visions of getting in there with my gold dredge and getting some pay. But it didn't work out that way. Everything had been swept pretty clean, either by the dragline that went through there, or some other gold dredge, suction dredge, that had gone in and gotten it. But anyway, I didn't do too well there.

Jim: How long did you spend there?

Ed: In Candle? I was over there for four summers altogether.

Jim: Did you have any exciting or threatening adventures out there, Ed?

Ed: The last spring I was there, before all the ice had gotten out of the river, I needed some drinking water. So I got this fellow to carry me out in the stream with his canoe, to get a bucket of water. And the balance on the canoe wasn't too good, so I reached over to get my bucket of water, and the canoe rolled over.

Jim: This sounds more like life-threatening than exciting.

Ed: It was. That was cold water and deep. This fellow climbed up on the canoe, and I pushed off and headed for shore. And I'm not sure I shoulda done that. Anyway, someone had to launch another canoe and come out and help me get out of the water.

Jim: Probably saved your life, didn't they.

Ed: Well, there's a good chance that I'd 'a' drowned if I hadn't gotten out—I was struggling.

Jim: Sorry to say, folks, we have run out of time. Ed Ashby, thank you so much for joining us on Alaska Gold Trails today. It's been a pleasure.

Ed: Well, thanks, Jim. I enjoyed it.

Jim Bell
with
Jim Madonna
April 13, 1989

Jim M.: Welcome to Alaska Gold Trails, ladies and gentlemen. This afternoon we have a very talented guest with us, a real live dance-hall piano player from the Palace Saloon, Mr. Jim Bell. Jim, welcome to the show.

Jim B.: Thank you very much.

Jim M.: Jim, you have had many interesting experiences in your life. Let's start with a little background on where you came from and your early history.

Jim B.: Okay. I'm originally from Milwaukee, Wisconsin, which is a town of over a million now. When I was growing up, it was only 800,000. It's a German beer town. Milwaukee and beer, it's a wonderful town to grow up in. We grew up in the burbs, the suburbs as they call it. There were lots of fields and ravines to play in, and it was lots of fun. And then I went to Northwestern University in Evanston, Illinois, and got a bachelor's degree in speech, starting me off on my career up here as a piano player in Alaska and a songwriter and director of shows at the Palace Saloon—now the Palace Theater and Saloon; we have a new title for the place. I came up here in the Army actually, Jim, in 1967. Uncle Sam sent me up here from Texas. I was having a wonderful time in Texas, and then I got orders for Alaska and thought of course it was the end of the world or a wasteland. I felt kind of forced to come up here, but the minute I sailed in over the skies of Fairbanks I said, "This is it!" I love this town, and I've been here ever since.

Jim M. It wasn't the end of the Earth after all, but the beginning of your career.

Jim B.: Absolutely not. It was the beginning of everything. You know, Alaska's the land of opportunity, right? And it certainly was for me. I walked into the Palace as a G.I. and I met my wife right there. She was one of the original can-can girls at the Palace Saloon at that time in 1967, which was a terrific year. That was the year we were celebrating the Centennial.

Jim M.: You mean to say you focused in on one of the can-can girls?

Jim B.: Absolutely. It was easy, those big blue eyes.

Jim M.: Love at first sight?

Jim B.: Yes, although I left for awhile then came back, and then we got together.

Jim M.: I see. You couldn't get her out of your mind.

Jim B.: That's right.

Jim M.: Where did you go?

Jim B.: I went back to Chicago. It was a city that I had of course had some contact with, having been at college at Northwestern in Evanston, Illinois. And Chicago was a great town. I was in advertising there. I was a copywriter for Leo Purnett Advertising Agency and I wrote copy for Kellogg's cereals and Shendley Liquors, Nestle Chocolate, Oldsmobile, you name it; the Jolly Green Giant, Charlie Tuna. It was fun but it just wasn't me, and I decided at one point I was going back to Alaska, and so I did.

Jim M.: That was a pretty high-level career that you left. It sounds like big time advertising for many major product lines.

Jim B.: It was so boring though compared to Alaska, where almost anything can happen at any time right?

Jim M.: At the Palace Saloon?

Jim B.: Almost anything happens at the Palace Saloon yes, nightly.

Jim M.: Tell us about the Palace Saloon.

Jim B.: Well, virtually everything has happened there short of the birth of a baby. Although, I think we have gotten as far as boiling water at some point. It's a fun place, and it's a family-oriented place. It's a place where entertainment and lighthearted comedy are the bywords, and it's been going on since 1967. I'm amazed at the number of people in town who I talk to and who say, "Why I've never been out there to Alaskaland." I can't imagine it. It's a 40-acre park completely devoted to not only the tourist industry but to the citizens of Alaska, and it's available for them to take advantage of, and only one of the many attractions at Alaskaland is the Palace Theater and Saloon. So I hope everybody comes out and sees what we've got going out there—the riverboat, airplanes, mining equipment and shops.

Jim M.: One of the new displays of mining equipment is a booming system that they installed in the pond. The booming system is an old-time piece of placer gold mining equipment, and I think that the old-time miners who have done any booming at all would enjoy taking a look at it. They actually have it in operation with water flow, and show how a limited amount of water can be used to wash placer gold bearing gravels through a sluicing system.

Jim B.: I think that is wonderful, and I'm also glad to hear that the mining village at Alaskaland is being developed further, because I think that is an attraction for people from the Lower 48. And it certainly is fun to go there and see that booming system sluicing water out there in the pond and see all the old machinery that the early miners used. You know, it's fascinating, and I think it is interesting for people from the Lower 48.

Jim M.: One thing that might be interesting to a lot of the old-timers is for them to take their friends out and they can nostalgically reminisce about the old days and explain how they used some of that older equipment. I sometimes go out there with my friends who are visiting and go through the booming system and the water flow systems and the stamp mills and the ore buckets and the different kinds of backhoes and explain how they were used in gold mining here in Alaska.

Jim B.: Absolutely. I am amazed that a lot of locals are not aware of what is going on at Alaskaland. In fact, you know the Harding Car has just been restored through Jack Williams and the Historical Commission, and the *Nenana* riverboat, which is the last wooden sternwheeler, has been declared a national historical landmark. So exciting things are happening in Alaskaland. There's all kinds of things going on. The shops are thriving. The Palace Saloon is jumping. The Alaska Salmon Bake is feeding lots of people with a delicious meal every night. So, Alaskaland is definitely a summer place and hopefully going to be a winter place in years to come.

Jim M.: When you speak about the winter place Jim, how do you see that developing?

Jim B.: Oh, I'd love to see Alaskaland become a winter fun place as part of the Ice Festival. They've had the snow sculpture out there, and I can just imagine a wonderful skating rink out there with beautiful music being plugged in and then people coming in maybe to the Palace for a hot toddy or hot chocolate, and perhaps cross-country ski trails. There's all kinds of possibilities for wintertime fun at Alaskaland, year-round fun.

Jim M.: I was aware of the snow carvings this year. You know, as we drove around town, the snow carvings and the ice carvings weren't just restricted to the Golden Heart Park area anymore. They could be seen all over town.

Jim B.: You're right. Yes, I think that's neat. It has become a real community thing. We went down one day at 11 o'clock at night and viewed the ice carvings down on the river. They were all lit up, and there were lots of people down there walking on the river and enjoying it. It was beautiful.

Jim M.: You know, the festival is a short period of time in Alaska winter, but it is becoming international, and I think it will perhaps grow to some outstanding level. We could see a lot of people come to visit Alaska during that period of time just for the ice art. If you think about it, it is a nice period of time when spring is just trying to get started.

Jim B.: Absolutely, the harbinger of spring, you bet.

Jim M.: We got ahead of ourselves. How many years were you up here in the service, Jim?

Jim B.: I was here for two years at Bassett Army Hospital on Fort Wainwright.

Jim M.: And what did you do there?

Jim B.: I was a clerk for the colonels who ran the hospital. It was really good duty. I made coffee and typed. It was terrific; I had a wonderful time. Then I played nights at the Palace Saloon. Played the rinky-tink piano. Why I ever left, I'll never know, because now I'm hooked on Alaska and Fairbanks of course.

Jim M.: How long have you been in Fairbanks, Jim?

Jim B.: About 22 years, 1967 to '89. This is home-sweet-home now.

Jim M.: You're pretty familiar with the place?

Jim B.: Well I think so.

Jim M.: We have a call, Jim. Hi. Welcome to Alaska Gold Trails. You're on the air.

Caller: Hi Jim?

Jim M.: Hi, do you have a question for Jim Bell?

Caller: Yeah, can you hear me?

Jim M.: Sure.

Caller: While we're still on 1967—1967 was kind of an interesting year for a lot of us around here. I just wondered what date you arrived.

Jim B.: I'm not sure of the exact date, but I know that I arrived three days before that earthquake that we had, and we had to evacuate the hospital.

Caller: So you enjoyed the flood too then, did you?

Jim B.: Oh the flood yes, I hauled a lot of sandbags.

Caller: I'm glad you didn't miss it.

Jim B.: No, I didn't miss that. I was involved.

Jim M.: Thanks for the call. You have had a lot of those memorable experiences, haven't you, Jim?

Jim B.: Yeah, it was pretty fascinating to come to a completely brand new territory as it was and then be subjected to first an earthquake and then a couple of weeks later—I think actually that earthquake was in June or July, and then in August—of course it was August 14th I think or 11th—that the flood came, and I was out at the base. It really was memorable because the hospital was slightly higher than most of the surrounding buildings, so a lot of canoes and rowboats were actually rowing up to the hospital and depositing sick children and pregnant women, and helicopters were flying in to the one high spot and landing patients, and then we'd do this cross-hand-carry business, where we'd carry people into the hospital through chest-deep water, you know. People say, "Oh, that's impossible," but it wasn't. It actually happened and it was fascinating. You know, the elevators gave out in the hospital, and the maternity wards were on the fourth floor, and we had to carry a lot of ladies. Every lady within 300 miles was delivering at that time, of course. It must have been due to the stress factor or something.

Jim M.: This sounds to me like you were doing a little bit more than just making coffee and typing.

Jim B.: Well, everybody did, during the flood, you know. Everybody just pitched in and helped everybody else because that was the name of the game at that point.

Jim M.: You bet. I think it still would be, wouldn't it?

Jim B.: I think so. I think Alaska still has that. I certainly hope so.

Jim M.: Aside from that, what other characteristics attracted you to Fairbanks at that time?

Jim B.: Oh gosh, I think it was, you know, everybody mentions the people and that certainly was one thing. People were instantly friendly to an outsider and to a beginner here in town, and that was attractive. And then just the kind of freedom that you get in Alaska that you don't get anywhere else. I think that still is attracting people up here despite the fact that we are growing and becoming bigger and changing. I think that there's a lot to be said for Alaska, and the Last Frontier is not a cliché as far as I'm concerned. It still exists.

Jim M.: It certainly does. Did you have any exciting experiences while you were at the hospital, other than having to carry pregnant ladies up four stories?

Jim B.: Well, the hospital was always fascinating because there was something going on all the time. I was at the headquarters there where we had the administrative colonel who ran the sort of executive portion of the hospital, and then a medical colonel, and I was clerk to both of those colonels. And so it was fascinating because everything that came through the hospital started there. It was sort of the heartbeat of the hospital, and at least I kept up with what was going on, and as I say, everyday, it changes. I don't regret that experience one bit.

Jim M.: Did you by any chance know some of the old-timers here in Fairbanks that were around during those days?

Jim B.: I met quite a few of them actually. I think some of them are actually forgotten now, and it's too bad. I met a lot of characters in the early days, down on First Avenue where there were a number of saloons that were interesting to me because I am a piano player. One of them was Blue Monday who is a wonderful old rag-time musician, and she befriended me and was very kind to me in the early days when I was first here in Alaska. And they even had some can-can girls down there in 1967. Yeah, there were lots of fascinating characters in those days, and I was kind of sorry to see some of that change downtown.

Jim M.: Tell us a little bit about Blue Monday.

Jim B.: Oh, she was a wonderful entertainer, and a wonderful ragtime musician, and also had a golden heart if you will, a big heart, and took in everybody from all walks of life and gave them a good time and ran a wonderful saloon down there. It was terrific. She was sort of a, if you will, the last of the red hot mamas. Wore feathers and a feather boa every night. She was terrific. She let me play on her breaks and I waited on tables and I think I got $12 a night at that point. I was delighted to have the job.

Jim M.: How did she happen to come to Fairbanks?

Jim B.: I'm not exactly sure, but I know that she was from Idaho and had somehow wangled her way up here and then later on in her life—in her 60s as a matter of fact—she went out to Bethel and taught school. First she went out to Idaho and got her teacher's degree at a very late age in her life, and then went to Bethel and taught school for several years, and then came back to Fairbanks. She was a very dynamic lady.

Jim M.: Very dedicated to Alaska, wouldn't you say?

Jim B.: Oh, absolutely!

Jim M.: And how old was she when you met her?

Jim B.: I think she was probably oh, 60 when I met her.

Jim M.: I see, and was that your first engagement playing piano?

Jim B.: Yes, downtown. It was the French Quarter, but before that it was the Club Bonanza. That's what it was called when Blue was down there. I don't know how many people can remember that or who hung out there. Downtown has changed a great deal.

Jim M.: I remember back in 1949—1950 I used to shine shoes there in front of the bar. It was big money.

Jim B.: Whoa, but you're a hometown boy aren't you? You can remember the history further back than a cheechako.

Jim M.: Well, off and on. I never heard of the piano player that you just described.

Jim B.: You didn't? You didn't hang out in the right places.

Jim M.: That's right. You have to remember I was only nine years old.

Jim B.: Oh well, you're forgiven. You wouldn't have been let in anyway.

Jim M.: Although the bartenders would always come out of the bar, and they'd put their shoes on the sidewalk for me so that I could shine them up, and then I'd put them inside the bar door, and that was kind of fun.

Jim B.: You were on your way to corruption at an early age.

Jim M.: Oh that's right, and I sold the Daily News-Miner at night. Of course, I had to collect a few coins there. That's when they were on Second Avenue. You know, Jim, I always liked working and staying busy. Anyway, is there anybody else?

Jim B.: Well, there was an old guy named Whitey, and Whitey would come in and he would play a fake trombone to *When You Wore a Tulip,* and he kind of sang in a funny voice like that and he played an air trombone, as it were. Whitey had been around for a great many years, and I heard that in his latter years, he would just walk out of his cabin in his birthday suit and put up the Alaskan flag every day at about 5:30 in the morning, and it became kind of a ritual for some of the night people who hung around downtown in those days to go to Whitey's place at 5:30 and watch him just walk starkers out of his cabin and put the Alaskan flag up on this flagpole, and salute it and go back inside.

Jim M.: Jim, we need to let our listening audience, especially those who have tuned in late, know that they are listening to Alaska Gold Trails on KFAR Radio in Fairbanks, Alaska, and our guest today is Jim Bell, who has made quite a name for himself as the piano player at the Palace Saloon. If you've got a question for Jim, the number is 479-TALK, 479-8255, Give us a call. Jim, was Fourth Avenue still alive when you came?

Jim B.: No, it wasn't. Unfortunately, I never got to check that out. But then, of course, there were the Pipeline days. That brought an influx of ladies of the night, which of course, is something that happens wherever gold is discovered. Isn't that true, Jim?

Jim M.: That's true, and it sure did happen in Fairbanks, Alaska, didn't it?

Jim B.: Absolutely, different kind of gold but....

Jim M.: Well, it's still the same story. Boy, it was a frontier town. You know Jim, there were two periods there. There was, well I guess the mid-70s up until the late-70s in which we had an influx of people, and that was the oil pipeline days. Fairbanks was a wild exciting town at that time. I saw things happen in Fairbanks that I couldn't believe. It was definitly frontiersy—real frontiersy. Probably some of the most interesting things—the food shelves at Safeway were running bare; there was no place to sleep; small sleeping cots in what would not be a respectable place to sleep would go for $20 a night; wages were astronomical. There was a lot of that kind of stress and tension in town looking for these places to live, along with the downtown area, which was jumping. I saw some activities going on there that were reminiscent of what one might expect in a gold rush town of the 1800s or when Fairbanks had its heyday in 1902—1907.

Jim B.: And got on the map.

Jim M.: You probably have a lot of experience with looking into the frontier history and coupling it with the activities going on at the Palace Saloon.

Jim B.: Well it is kind of fascinating. We, of course, have taken a humorous look at the mining industry in a very cursory way, really. We have our character, Felix Pedro, of course, and he discovers gold. However, he doesn't suffer at all. He perhaps suffers with the mosquitoes for maybe 10 seconds musically and then he just sits down on a gold nugget the size of oh, a good baked potato, and his future is made. So really, our look at the mining industry is just strictly for fun. And he sings a song called, "I gotta de gold" in an Italian accent because, in fact, he was of Italian extraction. So anyway, that's the kind of a point of view we take on the mining industry out at the Palace Saloon. It's just for fun, so that after you've struck gold out on your claim, and you come to town to get your bath and cash in your nuggets for real greenies, then you can bring them to the palace saloon and take a light-hearted look at what's going on there.

Jim M.: What you're saying is that the miners, after cashing in their gold, go over and listen to Jim Bell at the Palace Saloon and have a good time, kick up their heels, and get ready to hit the field again. Is that it?

Jim B.: You got it. That's it.

Jim M.: That's the common cycle and you know. That's precisely what happened during Pipeline years. The next step, Jim, was the price of gold spiraled up to $850 in the early 80's and we had an influx of people looking at placer mining here, and there was a gold rush into Alaska, especially the Interior. That helped Fairbanks once again have a boom. Believe me, the excitement over the thought of striking it rich in a placer gold mining operation was phenomenal here in town. I'm sure a lot of the people made their way with their pokes over to the Palace Saloon.

Jim B.: Well, let's hope so.

Jim M.: Jim, we have a call here for you. Hi. You're on the air.

Caller: Hi, Jim Bell.

Jim B.: Yes.

Caller: I may be one of your biggest fans since you hit the country.

Jim B.: Is that right?

Caller: Yeah, Bob Tremble here, seen your show about a thousand times, and a thousand more wouldn't be enough.

Jim B.: Well that's wonderful. Thank you. I appreciate it.

Caller: Now, when you were talking about Alaskaland, by golly, as an attraction, we got The Big Stampede show and the museum.

Jim B.: You bet you do and it's very well worth seeing. I have some relatives coming up, Bob, and I'm going to send them right over there to see your show.

Caller: There's something else. The Pioneers during the winter got onto a dredge upcountry that's a whole lot smaller version than your great big huge bucket-line gold dredge. You know what I mean?

Jim B.: Yes.

Caller: And I believe it was at one of the meetings this fellow said he got his hooks into it someway and it could be transported to town on a lowboy and we could get it out there in the park.

Jim B.: Well, let's bring it in.

Caller: If you can find a spot for it around Gold Mine Valley. The Pioneers might want to restore that dredge to the extent that it could be a working one, and show tourists how they operated.

Jim B.: Well, I think it's terrific.

Caller: Yeah, that's the way they would like to go, and it would fit right in.

Jim B.: I know it, and it's a terrific place to visit.

Caller: I hope they follow through on that.

Jim B.: Alright, keep it going.

Caller: You bet. It's good to hear you on the air.

Jim B.: Well thank you. It's nice of you to call.

Caller: See you at the park, Jim.

Jim B: Okay Bob.

Jim M.: Another call, Jim. Hi, you're on the air. Lost them. Nuts!

Jim B.: And there's nobody there. That's the story of my life.

Jim M.: Singing to an empty room?

Jim B.: That's right.

Jim M.: How are you affiliated with the Palace Saloon? I remember you playing there years ago. How long have you been there?

Jim B.: This is my 20th season at the Palace.

Jim M.: Are you going to stay?

Jim B.: Yes, I've taken some time off here and there. As I said, I went to Chicago, and then for awhile I ran a theatrical company here in town with Lee Salisbury and Walter Ensign called the Laughing Stock Company Limited, over at the Fairbanks Inn, and we did musical melodramas there. But essentially my career has been at the Palace Theater and Saloon. This will be my 20th season, and I'm pulling out all the stops this year, because I have relatives coming up, and I'm doing kind of a nostalgic show; going back and taking a look at tunes from the past that we've done at the Palace. All original material. Also, of course, some brand new stuff for this year. So we're excited about the '89 season.

Jim M.: You are stimulated by your relatives coming up, I think.

Jim B.: I think that did it, you know. I have to put my best foot forward for the family.

Jim M.: Tell us how it evolved from the time you first started. You started out as a piano player?

Jim B.: When I started at the Palace, they had a little show actually. It was about 10 minutes and it had been thrown together by the bartenders and the can-can girls and it was lots of fun. It was a little World War I review, and they did "Over There" and "Wave the Flag" and stuff. It was great fun and it just evolved out of that very slowly through different changes of management. With each change of management at the Palace, there was more encouragement for doing longer and longer shows. Now I'm working for Mr. Rick Winther, who also owns the Salmon Bake at Alaskaland. It's just thrilling because he's solidly behind doing these shows for the public and for our visitors from the Lower 48. We're doing "Good as Gold." You know, it's got the word gold in it, so your ears should just be twinkling over there. This is our fourth season doing that. It's a good show not only for the visitors, but for locals as well. We take a humorous look at what's been going on in Fairbanks over the last 80 years. It was written by Richard Ussery, Melinda Mattson and Tim Ames the original script, and then I contributed the musical score. It's delightful. It runs 59 minutes. You can't possibly get twitchy in your seat, because it's just 59 minutes long and it's good fun—a fast-paced show about Fairbanks and its environs, all the way from the gold rush days right up to the present time.

Jim M.: Does it take into account our problems in a humor-oriented way?

Jim B.: Right. We try to hit not only the problems but just some of the quirky things.

Jim M.: That's what I meant.

Jim B.: The way we dress up here, the way we act, how we spend our leisure time and so on, you know, and I think that people get a hoot out of seeing themselves reflected in the mirror.

Jim M.: Tell us about tourists that come to see you.

Jim B.: Oh, they're wonderful. I mean, you can't imagine how much fun they are. They come from the Lower 48 and they are beleaguered and they're harassed everywhere they go, and we try to provide at least one hour when they don't have to think about the next deadline, and the next place they have to go to, but just sit back and relax and eat some popcorn, maybe drink a beer or have a cup of coffee, whatever, and watch the show. It's lighthearted family entertainment, and we make sure they get to their next destination on time. The tourists are wonderful and we rely on them of course, you know, for a lot of our revenue. We're looking forward to a lot more traffic this year. Everybody says, "What about this terrible oil spill?" Of course, it is a tragedy in Alaska, but I don't think that it's going to diminish the tourist trade this summer.

Jim M.: Well, we're hoping that we have just as good a turnout this year as we had in past years. Fact is, I think our visitor's center is doing a marvelous job in attracting people to the Interior of Alaska and to Fairbanks.

Jim B.: They sure are. The Fairbanks Convention and Visitor's Bureau is encouraging year-round tourism in Alaska, and I think there are some real lively possibilities there. By the way, Jim, do we have time here to get in a little plug about when we're opening?

Jim M.: Oh, you bet! Let's talk about that.

Jim B.: Oh great! We've got our grand opening out at the Palace Theater and Saloon on Friday and Saturday, May 26th and 27th, with "Good as Gold" at 7:30 and 9 p.m., and the "After Hours" show—brand new for 1989—at 10:30 p.m. Although we do have a half price sneak preview.

Jim M.: Expand on the sneak preview.

Jim B.: Oh, you get to sneak in, as it were, on tiptoe and check out what we're doing this summer, and that's Tuesday, Wednesday and Thursday, May 23rd, 24th and 25th—half price at the Palace to see the show. And then, coincidentally, the Salmon Bake is opening Tuesday, May 23rd through Sunday, May 28th. The first six nights is just $6.95 for the Salmon Bake, and that's a wonderful deal and an absolutely terrific meal served outdoors—ribs and halibut and steaks and all the trimmings that go with that. You just can't beat it. So you can make a whole evening out of it. You can go to the Alaska Salmon Bake and have dinner and then come over to the Palace Theater and Saloon and check out our action this summer. We'd like to see you.

Jim M.: Well look, I'm sure there's a lot of people that are interested in the activities that are going on over there. Jim, once again, when is the Palace opening?

Jim B.: May 26th and 27th is our grand opening weekend.

Jim M.: The time has vanished. I want to thank you for joining us on Alaska Gold Trails today, Jim.

Jim B.: Thank you for inviting me, Jim.

Jim M.: It's been a real pleasure. Once again folks, time slipped away on us. I want to thank our guest today, Jim Bell, for sharing the time. I also want to thank you, the listening audience, for taking part in the program. This is Jim Madonna on Alaska Gold Trails. See you next week.

Bob Cowgill
with
Jim Madonna
November 17, 1988

Jim: We are here today with our guest, Bob Cowgill. Good afternoon, Bob, and how are you today?

Bob: Pretty well, Jim, and thank you for inviting me as a guest on Alaska Gold Trails.

Jim: Well, it's our pleasure to have you on the show, Bob. As you may know, many of the people that come on this show are a little shy about telling us what year they were born and some of their intimate background. Do you mind telling us the year you were born and the kind of area you were raised and the size of the town, and so forth?

Bob: I was born in Spokane, Washington, before the beginning of time. I'm not that reticent, Jim; 1909 was the year. As I grew up in the early years, my family and I spent our time in northeastern Washington, northern Idaho and even into Montana, fishing and hunting. Work requirements and food needs and those sort of things were taken into consideration, but we spent most of our spare time outdoors.

Jim: Sounds like you were an outdoor kind of family.

Bob: That is correct. We spent my early years in Coeur d'Alene, Idaho.

Jim: In 1909, what was the size of Coeur d'Alene?

Bob: Coeur d'Alene, Idaho? I would guess it had six or seven thousand people, mostly associated in lumbering, which was the industry there. It was also the gateway to Coeur d'Alene's famous mining district.

Jim: After you spent your time in Coeur d'Alene, where did your family move?

Bob: Well, we moved first to Wallace, Idaho. World War One was going on, and the mines were calling for men. There was lots of work. My family moved to Wallace and we spent 1918 and the early part of 1919 in Wallace, Idaho, the home of a number of big names in zinc, lead and copper mining.

Jim: You started working pretty young, didn't you?

Bob: Well, it wasn't really a matter of necessity, but I liked to have more than a nickel that I got each Sunday from my mother for the collection plate at Sunday school, so I worked with newspapers. As a matter of fact, it was quite a lucrative thing for a kid during the WWI activity. There were lots of extras every day, and people, sometimes the same people bought the same newspaper with a different headline, several times a day.

Jim: Changes were that fast during the war period?

Bob: Yes they were. I can remember one headline that really sold a lot of papers: "The Germans Have Fired Artillery into the City of Paris."

Jim: That was one of the biggest stories?

Bob: That was from Big Bertha.

Jim: Tell us, after you grew up, you also held some positions other than selling newspapers. What did your father do?

Bob: After moving to Bremerton, Washington, my father became a welder for the Navy in the Navy shipyard. When the war activity slacked off and they cut staff, he became the manager of one of the first self-service food stores in the nation.

Jim: What was a self-service food store, compared to what we have today?

Bob: It wasn't the first, Jim, but it was one of the first. The Munson Brothers opened up several groceteria stores in the Puget Sound area. Prior to that, people were mostly waited on. Generally in service retail stores, the clerks and all the employees, carried a little sales book and wrote down the grocery list and filled the order and passed it over. Lindy's Grocery, for instance, in Fairbanks, was still operating in that fashion when I came to Fairbanks.

Jim: And so they would actually help ladle out the material and package it up according to the person's request.

Bob: That's correct.

Jim: I see. And then, when you said it was the first self-service, that meant things were prepackaged for the people? Is that right?

Bob: Many items that are now packaged in cellophane or other cartons and so on, were bulk in those days. The advent of cellophane provided us with containers to pre-package many items.

Jim: You also went to work in the grocery store, after you sold newspapers, is that correct?

Bob: That is correct. I worked after school and on Saturdays.

Jim: And what was your job. You said your dad managed a lot of grocery stores. Did you work in the same stores with your father?

Bob: Yes, I worked pretty hard because he demanded more of me than he did the other boys he hired, which could be expected, of course.

Jim: Sure. He had to put that show on. Tell us about some of your duties in the grocery store.

Bob: Well, anyone who was in the grocery field in those days knows what a chore it was to bag a barrel of powdered sugar in small resale packages. A barrel of cocoa, similarly, in cellophane bags, and well, there was just a lot of bagging to do—beans, rice, macaroni. We were very happy when pre-packaged merchandise began to seep into the grocery field.

Jim: That eliminated a lot of your hard work, is that right?

Bob: That sent me home earlier at night. Previously, to tackle a little bagging job for the next day sometimes would take me until 10 or 11 o'clock at night.

Jim: What time would you start to work?

Bob: We had a general opening. It varied from time to time and from store to store. But as early as seven, but never later than eight. Quitting time was when the work was done.

Jim: I see. Let's change gears here, Bob. When did you get married?

Bob: I was first married in 1935, in Yakima, Washington.

Jim: Can you give us a little background on what exactly attracted you to Alaska and some of the experiences you had just prior to coming.

Bob: Well, following my having worked for the groceteria, Piggly Wiggly was formed, and my dad managed Piggly Wiggly stores, and I likewise worked in Piggly Wiggly stores. Later, after a couple of years in the wholesale grocery business as a salesman, things were pretty tough back in those days. I hope most of you are young enough that you don't remember. My job finished up along about 1933. I then went to work for KVOS Radio, in Bellingham, Washington.

Jim: What exactly did you do with KVOS?

Bob: Well, what you are doing right now, and actually I did almost everything there was to do in that station, because it took me from about 6:30 in the morning, until sometimes 11 o'clock at night, which was sign-off time. I wrote copy—we had to have written copy for every announcement, in those days. I was fortunate enough to get some air time, they gave me an hour and a half in the morning, after the news, and an hour and a half in the late afternoon, with a request program, which we called the Classified Ad Program of the Air.

Jim: Well, we've got a request right now, Bob, we've; got a phone call for you. Hi, welcome to Alaska Gold Trails. You're on the air with Bob Cowgill.

Caller: Well, good morning, or is it afternoon.

Jim: It's afternoon. Matter of fact, my clock here says it's 1:40 and 57 seconds.

Caller: Well, I'm looking at my little clock radio and the time is not right. You know, I know Bob and his lovely wife, and what a wonderful couple they are. Bob, you were talking about Piggly Wiggly. Now was that on Second Street? Was Earl Houseman running the Piggly Wiggly store at that time?

Bob: He was running the Piggly Wiggly store in Fairbanks at the time I came to Fairbanks. I never worked for Earl.

Caller: I don't remember what year that was. I think it was in the early '50s, wasn't it?

Bob: Well, I came into the country about 1949. Jim had earlier asked me what motivated me to seek out Alaska. I had two offers, in my grocery selling years, to come to Alaska to manage Piggly Wiggly stores—one in Ketchikan and the other in Fairbanks. That was prior to Earl Houseman's arrival. Following my first wife's death in 1949, I felt the need—the absolute dire need, because of the debts that I had run up for her year-and-a-half of care after becoming terminally ill—and Alaska was the answer.

Caller: Well, Bob, I'm very happy that Jim has you on today, and you're very informative. You know the old days here, years ago. Do you remember the cold? How low did the temperature drop in the early years that you were here? Do you remember that?

Bob: Well, I can remember one time when I was the manager and operator of Alaska Distributors Company, and we were in the Fidelity warehouse, and my thermometer outside the service door said 69 below and I thought that was pretty low, but another gentleman stopped in and said, "That's nothing. Over at the MUS coal dump, which is just kitty-corner across the yard there from us, it's 71 below."

Caller: I believe that. Because I remember many of those cold winters since I have been here. However, the weather has warmed up somewhat since. There was another question, Bob. Did you remember, during that time when Mr. Houseman was here, do you remember anything about the old country club out at the golf course?

Bob: Very well. Very well, because Mr. Ing operated the club, or leased it from the Country Club Association, and operated it for a period of time, which was sadly interrupted by fire. And Mr. Houseman, as I recall, operated it briefly. He had an excellent chef there. It was a fine place to eat.

Caller: It certainly was. And how well I remember some of the lovely evening dinners and the orchestras that they used to have out there, at some of the most marvelous functions. I have another question, Bob. Do you remember the All-Spruce Burls? I believe it was over there in Hamilton Acres somewhere.

Bob: It was over about at the extension of Third Avenue in the Graehl area, and they had excellent dinners. It was a small cozy place, and I frequented it from time to time in the course of conducting my business.

Caller: Well, thank you so much, Bob, and my love to Janet.

Bob: Thank you.

Jim: Thank you very much for the call. Bob, we appreciate the questions of our previous phone caller, that brought us up to the point of when and where you arrived in Alaska. When you came to Alaska, exactly what kind of work did you enter into?

Bob: Well, I was a salesman, Jim, having had some experience through the years as a traveling salesman. But I came to Alaska and joined an outfit called the Covey Brokerage Company. We had a fine line of grocery items, as well as the Alaska Distributors Company line. I traveled widely through the bush communities, selling groceries by single-engine aircraft, generally. I did that for about three years, finally tiring of it, however. Well, actually one morning about two o'clock, when I was in a place for business purposes in Kodiak, I got a phone call offering me a job in Fairbanks, and I quit my job of traveling; it was just getting too much for me—I was gone all the time, and collections being what they were at that time, it was a beastly job—and I quit and came into the retail liquor field in Fairbanks.

Jim: Well, then you got quite a bit of experience in the bush areas of Alaska.

Bob: The only villages that I hadn't made were those that had local option and were dry, and therefore one couldn't make all those stops and pay for them.

Jim: I see. Then, when you came back into Fairbanks you began working in retail liquor?

Bob: Well, I had a brief stint as the general manager of Jimmy Ing's liquor operations. He had five, I think, at the time, and he put his efforts to other things. I did that for about three months, and then he and I had some differences because we lived by different codes.

Jim: Tell us a little bit about Jimmy Ing.

Bob: Well, he was one of the most astute businessmen that I have ever been associated with.

Jim: What nationality was he?

Bob: I really don't know. He came out of Illinois. I think he came out of Joliet, but he had a criminal background, and we didn't see eye-to-eye on many things. I stayed three months, and then Alaska Distributors, who was our principle supplier, decided to open up a warehouse in Fairbanks, and they asked me to be their manager, which I did until my retirement in 1978.

Jim: What kind of things was Jimmy Ing into?

Bob: Well, some of the things made the newspaper. His Morrison-Knutsen payroll check caper.

Jim: What would that be?

Bob: He imported a couple of his ex-associates at Joliet, and they cooked up a thing, having stolen some Morrison-Knutsen payroll checks; had them made out to fictitious characters, and set up a five-or six-man team, apparently, to merchandise them around the retail stores of Anchorage and Fairbanks, and on the highway too. One team came up the highway. One person was caught, convicted and sentenced. However, there was not enough evidence to really put Jimmy away. He slipped out of that one.

Jim: Well, as you were explaining to the caller, Jimmy Ing had some affiliation with the club out here at Fairbanks.

Bob: The country club.

Jim: Yes. He also, if I recall correctly, owned a couple of businesses around town?

Bob: He had, all together, three or four. My memory fails me as to just everything that he had. He operated the skating rink at six-mile. He had the Town Club Bar, downtown on Second Avenue. He operated the country club. He had a liquor store in the Polaris Hotel building, which had been constructed by that time. He had a liquor store on First Avenue. And I think that he was connected with two or three other things, but nothing that I had any connection with.

Jim: Bob, you retired back in early '78. Tell us the sequence of events that led up to your retirement, and what you're doing now.

Bob: Well, for many years I have been interested in the American Cancer Society, since they function beautifully and gave me a great deal of assistance in 1945-46, when my first wife developed cancer. When she passed away, of course, I was left with large debts. I came to Alaska and became acquainted with the folks who were running the American Cancer Society operation here. We urge everybody to look kindly upon the American Cancer Society. We are all volunteers and happy to give you any information, if you have any questions.

Jim: Tell us a little bit about the "closet" and what you have available for people there.

Bob: Many people don't realize, but we do have many items available in what we call the "closet" for bedridden and home care patients. Hospital-type beds, wheelchairs, walkers, commodes. We have a few oxygen concentrators, which are much in demand, and they are busy all of the time. So give us a call, if you need it.

Jim: Give us the number, Bob?

Bob: 456-4575.

Jim: Well, the time has slipped away, Bob. I want to thank you very much for sharing your time with me and the listening audience on Alaska Gold Trails, today.

Bob: I enjoyed it. Thank you for inviting me, Jim.

Janet Cowgill
with
Jim Madonna
November 10, 1988

Jim: We are here this afternoon with Janet Cowgill. Janet, welcome to Alaska Gold Trails, and thank you so much for joining us today.

Janet: Thank you. I don't think I had a choice did I?

Jim: As a matter of fact, no, you didn't have a choice. I kind of roped you into this. Janet, just so that all the folks out there know what your background is, where were you born?

Janet: I was born in Tennessee.

Jim: You came a long way. Where in Tennessee, Janet?

Janet: Harrogate. It's a little university town. Actually, I wasn't in town. I was born and raised way back in the country.

Jim: What do you mean, "way back in the country?" Were you a farm girl, or what?

Janet: Oh yes. Back on the farms. So far back you smelled like cordwood when you got out.

Jim: Janet, tell me something. If you were that far back, how did you go to school? Did they teach you at home?

Janet: Oh no. We had a one-room school that we had to walk a little over a mile to, morning and night, of course. And then after I entered high school, we had to go five miles; the teacher would come and pick us up and take us to school, for the first year, and then after that we had a school bus.

Jim: What year were you born? Can I ask that question and get away with it? Or is that classified information?

Janet: Well, we'll say 21. That's my age.

Jim: I see. So, the school bus in 1921 must've been a rather, well as modern as the time, right?

Janet: Oh yes, it was a new school bus, and it was modern at the time. I don't know what it'd look like today.

Jim: Collector's item. Oh, excuse me.

Janet: Sort of. Yes.

Jim: When did you leave Tennessee?

Janet: 1938.

Jim: Well, that's a memorable year—the year I was born. Where did you go?

Janet: I left and went to Detroit. My brother lived there then.

Jim: And what did you do in Detroit?

Janet: I worked there, but I was also married, the first time, in Detroit.

Jim: And what did you do when you worked there in Detroit?

Janet: I worked on the B-29 wing.

Jim: Were you a Rosie?

Janet: Yeah, I was Rosie the Riveter, except they called me Honey-Chile all the time, 'cause I called everybody Honey.

Jim: You called everybody Honey? You still do. Rosie the Riveter, I've never met a Rosie the Riveter before.

Janet: Yeah. I worked for Hudson Motor Company.

Jim: Is that right? Was that a fun job?

Janet: Oh, yeah. That was really nice.

Jim: You remind me of a Honey-Child. Tell us, how long did you work as Rosie the Riveter?

Janet: Oh, a couple years, I think ... about a year and a half.

Jim: What did you do after that, Janet?

Janet: Well, I had a baby.

Jim: Well, that's interesting. You had a baby. You have a boy baby or a girl?

Janet: I had a girl.

Jim: You had a girl.

Janet: Right. And she lives here in Fairbanks, now.

Jim: And did you just become a housewife?

Janet: For a while, yes.

Jim: Then following that period of time, what did you do?

Janet: Well, we moved down to Kentucky, and we went into the restaurant business—owned two restaurants. And then I sold one to my brother, and I kept half in another one, and then I moved back to Detroit. My husband and I were separated, so I opened up another restaurant, and I stayed there two years, and then I moved back to Kentucky. My father had cancer and he soon passed away. That is when I decided to come to Alaska.

Jim: Well, what was the attraction in Alaska?

Janet: To meet you.

Jim: Oh, why you little devil. Now that we know why you came to Alaska, tell us a little bit about some of your first activities. You worked in the restaurant business here, when you first came, is that correct?

Janet: Yes. I first worked at Aurel's Cafe, and I worked for Booth Miller, he had a little Gaffney Lunch restaurant out at the Johnson-Ducker Building and I ran that for a little while, for him. Then what? I forgot what I did after that.

Jim: Hon, if you don't know what you did, I'm afraid I'm at a loss for words.

Janet: But I also worked at the Model.

Jim: At the Model?

Janet: At the Model Cafe.

Jim: Did you work there when Mary Hanson was there?

Janet: Yes, I did.

Jim: She was on the show last year. We had an interesting chat. She's quite a lady and had done a lot of outdoor activities.

Janet: Oh, yeah. She knows a lot of history of Alaska, I'm sure of that.

Jim: And how long did you work at the Model?

Janet: Oh, between Aurel's and the Model, I worked about two years, and then Bob and I got married.

Jim: Bob. Oh, that dashing, daring devil that lives with you across the street from me?

Janet: Oh yes, that's him. That's your neighbor. And then we left here in '50 and moved down to Anchorage, until '52, and then we came back. And we've lived here ever since.

Jim: Well, you've been pretty active in civic-type activities here, in the area, and you belong to a number of clubs and so forth, in the state of Alaska. You also belong to the Pioneers, don't you.

Janet: Right.

Jim: In summary, you came to Alaska in about 1948, with your daughter Pat. Then you met and married Bob Cowgill. Did you have any more children?

Janet: Bob and I have a son, Bob. And he's a first officer with American Airlines.

Jim: Oh, is that right. A pilot type.

Janet: Yes, and he loves it. He's in Washington, DC.

Jim: Some of the activities that you entered into when you came to Alaska, that were more or less, I don't know, kind of colorful activities. You think about stewardesses on airplanes today, and you think about rolling carts up and down aisles, serving Coca-Colas, and sandwiches and hot dinners and things of that nature. You were a stewardess, weren't you?

Janet: Oh, Golden North was an unscheduled flight. They traveled to Seattle, and I used to play stewardess for them. Of course, we had box lunches and I served coffee, and it was a lot of fun. It got me away for the weekend or for the week. And all I had to do is just go with them, and Milo Gaffey was one of the pilots. We flew out of Wien Airport, which is out there where the library is now—part of it, anyway.

Jim: And how long did you do that?

Janet: Oh, I only went on occasions.

Jim: Tell us, when you were the stewardess and went down to Seattle, how much was the fare to Seattle?

Janet: I believe it was around 55 or 65 dollars, something like that.

Jim: Big money in those days.

Janet: Yes. That was a one-way fare.

Jim: Yes, it's a little higher than that today. You worked extensively in a lot of activities around.

Janet: Oh yes.

Jim: Tell us about working with the Girl scouts.

Janet: Right. I was camp chairman. That was in '53 that we were building the kitchen—it was a house. I would take my car, and Bob would take his car, and we'd take volunteers out there to work. We finally got a kitchen built for the Girl Scouts. And that was a lot of fun.

Jim: How long did you work with the Girl Scouts?

Janet: Oh, off and on for quite a few years, but I was only camp chairman until we got the building built.

Jim: And you've also served as president and past-president of the VFW Auxiliary. What does that mean? What is a VFW Auxiliary?

Janet: Well, we are just the auxiliary. We have a post home at 3535 Hoch Road; it's right off of Van Horn Road. And all of the service people, the veterans and all, are invited to come out. At this time they are preparing for a move downtown. Hopefully, they'll be able to do a little more business. They'll be making that move by the first of January.

Jim: Carrying on with your participation in different kinds of social clubs, I noticed that in one case, you of course are a life member of Auxiliary #8, Pioneers of Alaska. What is the criteria for becoming a member of the Pioneers of Alaska? And then I want to take that a step farther, because you're also a member of the Alaska-Yukon Pioneers. But right now, let's just talk about being a member of Pioneers of Alaska.

Janet: Well, to be a member of the Pioneers of Alaska, you have to live here 30 years.

Jim: And so, then what do you do after that 30 years?

Janet: You're just one of the old-timers.

Jim: How many old-timers do you have in the organization?

Janet: Oh, there's hundreds of them.

Jim: That's hundreds in Fairbanks?

Janet: Yes. Hundreds in Fairbanks. There's a lot of Pioneers and they all stick together. They're all good friends. And they're people that have been here for years and helped Alaska grow. And most of them are older people and they don't really want to ever leave this country.

Jim: You know, I had a rare opportunity here a couple of years ago—well actually it was last year. I was down at Swede Wasvick's and he's from Petersburg, and he was the past-president—that was in 1986—President of the Pioneers, statewide, and he gave me quite a chat on the Pioneers from his perspective. How is it from your perspective? You all stick together. You have a good time. Do you have meetings?

Janet: Oh yes. They have two meetings, I believe, a month now, and then they have the Pioneer Picnic somewhere, and then they have a sort of a convention once a year, at different towns. I went to the picnic last year. This year I didn't get to go, but last year I went, and we had lots of fun.

Jim: When you go to the picnic, is that held in the same place each year, or does it rotate around the state, or how does that work?

Janet: I'm not really sure about that. But it was in Wasilla last year, and they have a park that was donated and dedicated to the Pioneers of Alaska, and its a gorgeous place to be. It really is nice.

Jim: Now, to take the Pioneers a step farther, they have local meetings. How about helping me out here. Anyone that would like to come and join me on KFAR on Alaska Gold Trails, and have some fun talking on the radio, and tell about their life and what they've done in Alaska, and what Alaska was like in the early years, I'd be happy to know about them. So if you'll lead them our way, here, we'll put them on the radio.

Janet: Well, thank you. If they can't get ahold of you, they can get ahold of me, and I'll holler at you across the street.

Jim: OK kid, I'd love that. Just for the listening audience, we're here with Janet. Cowgill, and she would like to have a phone call from you, if you have a question or would just like to talk to her. The number 456- 8255.

Janet: Not me.

Jim: Scared of that phone, are you, Janet? Janet, there's a couple of activities that you entered into in the earlier days, and we have talked about them many times in casual conversation. You came to Alaska in 1948. One of the things, and I want to go into a lot of detail here, was the winter carnival. That was a real big activity back in the early days when you arrived, and I think it increased in magnitude, during your participation.

Janet: Oh yes.

Jim: Tell us about that.

Janet: Well, in 1953, the Junior Chamber of Commerce was trying to get the winter carnival going again, because it had stopped for a couple of years, or maybe three years, but two years for sure. So I knew most of the fellows in the Junior Chamber of Commerce, and they were all real nice guys, and we had been friends for some time. And Bill Fitzgerald, we knew him real well; my husband did business with him, and he was the ice man. So we got to talking and he agreed that he would go out and cut the ice, just for the price of whatever he had to spend to cut it, which was very little. So, we all worked together, and we had our office down in the Grauman building. And we gave a car away that year, and we had lots of fun doing that. But we started the winter carnival again. And we had it on the ice, and they can't do that any more, but it was on the ice. It was right down there between Wendell and the Cushman Bridge.

Jim: I was here the particular year that they had the big carnival, and I recall that on the ice they also had dog races down the Chena. Didn't they even have automobile races on the ice during that period of time?

Janet: I'm not sure.

Jim: They just had all kinds of activities going on. It was all conducted on the river ice, there off of First Avenue, wasn't it.

Janet: Oh yes. It used to be very thick. But the year I was the office manager, we were able to bring the reindeer—Wien Airlines brought up the reindeer—and we brought up a bunch of natives from the villages, and we paid their way. And they would eat at the Model and charge their food, and then we picked up the bill for them.

Jim: I know about the ice throne. Let me just jump back a little bit. Bill Fitzgerald brought in the ice, is that correct?

Janet: Yes.

Jim: And how big was the ice throne?

Janet: Well he would cut it himself. He has a cutter. And I believe he has donated it to the Winter Carnival Association, if they will use it. It's big—

I don't know, really, how big, but there are pictures of all the thrones, and they're quite large.

Jim: Tell us, then. Who was the queen?

Janet: Merle Hagbert. She was a beautiful girl, and she still is. I saw her at her mother's 80th birthday party, and she's just a pretty now as she was then.

Jim: And at the time, of course, you had participation from the people at Ladd Air Force Base.

Janet: Oh yes.

Jim: You know, a lot of people in Fairbanks don't know what the previous name of Fort Wainwright was.

Janet: I always liked Ladd, myself. They helped in many ways. I know when I was camp chairman of the Girl Scouts, they helped me an awful lot. I would go out and get food. I think that's the first time in history they ever let food get off of that base for a club or organization.

Jim: Janet, you did and do a lot of work with the Cancer Society. Tell us a little bit about the Cancer Society.

Janet: Well, at American Cancer Society, we have a loan closet. Aconna Kopf is in charge of that. And we have been able to get quite a bit of equipment. We help everyone that we can. Right now I am the state memorial chairman.

Jim: How long have you been with the American Cancer Society?

Janet: Oh, about 20-some years. In fact I've been with all of these organizations for around 25 years. I'm also a past president of the Emblem Club, which was in 1970. But I belong to the Moose and the Eagles and the Eastern Star and I don't know what all.

Jim: Well, is there any club that you don't belong to, Janet?

Janet: Well, I joined them back many years ago and I just kept paying my dues. I'm not active in all of these. I am active in the VFW and American Cancer Society, and I try to help out in the others, now and then.

Jim: Well, Janet, I think you've been extremely helpful in all areas here in the Fairbanks area, and you've contributed significantly to the benefit and growth of our community. And I, of course, want to thank you for participating with us here today on Alaska Gold Trails.

Janet: Thank you, Jim. I've enjoyed it.

Bob Hamilton
with
Jim Madonna
December 22, 1988

Jim: Welcome to Alaska Gold Trails, ladies and gentlemen. This afternoon our special guest is Bob Hamilton. Welcome to Alaska Gold Trails, Bob.

Bob: Thank you, Jim.

Jim: Bob, tell us a little about your youth, where were you born and what kind of area were you raised in?

Bob: I was born in Kentucky, in 1933, and was raised on a farm.

Jim: How long did you live in Kentucky?

Bob: 'Til I was 16.

Jim: And did you complete high school in Kentucky?

Bob: Yes. I completed high school in Kentucky before I came to Alaska.

Jim: What kind of farming were you doing?

Bob: Diversified. Corn, sheep, hogs, hay, tobacco.

Jim: So you raised animals and you raised crops at the same time.

Bob: Yes.

Jim: And what, then, your family decided to move?

Bob: To Alaska, yes.

Jim: What made your family decide to move to Alaska, Bob?

Bob: Well, partly curiosity, and in the hopes that the financial situation for us would be better here than it had been in Kentucky.

Jim: What was the financial situation there?

Bob: Well, Kentucky was very poor. My father was involved not only with farming, but with school work, and school teachers and administrators weren't very well paid there at that time. So my parents were looking for a better life.

Jim: Well, your family knew Alaska was a frontier when they came up here. What made them think that there would be a better life in a frontier?

Bob: Well, things were quite poor where we came from. It couldn't get any worse.

Jim: Did your dad and your family have a plan when they came up here?

Bob: Well, we planned to stay at least two years and see if we liked it, and if we did then we would stay, but we thought we'd give it a two-year test. And we must've liked it because we're still here.

Jim: How long have you been here, Bob?

Bob: It's going on 40 years now.

Jim: It's always interesting to know how a person decided to come up to Alaska. Whether they just said, "All right," and dropped everything they were doing and picked up as much cash as they could put in their pocket and just came to Alaska, or whether or not they came up for a job or they came up because they were gold prospecting and mining, or whatever the reason.

Bob: Well, what happened was, there was an article in our local newspaper about Alaska—just a general article—and that caused the family to talk about Alaska, and then my parents thought they might like to try that, so they applied for schoolteaching jobs in Alaska and were hired, and they had their jobs when they came up.

Jim: Oh, I see. Where did they teach?

Bob: They went to Unalakleet when they first came up.

Jim: Did the Unalakleet school take students all the way up through high school?

Bob: No, it was only kindergarten through the eighth grade.

Jim: From there where did students go to high school?

Bob: To Mt. Edgecombe.

Jim: How long did you stay in Unalakleet.

Bob: Less than a year, and then I came to Fairbanks to attend the University of Alaska.

Jim: Did you have a particular discipline that you wanted to get into, such as mining or agriculture?

Bob: Well, I was interested in engineering at the time. I didn't get too far with that before I changed, but I started out to be an engineering student.

Jim: What happened to change your plans?

Bob: Well, it lasted for probably a year-and-a-half, and then I was in the Army for a while, and was taking night classes, and a lot of the night classes were education classes. And then after I was out of the Army, I took business administration.

Jim: What caused you to change direction?

Bob: Well, for one thing, the night-class programs at that time were very limited. The few things they had were education courses.

Jim: Well, in a previous conversation, we talked about your parents. You came to Fairbanks, you started to school, went into the service, but when you came to Fairbanks to go to school, your father and mother stayed at Unalakleet, is that correct?

Bob: Yes, that's right.

Jim: I knew your father, and I was just wondering what brought your family to Fairbanks?

Bob: Well, for one thing, my sisters were going to be of an age where they needed to go to high school, and the whole family wanted more social activities available. Unalakleet was nice, but the family wanted to be involved in a larger city.

Jim: Perhaps it might be interesting to the listening audience if you described exactly where the geographic location of Unalakleet is.

Bob: It's on the Seward Peninsula, close to Nome, Alaska. I think it's about 375 miles west of Fairbanks, something like that. It was a small town. At that time it was probably about 550 people, something like that. Now it's about 750 people.

Jim: Now, you say that the students that finished school at Unalakleet went to Mt. Edgecombe?

Bob: Mt. Edgecombe, down in Sitka. There was a boarding school for high school students.

Jim: Oh, I see. It certainly was a long ways off. Nome High School was probably in the same predicament.

Bob: Well, Nome had its own high school, but the students from Unalakleet didn't go there, because it wasn't large enough to take in extra students.

Jim: Oh, I see. Well, let's talk a little bit more about your father and your family coming into Fairbanks. As I recall from a previous conversation, your sister and your mother came up to Fairbanks first.

Bob: Yes. They came for a visit here in the summer of '51, and I didn't have any place to put them. So I went to see Eva McGown—they called her the Fairbanks Hostess at the time—and she called around and found a family that had a spare bedroom that they weren't using, so I'd have a place for my mother and sister to stay while they visited me. And I always appreciated the favor she had done for me. She did a lot of nice things like that for a lot of people.

Jim: She played a big role as a hostess for Fairbanks, Alaska, didn't she? Can you give us a little background on Eva?

Bob: Well, she had been here a long time, and if I remember correctly, she was a widow, and her husband had been involved with mining in Alaska. I'm not too familiar with all the stories. She had an office in the Nordale Hotel for quite a while there, where she lived, and she was able to help make arrangements for people when they would come to town and all the hotels would be full. She would get on the telephone and call up somebody until she could find some place for them to stay. Unfortunately, she died in the fire when the Nordale Hotel burned down.

Jim: And that was what, in '73?

Bob: I forget the exact year, but it may have been... It was at least that far back. It might have been.. I was going to say '73, but '72-'73, somewhere in there.

Jim: Yes, it was right in there. I remember it was when I first started college work on my master's degree; it might have been '72. I was staying in one of the dormitories, and I could see the flames from the dorm window. Anyway, your folks then came up to visit you. What did they think about your lifestyle?

Bob: Well, my mother wasn't too fond of the way I was keeping house, so I don't know if that was the exact reason, but soon the rest of the family was moved over to Fairbanks and my mother and I have lived here ever since. My dad died in 1981 and is buried up on Birch Hill, and one of my sisters is still in Alaska; she lives in Kotzebue, but the other sister married a boy that got homesick for Kentucky and they moved back to Kentucky.

Jim: After leaving Unalakleet, what did your father do?

Bob: He worked in some education programs for the Air Force and the Army on the bases, and also he did some teaching in night classes for the University of Alaska, until '58, and then he got involved in a gas station here in town.

Jim: Tell the listening audience what your mother's and father's full names were.

Bob: Well, my mother's full name was Mary Edith Hamilton and my father's name was Robert William, and that's my name; I'm a junior and he was senior.

Jim: I see. Didn't he also work for the mining company?

Bob: Yes. He worked for the USSR&M (United States Smelting Refining and Mining Company), what we call the old FE Company, out at Ester, on the conveyor system for the big Number 10 dredge. That was after education but before the service station.

Jim: And just exactly what was his job on the conveyor?

Bob: He was the operator of the grizzly, which is where the dragline dumped the material that it picked up and the larger boulders were separated from the finer material that the conveyor could haul away.

Jim: I can't remember the size of that dragline, but I understand that at that time, which was probably in the '50s, it was one of the largest draglines of its time.

Bob: At the time it was built there wasn't anything any larger. Now, by that time there may have been some larger things built, but originally it was as large as any machine that existed.

Jim: When we think about this gold mining that was taking place, we're thinking about something like Goldstream Valley there, out by what, Gold Hill Liquor, or somewhere around in that area, and stripping that muck and vegetation and all kinds of debris.

Bob: And in some places they washed a lot of that downstream and in some places they had to move it with Cats, or in some places they used draglines and conveyors. There was also a large dragline used out at Chatanika.

Jim: The purpose of this dragline, then, was to pick up that muck and other worthless material.

Bob: Right. To get it down to where there was pay dirt that the dredge could work on.

Jim: And once they picked this material up it was dropped onto a grizzly.

Bob: Yes. And the reason for that was the conveyor belt couldn't handle trees and large things, so the large pieces of waste were moved off of the grizzly mechanism, so that a Cat could push it away, but all the silt and worthless material that could be moved on a conveyor belt was stacked at some distance out of the way so that the dredge could function.

Jim: How long did your dad do this type of work, Bob?

Bob: He only worked on that one year.

Jim: Then he went into the service station business?

Bob: Yes.

Jim: Did he stay at the same location forever?

Bob: For a long time. He was there with some breaks when he was sick a time or two and when there were some problems with gasoline supply, but he was there until he died at the end of '81.

Jim: I remember that every time we used to pull in there for gas I always got a free stick of gum.

Bob: That was his trademark. We still have a lot of stuff around the house that's stored in old Juicy Fruit boxes.

Jim: Juicy Fruit. Right. It was always Juicy Fruit. Tell us, Bob, your parents came in, they talked to you about your living conditions, they moved into the area and then ultimately your father bought the service station and that service station was located where?

Bob: At 400 College Road.

Jim: Right next door to me.

Bob: Yes.

Jim: And the service station still stands there. What's there now?

Bob: It's a place called Car Tunes now, where they install automobile stereo components and things.

Jim: No longer a service station.

Bob: No. It's no longer a service station.

Jim: I see. And I think that service station, for the most part, if I recall, never did have the same flavor that it had when your dad was operating it.

Bob: Well, that's not to say that it was something good or bad, it's just that it was different. It was never the same after that.

Jim: Right. He had a personality that drew people in there.

Bob: Well I think so.

Jim: Bob, let's change gears here. Tell us about your personal prospecting adventures in the state of Alaska.

Bob: Well, I've been prospecting for several years, since 1962, in the Ladue Valley. That's between the Taylor Highway and the Canadian border. I've spent a lot of time and energy over there. I certainly haven't gotten rich or even broken even on it, but then a part of prospecting is the fun. I think there are some prospectors that would be disappointed if they really found a get-rich-quick place, because then they'd have to go to mining and wouldn't be able to prospect anymore.

Jim: And in your adventures over there in the Fortymile area or in that part of the country, were you successful or not?

Bob: Well, partly so, at least. I have found some places that I've given up on, but there's some places there that I want to do a little more work on when I have the time and the energy.

Jim: Now when you say that there are some places there that you'd like to do a little bit more work on, that leads me to believe that you found something worth putting more time and energy into.

Bob: Yes. It's called the Prudent Man Concept. In other words, if you find something that a prudent man would be willing to work on, why then it's considered to be of some interest or value perhaps.

Jim: And you, being a prudent man, feel that it's worth putting more time and money into a couple of these sites that you've discovered while out prospecting.

Bob: Yes. There are some places like that. There's one place that was of particular interest to me that I've abandoned my interest in. But there's a couple of other places that I would like to look at in greater depth.

Jim: I don't know if I should ask this question or not. How many square miles are we talking about over there on the northeast side of the Taylor Highway?

Bob: We're talking about an area that's larger than some of our smaller states back East.

Jim: Well, with that in mind, are you going to help us out by giving us some small hints as to exactly where these prudent-man-rule sites might be? Or are you going to keep that a secret for yourself?

Bob: Well, I'm not getting ready to make that public information at this time.

Jim: I want to peak our listeners interest but I don't want to lock you in too much, here, but you know the highway splits and part of it goes to Eagle and the other part goes to Dawson. Now, the question I have is, are your finds encompassed within that area between the Taylor Highway, the Alaska Highway and the highway that goes to Dawson?

Bob: Yes.

Jim: Well, I think that's good enough. If people would like to have more information about that, they might want to look in the literature for some of the potential hot spots that are encompassed by those road systems in Alaska.

Bob: There's a lot of good geological reports on that area, dating clear back to Brooks.

Jim: Brooks was running around during the 1899 gold rush to Nome. That's dating way back.

Bob: He went through there in '98, I believe.

Jim: Now, Ladue is in Canada, isn't it?

Bob: Well, it's in Canada and Alaska both. It runs across the border.

Jim: I see. And Joe Ladue was one of the big figures during the '98 gold rush.

Bob: Right, during the Dawson Gold Rush. He staked the townsite at Dawson. And he made his biggest money, or his only big money, out of selling the lots in the city of Dawson.

Jim: Yes, If I'm not mistaken didn't he die from tuberculosis?

Bob: Tuberculosis, yes.

Jim: But prior to that time Ladue was a trader and had several trading posts up and down the Yukon River and some of its tributaries. And there are a couple of other names in there too. I think McQueston.

Bob: Yes, McQueston and Harper.

Jim: Harper. Right. Anyway, so we have the general idea. Bob, we've got a call here. Hi, you're on the air with Bob Hamilton.

Caller: Yeah, I was wondering here, they advertise those metal detectors. They say they'll detect gold. Is that true there?

Jim: Yes, it is. As a matter of fact we had an interesting experience here in Alaska, not this summer but last summer. Well, we had several interesting experiences with metal detectors, finding gold this summer as well. But last summer, we had a fellow come up from Minnesota, and interestingly he had no arms. But he had learned to manipulate his metal detector and he went up to one of the recreational areas called Paradise Valley and he discovered a five-ounce nugget with his metal detector. And I think that indicates clearly that metal detectors do have a place in at least recreational mining, if not mining for the small prospector. One other comment that I should bring out is that personally I've never believed in metal detectors as an efficient prospecting tool. However, there have been a couple of cases where people under the right conditions have made nice discoveries. One of the applications that's been used quite successfully I might add, is the use of a metal detector on the bedrock, after the mining operation has pushed the material into the sluicing system and the processing plant. By going along the bedrock, it's sometimes possible to pick up small nuggets that have lodged themselves in the cracks and crevices of bedrock. Now the reason I learned about this is because a fellow, a miner, came in and bought a metal detector to perform that duty because he had visibly found gold nuggets on the bedrock. So he went in and he tried it and he came back and he commented that he had found about a dozen nuggets with that particular metal detector. So then he purchased four more metal detectors, all the same kind, and his whole crew went out every evening, after they had mined, and they'd go over the cut and over the bedrock, picking up these nuggets to add to the collection. So, that lent some credibility. The fact is, in the first case I was dubious, but when he bought four more detectors it made a believer out of me. So that's enough of that. I think that answered the question. Now where were we? Oh yes, we were trying to get Bob to tell us where his gold mine is.

Bob: Well, you'll just have to follow me and find out, Jim.

Jim: OK. The kidding aside. Let's cover the effort required to get into some of these remote but valuable mineralized areas. This is back bush country, isn't it.

Bob: Yes.

Jim: It's not something you just easily take your standard four-wheel drive into.

Bob: No, it's not regular four-wheel drive country. You can get there by walking or pack horse or helicopter, or if you've got a specialized track vehicle or four-wheel-drive but the regular four-wheel drive pickup won't get there.

Jim: Have you taken helicopters in?

Bob: Yes. But that's so expensive that I can't do very much of that. I went broke in a big hurry with that process.

Jim: Well, with the understanding that helicopter support is very expensive, a prospector must have something very attractive to put that kind of time and money into the venture.

Bob: I will say this for the helicopter. It will allow you to get a lot of work done in a hurry. It'll let you get in and out of a lot of places in a short period of time, and you can do sometimes in a few days what might take you months to do otherwise.

Jim: Well, it is nice to know someone who has been successful in their prospecting activities, Bob. Tell us, if somebody came up to you and said, "Look Bob, I know you've had some prospecting experience. How would you outline a program for me? I want to go prospecting." What would you tell them to do in terms of preparing himself to go out into the bush? Just in outline form.

Bob: Well, if a person was interested in becoming a prospector, one of the first things I would suggest that he do, unless he already had some experience and knowledge, would be to take some of the mining short courses from the University of Alaska.

Jim: Well, that's not where I was thinking to begin but it is certainly the right place to start. Why didn't I think of that?

Bob: I thought that would get a comment from Jim. And then the other thing to do would be to search the literature and learn as much about that particular country as they could, then go wandering around over it and take a look at it and see what kind of equipment would be needed, and what sort of supplies and what kind of support systems and everything they would need for that particular area. That can vary from place to place in this country.

Jim: What's interesting too, is that sometimes you think that because the snow is gone by the first of June one year, it may not be gone until the end of June the following year.

Bob: Very true. Particularly on the north sides of some high hills.

Jim: And you think a literature search is very important.

Bob: Yes. There's various offices and libraries where you can search through the literature, and then also it could be helpful talking to the old-timers.

We're starting to run out of old-timers, but I found that they are not only interesting but very informative to talk to. A lot of the old-timers have been out in various places in the bush country, and they can provide a lot of information. Not necessarily to find the precise spot to go dig a hole, but about how to exist in the country and how to get through the country and how to do what you needed to do—what you needed to take and all that sort of thing.

Jim: One thing that a person doesn't want to forget, and that's mosquito repellent.

Bob: That and a net, also. I not only carry repellent, but I also carry a mosquito net.

Jim: And is there any other vital component? Did you ever have any bear problems over there?

Bob: Well, I've come close to having bear troubles, but I've never really had a serious bear problem, but I've been borderline a few times. So one wants to be careful about bears, and you also need to carry something—probably, if nothing else, a 12-gauge shotgun or something to deal with bears.

Jim: It gives you a sense of security, is that it?

Bob: Well, yes, but the bears still look a lot larger than the shotgun.

Jim: Well, the on-site prospecting generally starts in the creeks, where you take a good look at the rocks and minerals.

Bob: Yes. There's different types of prospecting. There's the digging holes in the creeks for placer gold, and there's wandering around chipping on rock outcroppings to see what they look like, and then there can be things such as geochemical or geophysical prospecting.

Jim: Did you perform most of these kinds of operations out there?

Bob: Yes, I have. To a different extent in different places.

Jim: Bob, we have run out of time. I want to thank you very much for participating on Alaska Gold Trails today, and perhaps we can get together again and delve in depth into some of your other activities.

Bob: That would be fine, Jim.

Jerry Hassel
with
Jim Madonna
December 8, 1988

Jim: Welcome to Alaska Gold Trails, ladies and gentlemen. Our guest today is Jerry Hassel, a long time Alaskan who came from a gold mining family. Hello, Jerry, how are you today?

Jerry: Just fine, Jim, and how are you?

Jim: Real good, Jerry. Say, Jerry, you know, I have to reflect back a few years to when I first came to Alaska. The first placer mine in Alaska that I ever visited was your father's placer mine out at Ester—that's Ready Bullion Creek, isn't it?

Jerry: Right.

Jim: And I guess that's where I got acquainted with the Hassel Family. Jerry, tell us, when did you come to Alaska?

Jerry: I came to Alaska in 1930, by way of St. Joseph's Hospital. I had a son that was born there 30 years later.

Jim: Oh is that right. Where was St. Joseph's Hospital located?

Jerry: Well, the building is still there. It is over on North Cushman, at the head of Illinois Street.

Jim: Right there by the Catholic Church.

Jerry: Yes.

Jim: Tell us, what was life like, growing up in Fairbanks in the 1930s. Was the town spread out as far as it's spread today? Were there a lot of cabins spread out throughout the wilderness surrounding Fairbanks, or was it all concentrated near the Chena River and the bridge area?

Jerry: I don't think anything went out much past Gaffney Road. In fact, past Gaffney, we'd go out there hunting rabbits.

Jim: Did you do any trapping, or did you just hunt, Jerry?

Jerry: No, no. We'd just go out there shootin' rabbits, out on the south end of town.

Jim: Were there a lot of rabbits in the area at that time?

Jerry: Oh yes.

Jim: Tell us, what did you do in terms of going to school? Did you go all through grammar school and high school here in Fairbanks?

Jerry: Yes, I started school here in the public school building, which I believe now is a borough building. That was in 1935. And I graduated from high school there in 1949—the same building.

Jim: You completed all your education right there, then.

Jerry: Yes. Except for one year I went out to Pittsburgh, Pennsylvania, at the invitation of Anna and Jim Hanlon. I stayed with them one year, my sophomore year of high school.

Jim: How did that compare to the Fairbanks school? Was it higher level, lower level, or what?

Jerry: Oh, I think it was about the same level. Everything was about the same then, as far as the level.

Jim: Did you like it on the Outside, or were you anxious to come back to Fairbanks?

Jerry: Well, of course, I was anxious to get back. I knew I wouldn't be there for too long a time, so it didn't make much difference. I was just glad to get back, I guess.

Jim: You like the frontier life, I suppose?

Jerry: Oh, yes.

Jim: When you were a young man, was there a lot of mining going on in the Fairbanks area and were you involved in any of it?

Jerry: I wasn't involved too much in it, no. In the earlier years, my father worked at the Cleary Hill mines. He was the power plant engineer, and of course, I spent my summers out there. Then when I was going to grade school, we lived on Eighth Avenue, between Noble and Lacey.

Jim: Your father worked out there and during the summer what did you do out there?

Jerry: I didn't participate much. I didn't do any mining, but I got to walkin' up and down around the hills—the dumps, they call them, which is the waste piles—and I'd pick up pieces of rocks. You could see gold in 'em. And I had a bucketful. The geologist at that time, I believe was Mr. Gebhart, said, "Well, geez, Jerry, you should start collecting these rocks and make a pile of them here and mill them at the end of the year and see what you get out of them." So, at the end of the season, I had a truckload of rocks, and I got a pretty good check for it.

Jim: You got a sizable check.

Jerry: I mean a "**really good check**" for the time.

Jim: You would walk around the tailing piles out there and you would pick up quartz that actually had visible gold in it. Is it possible today to walk around tailing piles and pick up quartz with visible gold in it?

Jerry: I'm sure they could. I don't know why not. The larger pieces go toward the bottom and that's the best place to walk. You just walk around the bottom and you usually find them.

Jim: Did you collect gold-bearing rocks just that one summer, or did you do it for several summers?

Jerry: I did that for a couple summers.

Jim: And you made pretty good money at it both summers.

Jerry: Oh yes.

Jim: What other kind of jobs did you do here in Fairbanks while you were growing up?

Jerry: Well, of course, they weren't mining-related. One was in about 1945, I worked for Max Reedy out at Fox. He had the Fox General Merchandise store, and at that time of course, Max ran it all by himself, but at this time, there were about 2000 military troops moved in. They camped right on the hillside, close to where the Fox Spring is now. But anyway, they would just swamp that store at nights, buying Coca-Cola and candy bars, so Max had to go to town several times a week to stock up his supplies. I know I was about 15 years old at the time, because AP Bob Brant was the only territorial policeman at that time in the area, and he kind of looked at the way I drove the pickup in, to pick up supplies. I'd always get 40-45 cases of Coca-Cola on the back of this truck. It seemed to me that was about the only soft drink at that time.

Jim: Did they have a bottling plant here?

Jerry: Yes, they had a bottling plant down about in the same building that the Salvation Army's in right now—on Barnnette Street.

Jim: So, we had Coca-Cola bottling, right here in Fairbanks, Alaska.

Jerry: Yes, and at that time I thought it was kind of funny. That Fox store is still there. It's the same building they have now for a dinner house, I believe.

Jim: The Fox Roadhouse?

Jerry: Yes, the Fox Roadhouse.

Jim: It's still there, and still has a fine reputation, and kind of a historic atmosphere about it.

Jerry: At the time these military fellows would call Max Reedy Mr. Fox. We had a dog named Foxy, There was another fellow they called Fox, and they called me Little Fox.

Jim: Nicknamed the four of you. Tell us, weren't you affiliated with the Daily News-Miner in the early years?

Jerry: Oh sure. I sold papers. Seemed like all the boys growing up in Fairbanks at that time sold papers at one time or another. I had a short route.

Jim: Was that in and around the Fairbanks area?

Jerry: Yes.

Jim: What were the conditions like? For example, were there a lot of log houses in Fairbanks, or were they just wood structures, frame-house type?

Jerry: No, in fact at that time, most of the houses were log houses. Some of them were frame, and then a lot of houses at that time, they'd put siding over the outside of their log house.

Jim: You have watched, over the years, as Fairbanks changed its style to a little more durable and more heat-retaining type materials. I just want to inject this here, briefly. I read an article recently regarding plating glass with gold. Now this is a strange use for gold. What they do is they plate a piece of glass with gold, and then they lay another piece of glass up next to it. And what happens is they place these two glass panels in the structure. And the way I understand it, during the winter months the gold reflects the heat back into the room and reverses itself in the summer months, when it's warm. It permits about 20% of the sun's heat to come into the room and about 80% of the heat is reflected away from the building. It's kind of an interesting modern use of gold. Anyway, getting back to our subject. Following the period of time that your father worked out at the Cleary Hill mine, he opened up a gold mine here, didn't he.

Jerry: Yes, that was after he left the Cleary Hill mine that he opened up this one. During the war, the gold mines were closed down. They were open longer than some of the other mines around here, because they had a tungsten discovery. You know, they couldn't mine during the war, but they kept their gold mine going a little longer because of the tungsten, which is a strategic metal. And then about 1946, he did mine over on Livengood, on Wilbur Creek, I believe it was, for a year or two.

Jim: Jerry, you commented on some of the minerals other than gold that were mined here in the Fairbanks area during the war. You mentioned scheelite, which is the ore of tungsten. Stibnite, the ore of antimony was also a strategic mineral mined here during the war. Following the time of stibnite and scheelite mining, did gold mining resume back in the late '40s?

Jerry: After '46, sure. It started again after the war.

Jim: When did your family—your father—go into the placer mining business out there at Ester?

Jerry: I think he acquired that property in 1946. That's when he first started mining there.

Jim: You commented that he was mining out of town prior to that. Give us a little background on that.

Jerry: Well, before Ester, he and a partner or two were placer mining over on Wilbur Creek, towards Livengood.

Jim: And how did they mine the placer deposit, Jerry?

Jerry: Well, they'd always use the hydraulics (high pressure water monitors) to strip the overburden, which is muck, you know. It'd flow, so I guess it was hydraulic mining.

Jim: After they stripped the muck away with the water monitors, it would expose the gold-bearing gravels, is that right?

Jerry: Usually, yeah, unless the gravels were not gold-bearing. They might have to strip off some of that. I know places out at Ester where they strip maybe 40 or 50 feet of muck off, and then the dragline came along later, and Cats, and they strip off another 30 or 40 or even 50 feet of gravel, before they get down to the gold-bearing dirt.

Jim: Interestingly, Jerry, there are a lot of drill logs around the Fairbanks area that indicate that the gold was concentrated at the last 5 to 10 feet above bedrock, and that the gravels that were thicker than that were probably not economical to mine.

Jerry: Right.

Jim: Your dad started mining on Ready Bullion Creek in 1946, is that right?

Jerry: Yes, about 1946.

Jim: Was that hydraulic mining?

Jerry: Oh yes. He used the water coming down Ready Bullion Creek for the reservoir on top, and into a pump, and stripped with high-pressure water.

Jim: So this particular mine, then, was totally hydraulic mining. The overlying silt material, similar to what can be seen on the hillsides around here, was stripped off the gravels with the water from the hydraulic monitors. Then was it necessary to strip a portion of the gravels at Ready Bullion Creek, or did they all contain gold?

Jerry: It depends on where you were on Ready Bullion Creek. Now, later on he started mining down at the mouth of Ready Bullion Creek, and over on the left limit it was about 50-60 feet of muck that extended right down to the gold-bearing gravel, about four feet of gravel to bedrock, which was all paydirt. And over maybe 100 feet to the south of that, there's closer to 40 feet of gravel that was paydirt, but not as good.

Jim: But it did pay to run all that through the box.

Jerry: Oh yes.

Jim: In the early days your dad used a single-channel sluice box, is that right?

Jerry: Yes.

Jim: Do you know the dimensions of that box?

Jerry: Well, this is the box my father had. It was a 30-inch-wide box, 40 feet long. And then he just had a mouthpiece and a slick plate in front and just washed the gravel in with the monitor. But first he would push the gravels up to the slick plate with a bulldozer, then wash it through using the high-pressure water from the hydraulic giant (monitor).

Jim: So he would just artfully move those boulders and all the gravel and slurry right into the sluice box mouth and it would wash down.

Jerry: Right. Then we would take a pitchfork and bend the forks, so we could pull the rocks through. Rocks would give us problems.

Jim: Every once in a while you had to get in there and bail them out, didn't you? Did you have gold losses, Jerry?

Jerry: Oh, I'm sure there were. Like I say, I talked with an old-timer the other day, and he says, "Boy, you've got to have at least $20-a-yard dirt to mine that ground out there." And I said, "Well, I can get $20-a-yard out of just the tailings that had already been washed through."

Jim: Tell us, Jerry. You're in the mining game today. Do you still use that same old sluice box?

Jerry: I've used it a couple times just for a water trough. Right now I have a Hector's multiple-channel box. It's a good one. It's small, but I like to keep it small.

Jim: You know, Hector is one of our sponsors. Jerry, back to the early days when your dad was stripping the muck overburden from atop the gravels, he also used draglines and Cats. What part of the mining operation were the draglines used in?

Jerry: Well, the draglines were only used in the sluicing operation. He had them on the tail end of the sluice box, and he always pushed into the mouth-piece with the dozer. And then he'd wash it through manually with the hydraulic nozzle. Then he would remove the tailings with the dragline.

Jim: Your father was a fairly successful miner out there, wasn't he.

Jerry: I think so.

Jim: When I went out there, back in 1971, I believe it was, that was the first day I met your father. And again, it was one of the first placer mines that I'd seen in Alaska, and it was fascinating to me to see all that equipment and actually see him working the mine. It was interesting, how he operated that particular kind of mine. It's a little different from some of the mining operations today, in that most of the mining operations have gone to stripping with Caterpiller and large earth-moving equipment and the gravel is then pushed up to a stockpile, then loaded into a hopper with perhaps a backhoe, and there's a lot of screening devices on-line today that you didn't have in your particular small-scale operation out there at Ester. You've modernized now a little bit with that Hector box.

Jerry: Well, I've modernized quite a bit with the Hector box, and also I've put a screening plant in front of the box to screen out the big rocks. We no longer have to pull them through with a rake. I've been keeping it very small. This is a two-man operation. So we can load the box and sluice and take the tailings away with no problem at all. If someone wants to see the overburden that covers the ground out here, they can drive out the Parks Highway and look close to where that Gold Hill Liquor Store is, and they will see the 100-foot muck banks on each side. Just imagine, those muck banks went from one side to the other side of the valley. That's how much muck has been moved out of there over the years, just with water.

Jim: That's interesting. And that was accomplished with high-pressure water from hydraulic monitors.

Jerry: All hydraulic.

Jim: Well, I believe it was in 1928 the FE Company (Fairbanks Exploration Company) started a drilling program out there to drill that area. You have some of those drill logs as well.

Jerry: Yes. I have some claims that have been drilled by the FE Company. I don't know just why they drilled them at the time, because the bedrock comes up too high for them to dredge. 'Course that's why they were never dredged.

Jim: And so your father stepped right in there and opened up. Tell us, how much ground do you have at Ready Bullion Creek that you think might be valuable reserves? Do you think it'll go up two claim lengths?

Jerry: Oh yes, it goes two claim lengths or more. I've got a couple claims at the bottom of Ready Bullion Creek that I'm sure will be pretty good. I don't know for sure, but these claims have been drift mined in the early days. So, I'm opening up a spot right now where you can walk out towards the middle of this hump and look down the shaft. This must've been a ventilation shaft, because it's too small for a man to climb down. So I'm sure there's a big open area exposed down there.

Jim: And you're going to look into that this next mining season, are you?

Jerry: This spring I'm going to start stripping it, and hope to have it stripped by summer. I'm going to do like Dr. Ernie Wolff taught us how not to do it. He says, "If you ever have an area you want to mine," he says, "but you're not sure if it'll be profitable or not," he says, "Take and mine it. Put everything you have into it. Really go to it. And he says, "If you go broke, then you know it wasn't profitable to mine."

Jim: That's one way to make an evaluation, Jerry. Do you subscribe to that point of view?

Jerry: Ernie Wolff says, "Don't tell anyone about this, because..."

Jim: If he's listening right now, he's red-faced. We were talking about mining in Alaska and your present operation out at Ester. But there was more to your story, Jerry. I think we took a quantum leap forward from 1946 when your father first started placer mining, up until the present day, and I think you had quite a history between 1946 and the present time. Jerry, tell us, what did you do, where did you work between 1946 and the present time?

Jerry: Well, I had several jobs around town. I was working at M&O Auto Parts for a time. Then in 1967, the year of the flood, I went to work for the MUS power-plant, and I worked there until 1986. May first of 1986 I retired from there. Since then I have been mining full-time.

Jim: Full-time mining. And the other question that I was really interested in— you know many of us in our life here in Alaska have had some scary, maybe not scary, but some interesting incidents that have occurred to us. And they're stories, kind of like the campfire stories that we heard the oldtimers tell when we were kids, and I wondered if you'd had any experiences that you might like to share with the audience today.

Jerry: No, I don't have any experiences as far as mining's concerned or anything, but the closest one I had was back about 1955 I had an airplane. I also had a partner in this airplane. We had a service station down here on Wendell and Noble, and quite often we'd get in the airplane and fly up to Chena Hot Springs and take a bath afterward. You know, it only took an hour—less than an hour—to fly up there. And we'd fly up, take a bath and then come back. Well, this one time, this partner didn't have a license, but I did. So, I thought I'd let him do the flying. I sat back and went to sleep. Well, he took off, and I don't know how long we'd been up in the air—more than an hour—and I woke up and says, "Where are we?" He says, "Well, I'm not too sure." So, if you ever tried to look at a map after you've been up in the air, and try to figure out where you're at, you know you've got problems. You feel so alone. So I said, "Well, all we can do is start following one of these rivers down. After quite a while—it seemed like quite a while, I looked and I says, "Jacques, I think these rivers are getting smaller." Sure enough, we were going up the river. So, we turned around and went down and we saw a little landing strip down below. We landed on it, and a fellow walked up to the side of the strip, and we asked, "Where are we?" He says, "You're at No Grub Creek." This is up the Salcha River. We says, "All right. Now we know where we're at, we'll be all right." So we took off for Fairbanks.

Jim: Jerry, I want to thank you for participating in Alaska Gold Trails with us today. Time seems to have slipped away.

Jerry: Thank you for inviting me, Jim. I enjoyed it.

Phil Holdsworth
with
Jim Madonna
at Anchorage, Alaska
October 9, 1988

Jim: Today our nomadic microphone has traveled the trail to Anchorage, Alaska, and the Alaska Miners' Association Conference, where we are interviewing Phil Holdsworth. Welcome to Alaska Gold Trails, Phil.

Phil: I am looking forward to this interview, Jim.

Jim: Phil, you have traveled a lot of trails in your life. You were an assayer, served in the armed forces, worked as a mining engineer and served as an official in the state government. These are only a few of the ways in which you have served the people of America, Alaska and the mineral industry, and we want to hear about these colorful adventures in detail. Perhaps we should start at the beginning with a little background on where you came from, where you were born, and just what kind of environment you were raised in.

Phil: Well, I was born in Grants Pass, Oregon, in 1910, and my dad was running a suction dredge on the Rogue River, downstream from Grants Pass.

Jim: That must have been one of the first suction dredges ever run in the world. That was with a venturi-type inductor system?

Phil: Well, yes. Well I didn't know much about dredging in those days of course. But three years later, in 1913, I spent my first winter in Alaska, at Moose Pass. My dad was building a mill and operating a mine at Moose Pass—what later became the Falls Creek Mine. I unfortunately got quite ill, and they had to take me out that spring.

Jim: Two questions here: What kind of mine was the Falls Creek Mine?

Phil: It was a gold mine.

Jim: The second question, what kind of illness did you have?

Phil: Well, I was given four months to live by the doctors.

Jim: I think you should have gotten a second opinion, Phil?

Phil: Well, it just didn't happen that's all, and I did get a second opinion when I was a young adult. I had a palm reader look at my palm and say, "Oh, you were supposed to have died at the age of three." I think that supported the doctors' position.

Jim: Where did you go to school, Phil?

Phil: Well, my dad was a mining engineer, chemist and geophysicist and was working in the Seattle area where I went to school.

Jim: Your dad seemed to have a deep mineral-industry-related background. Is that where you first got your interest in mining?

Phil: Well, I always knew that I was going to go into mining. I worked for him over in the B.C. side when I was, oh I guess 15 years old, and got a little milling experience and worked underground.

Jim: That was in British Columbia, Canada?

Phil: Yes.

Jim: And what kind of mine was that, Phil?

Phil: That was a hardrock gold mine. I worked there during the summertime while I finished high school. When I graduated, I entered the University of Washington; that was in the fall of 1928 that I started my first year there. I stayed out after high school for a year and worked to save the money for college.

Jim: In those days, a lot of the pioneers that I have interviewed, who obtained higher level degrees, report that it was typical for them to have to do a lot of hard work to earn the money to get that education. Some suggest that it took them a little longer than normal to get that degree because they had to stay out and work to save the money for their education.

Phil: Well, I was nine years getting through college. I had one year in, and then at nights I learned assaying from A.L. Glover, Art Glover's dad. He was the umpire assayer for the mines at the Tacoma smelter and all the Alaskan mines. I took a break from college when I was hired by the Nabesna Mining Corporation to go up there as an assayer in the spring of 1931. I got on the boat and the mill superintendent they'd hired was with me. The Nabesna mine had just been discovered, and they had done a little exploration and were installing the mill, which had been designed by a metallurgist who based the design on about 40 pounds of very unrepresentative rock. So I got there when they were starting to set up that mill. We had a little sawmill there to cut our timbers and all, but nobody could read the blueprint for the rock mill, not even the mill superintendent. I was the only one who could read the blueprint, so I had to set up the mill. It was supposed to be a 40-ton mill—40 tons a day. The mill feed was four and a half ounces to the ton in gold. The original ore came from the oxidized zone up on the surface.

Jim: That's a tremendous amount of gold per ton, Phil.

Phil: It is.

Jim: Did you have a by-product as well?

Phil: There was copper and a very small amount of silver that was alloyed with the gold. The ore was from the upper levels near the surface, which was of course the oxidized zone. It should be understood that the solid rock was below freezing temperature, and when we got inside the mountain—we had to get 200 feet away from the surface before we got into ground that wasn't frozen—wasn't below 32 degrees. The surface ore from the oxidized zone was coming down in frozen chunks. We were having a hard time getting it thawed and getting it through the mill.

Jim: Did that have an effect on gold recovery?

Phil: Yes. The mill superintendent they'd hired had been corking sewers in Seattle for the past eight years, and hadn't seen any milling equipment since the old styles used in the Cripple Creek, Colorado, days. He was an elderly man and not up-to-date on milling procedures. He could only get 20 tons a day through the mill, with a 25 percent recovery; he didn't know how to build a tailings pond and was losing 75 percent of that four and a half ounces, as rich tailings went down the tailrace, without even storing it for re-treatment. I'd try to make suggestions based on the experience I had working with my dad over on the Canadian side. So I'd suggest—I'd say, "Hey Ed, why don't you try this?" I don't know whether I'd put this on tape or not, but he was a rough, tough mule skinner from the Cripple Creek days. He'd say, "Oh, you're just a young punk kid. You wouldn't know how to pour piss out of a boot with the directions on the heel." Anyway, he took sick and had to go out for an operation and medical care. So Carl (Quittem??), who was the prospector that found the mine and who was running the show, came to me and said, "Phil, it looks like we'll have to shut down until next year, until we can hire another mill superintendent, or would you like to try it?" I said, "Sure, I'd be happy to." In 10 days, I had 75 percent recovery. I had 40 tons going through the mill and had a tailings pond collecting the tailings. So the job was mine from then on.

Jim: You were collecting about three and a half ounces per ton. Did you turn that into a miners' bar for shipment?

Phil: No we didn't; we just shipped concentrates.

Jim: Oh, you left it to the smelters and refiners to extract the gold from the concentrates.

Phil: I've forgotten now, but it was something like—at $20-per-ounce gold— a thousand ounces per ton.

Jim: A thousand ounces.

Phil: We shipped the rich concentrates in real nice tight canvas bags. We put three of those bags in a big burlap bag and then shipped these burlap bags by air to the Tacoma smelter. Our other concentrates, which were lower grade, were bagged just in the regular burlap bags and eventually went to the Tacoma smelter but were first stored until we could get them out overland.

Jim: Tell us a little about the history of Nabesna.

Phil: When we first went in there, there was no road from Slana in. There was just the mining camp. It was three years later, in 1933, before we got a road built in there.

Jim: The government put the roads in, in those days, didn't they?

Phil: Well, yes. They built within five miles of the mine and the mine paid for the last five miles. Until we put that road in we were using 40-horsepower gas Cats and double-ender sleds for overland transport.

Jim: How long did the Nabesna mine operate?.

Phil: It operated from 1931 until 1938. At $20 gold they produced about two million dollars worth of gold.

Jim: And this was a seasonal operation?

Phil: It was seasonal for the first three years.

Jim: What did you do then, Phil?

Phil: I worked up there during the season, and during the off-season I went back to the university and got in a degree or two.

Jim: This was the University of Washington?

Phil: Yes, the University of Washington. Nabesna was a bachelor camp and I wanted to get married. Besides, I had only one more quarter to get my degree and had been out three years. So I worked it all out and concluded it by getting married in Fairbanks.

Jim: That was a whirlwind, Phil. You accomplished both things at one time in that quarter? You better give us some details.

Phil: I got married in Fairbanks on what I like to call the longest night of the year, December 22nd, at 44 below—it was a good time to get married. Bill Growden was the commissioner; he married us. Alice Nordale and Bobby Sheldon stood up for us. Then we went to Seattle and I took my last quarter. Among the subject matter was ore dressing, and the old dean said, "Well, we've got a student in the class this year that knows more about ore dressing than I ever will and he's going to teach the course." So, he called on me.

Jim: Oh, is that right? What an honor.

Phil: It was the first time the students ever got real hands-on practical instruction. Previously the dean gave the course. He was a Stanford graduate and his only-hands on experience was drilling three placer holes down on the Kenai (Peninsula)—that was his total practical mining background. He'd have the students sit down and draw a picture of a crusher, a picture of this and that, with no discussion about how these things worked. But they got the full instruction in the milling process the year I was there teaching.

Jim: Knowing you, I would say they did and then some. After the degree what did you do, Phil?

Phil: After the degree, I decided to go over to the Philippines on a honeymoon.

Jim: Well, that must have been a memorable adventure.

Phil: I'll say it was. Mining was going strong over there. We put our car on the ship and sailed over there for our honeymoon. When we got there we checked in at the Onetta Hotel. The manager said, "What's your business? What do you do?" I said, "Well, I'm a mining engineer." He said, "Well, I'd suggest you go down and talk to Engineering and Equipment Supply; they are looking for someone with your background and experience." So, 10 o'clock the next morning, I went down there and went right to work.

Jim: Is that so? Some honeymoon that was!

Phil: They were building a mill down on a gold property. They had a metallurgist up there running the tests in their lab. They were an equipment and construction company that represented Denver Equipment Company over there in the Philippines. But they had never done anything in mining. One of the brothers of the company was down building the mill based upon the design. I ran some tests with the metallurgist in the lab for about 10 days, then they sent me down there to finish construction of the mill. I saw right away that the metallurgist was fudging the settling rates on the ore. The wall rock was andesite and the feldspars had altered to clay. They had 50-foot thickeners, and it was supposed to be a 200-ton mill. The stuff wouldn't settle out; the thickeners didn't have the capacity to give a clear overflow.

Jim: Was this all related to the fact that the feldspars had altered to clay?

Phil: Yes, that was the whole problem. So, the stockholders got dissatisfied with it and sent a consulting engineer down. He came to me and said, "Phil, we know this isn't a 200-ton mill. How would you make it run?" My answer was based on my experience at the A-J (Alaska-Juneau Mine), where they hand-sorted the waste rock from the ore. The result, at the A-J was that they mined 12,000 tons a day, but after hand-sorting they only milled 5,500 tons of that; the rest went on the rock dump. Fred Bradley came up with that idea, and that's when they started making a profit.

Jim: Sure, they were handpicking all of that ore, weren't they?

Phil: Well, yes. They had men up there picking up the white quartz from the black country rock.

Jim: Did you do that then? Did you install a handpicking method?

Phil: That's exactly what I did. We put a trommel with two hole sizes where the ore came out of the ore bin. The extreme lightweight fines (clay) were separated out. We had seven Philippino women there picking out the lighter-colored wall rock. You could see the difference between that and the rest of the stuff. They picked out 22 percent of the mine delivery. That's all I had to do, and it cost us $7,000. We built everything right there, and we had a 200-ton-a-day mill.

Jim: For that they must have made you part owner.

Phil: Not quite, but they did send me back to the United States before the war broke out to get the equipment to make a 400-ton mill out of it. Then I came back as mill superintendent, and in fact got that 400-ton-a-day mill set up just as Pearl Harbor was hit.

Jim: Oh, I see.

Phil: Yeah, when Pearl Harbor was hit, we shut the plant and mine down. Then we took all the women and children up into an evacuation camp in the middle of the island. It was 60 kilometers south and two days by launch up the river to an old mine. Then I offered my services to the Army, and because I had ROTC I was given a field commission.

Jim: That's where the military service came in. How long were you there?

Phil: Well, I was with that until Wainwright's surrender orders came through. Those orders were that all the troops in the islands were to voluntarily surrender, stack their arms and surrender at certain collection points. The Japanese weren't even anywhere near where we were. They had landed on the southern part of the island, but they hadn't come up in our area. There were five producing mines in the area and I couldn't see any sense in surrendering, so I went to the C.O. and said, "Well, I don't want to surrender. What can you do about it?" He said, "Well, I'll write you out a release from active duty and date it prior to the surrender date and you're on your own." I said, "That's fine with me." I went out and formed a group of guerrillas with my Philippino miners and we got kind of organized and set and waited for the Japanese to get up there, and tried to harass them to see that they didn't take advantage of the supplies and things that we had in the mines up there. A stool pigeon went into their headquarters when they finally got up there at Surigan. They were looking for me because they had an informer that was telling them that I hadn't shown up, and neither had my car, which the army had requisitioned. In the beginning, they needed all of the rolling stock they could get. Before we were told to surrender, I was the demolition's officer in G2 for the area and they sent me down a command car from headquarters in the middle of the island. They wanted me to make an armored car for them. So, they sent me an air-cooled, 50-caliber machine gun off a B-17 and three pieces of 5/8-inch armor plate. I'd never seen an armored car. They have a rail that the muzzle can rest on, which is above the driver station. Of course, I didn't know that. I knew that you could take 3/16-inch steel plate, if you put two plates of 3/16-inch steel together at an angle, at point-blank fire, the bullet will go through the first one, but it would be deflected enough that the next one will stop it. So I built that whole thing, and I put more springs on the car, and I put the plate around the engine and the driver. Jim, it was the most honest-to-goodness abortion you ever saw with these broken, odd sections of these steel panels going all around it. Then I mounted the machine gun. It would swivel 360 degrees and it could turn almost straight up. They had sent the driver up with it, Lieutenant Mitchell, and he drove it back and got it up on the Malaybalay airstrip. They were being strafed by Zero airplanes on that field all of the time. They were going to see if they couldn't take out some of those Zeros.

Jim: That was before the orders to surrender. You were saying that after those orders you and your crew were harassing the Japanese and there was an informer telling them of your existence. What went on there?

Phil: They were looking for me. Finally, the informer was the one who found out where I was. He went into the headquarters and told them that he knew where I was. Fortunately for them, they locked him up so he couldn't talk around town, because I would have been advised right away. When they caught me, I was 12 kilometers out and back off the road a ways in a tree-shack with my wife.

Jim: What an experience, Phil. You must have been concerned about the welfare of your wife. When did they release you?

Phil: Well, we were finally released from prison camp in 1945. We went back to Seattle. Not long after that the Independence people hired me as general superintendent to reopen the Independence Mine.

Jim: It doesn't seem like there was much of a break. What year was that?

Phil: That was 1946.

Jim: Give us some background on the Independence Mine.

Phil: The Independence Mine produced from the 1920s up until the war. Anyway, following the war it was under new management, stockholders and new officers. I'd done consulting for some of them in the past. They knew my record and consequently hired me to go up and reopen the mine. We got a crew up there and got started and there was no ore in evidence whatsoever. We were scratching around trying to find some ore. In the meantime, the U.S. Department of Labor had filed a lawsuit against the company for not properly paying overtime prior to the war.

Jim: Sounds like bad news.

Phil: The suit was settled right after I got up there. The company lost the case and they had to pay a real big fine and it just took all of their exploration money. Here, in the middle of winter, with 15 people up there and 15 feet of snow, I got a wire, "You'll have to shut down and get out of there. Our money is gone." At that time a big slide just above Little Susitna Lodge took out a piece of the road. So I wired back, "Well, these people will stay on the payroll until I can get them out of here." We had to shuttle down with a double-ender sled to get their stuff down, then hand-carry the stuff around that slide area.

Jim: How long did the Independence Mine run?

Phil: We only ran that short period. I think I put something like 1,500 tons through the mill. Then there was kind of a break in my work. I went down to a homestead near Wasilla and constructed a log cabin. Interesting thing about that homestead and that cabin. I used to drop supplies to my wife as I flew over in a little single-engine airplane that I had. I got so good at it I could almost put the stuff right in her hand. The homestead was enjoyable but I wanted to get back into mining.

Jim: You have mining in your blood, don't you, Phil?

Phil: Yes I do. So I went to work at the Snowbird Mine in the Illinois Creek District, which is up Reed Creek, near the Fern Mine. You're probably not familiar with it.

Jim: I'm familiar with the district, but not the different mines around that area.

Phil: They had done a lot of drilling. They'd spent $300,000 in driving an adit on this Snowbird Mine, quite high up in the mountains. The camp was below; they had a 5,000-foot aerial tramway with four support towers running from the lower camp up to the upper camp and mine site. In addition, they had an aerial jig-back tram, which was used to haul ore from the mine down to the mill and upper camp, which was between a thousand and two thousand feet below the mine. The upper camp also had a bunkhouse and cookhouse. The mine entry was high up on the mountain. A well-known fellow by the name of Bill Dunkle, who had run the Lucky Shot Mine, was the mining engineer.

Jim: Oh, he got around this state too, didn't he?

Phil: Yeah, he was on the Golden Zone, and the coal too. Anyway, he made an examination for the owners of the Snowbird and he said, "You're ready for a mill." He figured he would get the job.

Jim: Something tells me he didn't get it.

Phil: Well, the management and stockholders wanted me for the job. After they decided they were going to open the mine, they issued some stock and raised some money. The Goodnews Bay people got in on it too. They wanted me to go up there and design the mill, power plant and the whole thing. So, I started working on it. They got a few guys up there, but they wouldn't let me put anybody underground. There was still snow on the ground during the spring. So I went underground and I went all through the workings and sampled, but I couldn't find any ore. I finally found one piece of quartz that I took down and assayed, that went two ounces to the ton, and that was the only piece that I could find anywhere in that mine. Dunkle had given them a report that the tonnage was there. I asked them about that. They said, "Well, there's lots of outcrops up there on the surface, wide veins and so on. That's what this is all based on." Of course, there was five or six feet of snow on top of it and I couldn't go up there and check that. I finally talked them into letting me put one shift underground. In the meantime, they wanted me to put the mill up there near the upper camp instead of down at the lower camp. Strange, snowslides had taken that upper camp out twice in a row, and they still wanted me to put the mill there. I set the mill up near where they wanted it but far enough out of the way of the snowslides so it would be safe. One more time, just so you get the lay of things, the mine and mine portal were high on a steep mountain. An old rickety tram ran from the mine to the mill and upper camp, and a second longer tram ran from the mine to the lower main camp, which was down the hill on Reed Creek. I built the power plant there where there was potential for inexpensive hydropower in the summer. Because there was water there I wanted to build the mill down there too. But, I was out-voted and had to build the mill up above. But I didn't build it exactly where they wanted it. I erected it out on a ridge away from the slide area. Because I put the mill there, it was not at the terminal of the old tram, so I put in an all-new jig-back tram, which ran from the mine portal down the mountain side to the new mill.

Jim: Tell us about this jig-back tram. How did it work?

Phil: Well, okay. The old jig-back tram was an old ramshackle deal. It was noisy and always in need of repair. Anyway, I put in a new one. Not only did it have Timken roller bearings, everything was nice and quiet and it had good brakes. I laid it out so that the bumper-log down at the lower end dumped the ore into the ore bin at the mill. The bucket went down that far before it was stopped, so it dumped.

Jim: The way I understand it, there are just two buckets on this tram, is that correct?

Phil: Yes, just one bucket each way. A jig-back tram is the only way you could do it because you had no power on it. The only real control was the brake.

Jim: So the full bucket traveled by gravity, down to the mill bin. As it approached, brakes were applied until it hit the bumper log at the end. The bumper-log then automatically forced the bucket to dump?

Phil: Yes, the bumper-log would kick a latch on the bucket, allowing it to swivel, and then force the bucket to dump. The first time we started running that thing, I was at the upper end, near the mine portal. The elderly fellow who had been operating the old tram, Ole, was hard of hearing. I think he was 65 years old. He could tell by the vibration on that old tram when it was going full speed, and could tell when it was slowing down. In both cases, he could see the bucket coming up the other side if the weather was clear. So I was up there, and we sent about four or five bucket loads of ore down this new tram. Each bucket could carry about 800 pounds of ore. I watched them going and how Ole operated it and so on. It got up to 60 miles an hour in the middle of that span and only took two and a half minutes to run the full bucket to the mill. It really surprised him; he couldn't hear that thing running it was so smooth, but he could see the buckets.

Jim: Ole wasn't quite used to that new tram, was he?

Phil: Not at all. After we ran several of those down, I climbed on top of the ore in the next bucket and started to ride down. Just about that time, a fog bank rolled in and Ole couldn't see the bucket after it got the first 100 feet down that cable, and I couldn't see anymore either—I was in the fog. I began to wonder whether they could see the bucket coming up the other side. Anyway, he had cut her loose and boy that bucket was traveling about 60 miles an hour in the middle of that span. Then of course it began to slow down. It was such a smooth running system, that the operator really had to put the brakes on to slow it down and get it stopped. I finally came out of the fog and here I could see I was almost down to the bumper log at the end, and Ole was not applying any brakes to the cable. Keep in mind that the bumper-log spanned across the top of the ore bin, and below and in front of that was a 15-foot-long, 5-foot-wide deck that butted up against the ore bin outer wall. On the other side of the ore bin was the wall of the mill building. We were rapidly approaching that bumper-log, and Ole was still not putting any brakes on. I saw what was about to happen so as I saw this bumper-log looming up. I just automatically swung my feet over the side. As I told you, I had a lot of good experience on timing, dropping parcels to the wife out at the homestead from a small single-engine aircraft; I would open the door and drop it right into her hands almost. So I just automatically swung my feet over the side and timed it and left that thing before it reached the deck. I landed on the approach of that 15-foot deck and threw myself flat on the wood surface, then began to slide. There was a four-by-four support timber standing up there and my left shoulder struck that and snapped it off. I didn't even know it. I continued sliding the distance and ended up with my scalp plastered against the wall on the other side. It took a chunk of my scalp. Meanwhile the bucket hit that bumper-log and it stretched the cable to the point where the bucket on the upper end went clear by the operator and sailed clear up into the excavation. But more than that, when that bucket hit the bumper-log it sent that 800 pounds of rock flying and it tore the side right out of the mill building. Of course, the bucket came off the cable. The guy who was standing along side of Ole up there at the controls said, "Ole, Phil must be hurt." Ole said, "Phil isn't hurt, he's dead." He was sure he'd killed me.

Jim: If you had stayed in that bucket he would have killed you.

Phil: I believe that to be true. Anyway, I got up and shook myself off, and here is this piece of scalp hanging out there. I went up to the cookhouse and the cook patched it up. I went back down and I helped them put the bucket back up. In the meantime, Ole came down the mountain. When he got down there and he saw me helping them put this bucket back on he almost had a heart attack—he was so shocked, so surprised. He was sure he had killed me.

Jim: It's a wonder you didn't get broken all apart with that kind of impact.

Phil: If I'd stayed on the bucket, I wouldn't have lived through it. By the time we got the bucket back on, I began to feel the pain in my left shoulder and arm, so, I went over to the tram leading to the lower camp and called my wife on the mine phone and said, "Will you go and start up the tram and bring me down." It had power on it—a gas engine—and I had taught her to crank up the engine and run the tram. She said, "What's the matter?" I said, "Not much, I just had a little accident up here." So she took me down and we went into Palmer to the doctor, and he took an Xray and found it was a shoulder separation. So he put my arm in a sling. He said, "We'll watch this to see if it's going to pull up all right, quite often they do." I went back to the mine. I was still trying to get a chance to get up on the mountainside with that snow up there to check these outcrops out.

Jim: For ore quality?

Phil: The ore quality in the outcrops. In the meantime I had visited the doctor once and my shoulder wasn't pulling up. The doctor said, "If that doesn't start coming up, were going to have to go in there with a wire suture and pull that up with surgery." A little later after the snow had melted I was wandering up there on the side hill with my arm in a sling and I slipped in a snow patch and fell. I hit right on that elbow. You know, when I fell on my elbow and jarred that, it must have activated that shoulder. The next time I went to see the doctor it was okay.

Jim: Strange things happen. Tell us again, where was the Snowbird Mine located, Phil?

Phil: It was near the Little Susitna River, on the road going up to the Independence Mine up over Hatcher Pass.

Jim: Were you successful in the Snowbird at all?

Phil: Well, when they finally allowed me to put a crew in the mine we ran into a little quartz pocket. It got to be about two feet wide.

Jim: What was the grade?

Phil: Well, the grade was about an ounce and a quarter per ton. Oh, it was good grade all right, but it was just this little pocket. When the snow got off up above—and of course I didn't get the mill started until after the snow was almost gone—then I went up and checked the outcrops. They were just plain barren bull quartz. I never got any mineralization at all.

Jim: Is there some characteristic that distinguishes bull quartz from mineralized quartz?

Phil: Well, sometimes you can find places that are pure white bull quartz with no sign of coloration or anything in them, but it is possible to follow along these veins and sometimes mineralization begins to show. In many cases the first sign of fine-grained sulfides will show up as black streaks in the striations or in the flow pattern of that quartz or in some cases alter to rusty surface coatings. That is about the only way the fresh white bull quartz can be distinguished from the mineralized quartz.

Jim: To the educated eye, there is a difference, isn't there? Well, after leaving the Snowbird, where did you go?

Phil: Well, following the Snowbird experience I went to work for the Army Corps of Engineers. I worked for them until 1952 when the commissioner of mines job opened up with the territory. My friends like Pat Ryan and others asked, "Why don't you apply for that job. We'd like to have you down there." The commissioner of mines was a dual federal/territorial position. Half the salary was paid by the territory as commissioner of mines and half was paid by the U.S. Geological Survey from the federal side. Well, when Leo Saarela took that job, the very first year he said, "This is too much for one man. We should separate this into a federal job and a territorial job." He wanted the federal job and they agreed to that. So that left the territorial job open. I had a good position and was making good money with the Corps at the time. We lived on 112 East Second, here in Anchorage. Pat Ryan was calling me on the phone all the time saying, "Why don't you file for this job? We want you down there in Juneau." I was saying "No, no." Peggy was in the other room listening, and I hung up finally, and she said, "Who were you talking to?" I said, "Pat Ryan." "What were you saying no about so much?" "Well," I said, "They want me to apply for the job as commissioner of mines for the territory down at Juneau." She said, "Well, that's back in mining, where you belong isn't it?" That's the first time I ever thought of it that way.

Jim: Your wife set the hook, didn't she?

Phil: Yes she did. I said, "Well, I'll take a look at it." So, I flew down to Juneau and I got a copy of the 1939 statutes to see what the responsibilities of the job were. Of course, the salary then was annually $7,000.

Jim: How much?

Phil: $7,000 annual salary. Of course, look what the guy in that position is getting from the state now.

Jim: Things change.

Phil: $40,000 at least, some of them higher than that.

Jim: Sure, now this became the Territorial Department of Mines?

Phil: Yes, the Territorial Department of Mines, it was a full-scale department. It was a cabinet-level position. Well, I took the position and remained in that job for seven years, up to statehood. Then, I was appointed the first commissioner of natural resources and I held that for nine years. Now that was a broad responsibility. That was everything but Fish and Game. It was timber, oil and gas. In fact, while I was commissioner of mines in the territorial days, I introduced the Oil and Gas Conservation Act. That was in 1955. It was passed unanimously by both houses and signed by the governor in two weeks. California, to this day, doesn't have an Oil and Gas Conservation Act. The Conservation Act limits a company on the amount of flare drilling they are allowed when they drill a well. Correlative rights are protected and well spacing is controlled. Anyway, I was commissioner of mines for seven years, then commissioner of natural resources. Interesting thing there, politically, I had never declared a party, and Ernest Gruening was governor and he was a strong Democrat. There was a Republican legislature in session. In fact, George Miscovich was speaker of the house. Anyway, everybody though I was a Democrat because Gruening appointed me. So he sent my name down. They wouldn't confirm me. The legislature wouldn't confirm my appointment. But in those days, under those laws, I just stayed on the job until the next session of the legislature. They didn't deny it, but they wouldn't confirm it. In the next session of the legislature, B. Frank Heinsen, former regional forester was the governor. These were federally-appointed governors. He was a Republican, but there was a Democratically-controlled legislature at that time. So he sent my name down, and they wouldn't confirm me. Finally, the third governor was Mike Stepovich from Fairbanks, and by that time they figured, "Well, you're doing a good job. We don't care." He sent my name down, and it finally got confirmed. I served three terms on that job without confirmation. I still to this day haven't declared a party. That's why I am so effective as a lobbyist, see, both parties claim me.

Jim: So anything you do good, each party claims. What about anything you do bad, Phil?

Phil: Well, they haven't found anything bad yet.

Jim: Well look, after you finished as commissioner of natural resources, who was the governor when you finished, Hickel?

Phil: Yeah, it was Hickel. I served eight years under Egan, his two full terms. Then, all of the commissioners were supposed to send in their resignation from these jobs when the new Governor comes, but Wally said, "No, I want to keep you. You're doing a good job." We always got along well. He said, "I have no intention of moving you, so you can be assured that you are going to be on the job for me." One by one, most of the others were replaced. I served for nine months under him. Tom Kelly's stepfather was Mike Halbouty, an internationally well-known petroleum geologist. Well, Tom had been up here from Texas, as a petroleum engineer, and he'd been on some other jobs up here for private industry. Mike Halbouty had contributed about a million dollars to Wally's campaign. Tom had come up for the inauguration when Wally took office there in Juneau and Wally offered him a job as executive assistant in the governor's office because he owed a political debt. Tom wasn't interested in that; he went back down to Texas. Wally kept writing him and phoning him because he owed this debt, and tried to get him to come up and take that job on the governor's staff. Finally, Tom said, "No, the only job I'll take is Phil's." We knew each other, see. So Wally took a trip over to Tokyo, and while he was gone he had his hatchet man in his office ask for my resignation. So I said, "Where's Wally?" He's in Tokyo. I said, "Well, I'll wait until he comes back and I'll give him my letter of resignation." So I had it written out. When he came back I went in and presented it to him.

Jim: That must have been a little painful after the guarantee that he'd given you.

Phil: Well, it was the best thing that could have happened to me. I got back into private enterprise where I belonged.

Jim: Now that you look back, it wasn't so painful. Hickel didn't finish that term as governor, did he?

Phil: No, he was appointed as secretary of the Interior about two years into his term.

Jim: Tell us about what you did after you resigned.

Phil: I did a little lobbying for the oil industry and helped them with their problems. Then I was hired as exploration manager for INESCO, it was then known as International Nuclear Corporation, and they eventually bought a couple of oil companies and changed their name to INESCO Oil Company. They were convinced by their oil man that had been up here during the period of time, that there was a lot of good mineral potential up here and they should have somebody up here representing their minerals. So I became their exploration manager for all of Alaska. They were drilling a well over on the west side of Cook Inlet where there is now a producing oil field. I was on that job for six years as exploration manager, we did a lot of work. We put three years in on the Kennicott copper belt. We did 75 miles of air color photography on that copper belt, all the way from one end of it to the other. That completed my consulting work for a time.

Jim: When you finished up with the oil and copper belt work, what was the next big adventure?

Phil: In 1973 I got seriously involved with lobbying and that is when I gave up a lot of consulting. The Alaska Miners' Association, Southeast Conference, Resource Development Council, and the Coal Association, those were my four clients. I finally dropped out of the Southeast Conference. They wanted to make that a combination executive director and lobbyist and I just didn't want that.

Jim: That would have locked you into a full-time position with them, wouldn't it?

Phil: Yeah, and it was pretty much out of mining.

Jim: More recently, if I'm not mistaken, you attempted to do something with the tailings out of the Alaska-Gastineau Mine.

Phil: Yes, the Alaska-Gastineau, down at D Street in Juneau. The one that was described in this morning's session. Did you hear it?

Jim: Yes, I heard that presentation. Those were the tailings you tested?

Phil: Yes, I was retained as a consultant to estimate the reserves and try to get an average grade of what was there and do metallurgical testing and identify the most economical method of recovery.

Jim: Phil, just a minute, I visualize this material as tailings, some of which is exposed, but most of which is under the water.

Phil: This is true.

Jim: How did you evaluate?

Phil: The tide differential—at extreme high tide the water almost covers the whole deposit, at low tide, it exposes it to about 35 feet down, to the old beach line.

Jim: What was the width of this? How far did it span?

Phil: Well, there are two claims, and these are 40-acre state claims because they are state tidal lands.

Jim: It was possible to estimate that you had 80 acres that was roughly 30 feet thick of this material?

Phil: Of course, you didn't know that, but you just had to assume that. In my report, I was very careful about stating that this was what I assumed to be the case.

Jim: How did you collect your samples?

Phil: I had a pipe sampler that I had made up. It's a soil sampler, in other words, two-and-a-half-inch metal tubing, eight feet long. I put down 24 holes to the maximum depth, distributed in a grid over the area. So I had to base my average on that information. This brings us to an interesting fact that people are just beginning to understand. In these types of deposits that are laid out in the tidelands, over a long period of time with tidal currents and wave action, you would expect it to act just like a placer deposit and work its way down to bedrock. It doesn't do that. The tidal action washes the slimes out and the gold stays there and concentrates on the surface. In most of these deposits along the coast in the Alaska Gulf and elsewhere, all of the values are concentrated in the top two feet. Sometimes it is only 12 inches. Below the tidal action, it remains as it was when it was first laid down. It hasn't been reconcentrated.

Jim: Have you examined some of these beaches, Phil, not just this specialized tailings pile we are dealing with here, but other beach deposits around the state of Alaska?

Phil: Oh yes, Icy Bay, Yakutat and Yakataga where the White River comes in. That is where the third generation family goes out after every storm reconcentrates the gold on the surface, and skims the gold right off the top. I've seen a Mason quart jar of the nicest, cleanest, fine gold you ever saw; they go out and get that much. I'm not saying it is easy, but there is three generations still doing it.

Jim: We got away from Juneau with that interesting bit of information. Back to Juneau. What was the next step in your evaluation? Now correct me if I am wrong but you were testing the tailings off of the mill, and while there was some free gold most of the gold was locked in the rock and mineral grains.

Phil: Yes, you're right. There was some gold that could be panned.

Jim: When you took those tailings and analyzed them ... now what was the step-by-step process that you used to determine the values.

Phil: Well, I got bulk samples. We finally shipped a bulk sample down to the equipment outfit that had the turn-key contract.

Jim: Was this in Washington?

Phil: No this was Yuma City, California. I put a backhoe out there at an extreme low-tide period and we put down three holes and got down to 10 feet in each one of them. After they got the hole dug down, then I cut a channel sample down for average and we shipped three 55-gallon drums down there, but in the meantime, the sampling that I did with the soil auger, was sent down to a lab where they tried all kinds of things—flotation and cyanide and gravity—and did a lot of detailed panning on the various end products. We got our results about the time we learned that a company had been called in there two years before to do an evaluation. They drilled it. They had the hollow-flight drills so they did get samples pretty well down into the bottom. They went to the Colorado School of Mines and did a lot of metallurgical testing and everything else. They knew their business. The report came back that it was not a viable operation.

Jim: That had already been put out and you didn't know about it?

Phil: I didn't know about it. The owners of the property had buried it and didn't show it to me. They were after the state loan, of course, the state wanted a qualified feasibility study. So they showed me some old reports, assay reports, nothing on any drilling or anything like that, hoping I would give them a favorable report.

Phil: When I finally got wind of the previous report, I had no way of confirming it. Anyway, that's the kind of people they were. I didn't realize it.

Jim: So apparently the project folded?

Phil: The equipment company insisted their plant would work. All of the equipment they built—the big trommel, 50-foot long, eight feet in diameter, and a dewatering screw that was supposed to dewater the tailings from centrifuges—it all began to deteriorate before they got it on site. That was an important point, the state wouldn't pay the bills without the equipment being on the spot. The company wanted their payment when they got a particular unit finished. So they were sending these things up. It was a confusing mess.

Jim: Did you ever get the whole plant operating?

Phil: Yes.

Jim: And what was the result?

Phil: It was sad, real sad.

Jim: Well Phil, looks like we have come to the end of the trail. It always saddens me to end an interesting interview like this one. Thank you for taking the time to join me on Alaska Gold Trails.

Phil: I thoroughly enjoyed talking over old times with you, Jim. Thank you for inviting me.

Bob Jacobs
with
Jim Madonna
November 9, 1989

Jim: Our guest this afternoon is Bob Jacobs. Welcome to Alaska Gold Trails, Bob.

Bob: Nice to be here, Jim.

Jim: First give us a little background on where you're from, when you were born and how you happened to come to Alaska.

Bob: I was raised in eastern Pennsylvania, in a little town called West Chester, with a population of about 14,000 people. I lived there until I was a senior in high school, then my family moved down to Wilmington, Delaware, where my father got a new job. I finished high school there in 1937. I was interested in aviation even when I was in high school, so I went to work for about a year at the Ballanca Aircraft Corporation, nine miles down the road at a little town called New Castle, on the Delaware River. In January of 1939, I went up to Newark, New Jersey, and attended school at one of the biggest mechanic schools in the world at that time. Later, during World War II, it became an Air Force mechanics' school, where they trained thousands of Air Force mechanics. I got an A and P (Airframe and Powerplant) license there in 1939, then got a job in South Carolina. Another fellow and I were instructing and we started a mechanics' school there for the government. We instructed there for a couple of years, until World War II, when the Japanese hit Pearl Harbor on December 7, 1941. A few days later I went up north to work in one of the big aircraft factories.

Jim: Where exactly was that, Bob?

Bob: Well, at that particular time, I went back to the same factory I had been working at in 1938, the Ballanca Aircraft Corporation in Newcastle. They had a big contract from Fairchild and were building bomber trainers for the military. They had converted their aircraft production to these military airplanes. In fact they built another plant there to take care of the large volume of airplanes that they had to produce. I worked there through the beginning of 1944. At that time, the Air Force was beginning to gear up for a big push into Japan. They were beginning to build the B-29s. The B-29s were put together in Detroit, and Fort Worth, Texas, and aircraft factories all over the United States quit producing other kinds of airplanes and went to making parts for the B-29s. I was in flight test at the time I left the Ballanca Corporation, so there weren't going to be any more airplanes to fly. We had just two more airplanes to test out, the weather was down, and I was waiting in the operations office, when I picked up a copy of the old Alaska Life Magazine. I picked out two of the airlines that were advertised in there and wrote them a letter. One was Alaska Coastal in Juneau and the other was Wien. Well, I got a letter back from Alaska Coastal right away, and they said, "Come up here. We need an A and P mechanic and we'll pay your way up here." So I gathered up my tools and threw some things in a suitcase and took off on the train, out to Seattle, and went down and got a steamship ticket. In those days they didn't have regular flights up the coast like they had a few years later, and most of the people that traveled back and forth traveled on the steamships. And so, I got a ticket on the old Alaska Steamship Company's, B*aranof.*

Jim: Did it stop at all the towns along the way?

Bob: This particular ship was hauling general cargo and hauling passengers, and it stopped at all the villages on the way up the coast to Juneau—stopped at Ketchikan, Wrangell, Petersburg and Juneau. And after it left Juneau it went to Sitka, and where it went from there I don't really know. But, it took us six days to get up to Juneau from Seattle, and in some places along the coast we unloaded freight sometimes for 24 hours.

Jim: Were there any incidents along the way that might be interesting?

Bob: Well, there was one thing that happened. The Coast Guard had put a deck gun on the back of this ship. I guess they figured they would use it against submarines, or anything else that might attack them, and coming up across Queen Charlotte Sound, why I fired one shot through the thing and it pretty near pulled itself out of the deck. The deck plates weren't strong enough to hold it, I guess. And that was the last shot ever fired out of that gun.

Jim: Bob, you went to work then in the aircraft industry in Juneau, is that right?

Bob: I was working as a mechanic for Alaska Coastal, at that time.

Jim: How long did you work there?

Bob: I only worked there for about a month.

Jim: That was kind of a short job, wasn't it?

Bob: Well, Alaska Airlines had their head of maintenance down in Seattle trying to find some A and P mechanics to work in Anchorage, and he couldn't find anybody down there. At that time in the war, why you couldn't find aircraft mechanics anywhere that weren't actually tied up in building airplanes and so forth. So, I went up there and talked to him. He was at the coffee shop in the Baranof Hotel, and he offered me twice as much money as I was making for Coastal, so I gave Coastal two weeks notice and went on up to Anchorage on Alaska Airlines two weeks later.

Jim: Exactly what did you do and how long did you serve as an aircraft mechanic in Anchorage?

Bob: They had me troubleshooting their planes out of Anchorage. Maybe an airplane would be down at Kodiak with a fuel pump out, or an airplane would be down at Bethel, or Homer, or wherever they went, and I'd go down there and get the airplane operating again and then go back to Anchorage, and by that time there'd be some other place to go. So, along in December the mail plane had gone down between Unalakleet and Stebbins, on the Bering Sea, and it had gone up on its nose and bent the propeller and bent its strut and the belly got torn out going across some ice; I think it was on skis—it could've been worse if it had been on wheels. Anyhow, they sent me up there with three mechanics and we patched the thing up and got it back. We had to change the engine out there. And '44 was one of those years when it was real cold, and we were out there on the ice. We had to change the engine and put another propeller on there and patch up the belly enough to get it over to Unalakleet, and we worked right out there in the cold, using firepots to keep warm. In those days, they hadn't gotten Herman Nelson heaters yet. Herman Nelson heaters were being used by the military, and airlines didn't get ahold of them 'til after the war. And so we were using these old plumbers, firepots for heat, and we finally got the plane patched up good enough to get it over to Unalakleet. We spent some time over at Unalakleet fixing it up good enough so we could fly it up to Nome. We put it in a hangar up there and rebuilt it. That was supposed to be a three-week job. Fourteen years later I left Nome.

Jim: Let's explore that fourteen years that you spent up on the Seward Peninsula, Bob, and your new lifestyle at Nome. Tell us a little bit about what you did at Nome. You were a mechanic for Alaska Airlines. Did you fly for them, and what other activities were you involved with?

Bob: When we got up there with the Travelair, I still had these three mechanics with me, and about the time we arrived the chief mechanic, a fellow by the name of Tony Johansen, quit Alaska Airlines, and he and some other fellows had bought a surplus DC-3 from the military, and they went into business flying from Seattle to Fairbanks. So right away I kind of fell into his job at Nome, and I spent the next couple of years working on airplanes there. There were planes there that were flying the mail runs all over western Alaska. They went as far north as Kotzebue—Deering, Candle, Kotzebue—and mail runs all over the Seward Peninsula. They had mail runs down the coast—there were nine stops between Nome and Unalakleet, and then they went on down to Bethel. And at that time Alaska Airlines had all the mail runs on the Yukon. Wein's kind of overlapped some of our mail runs, like Nome to Kotzebue and some of the mail runs on the Yukon, but Alaska Airlines was pretty well established all over. And then of course they had the schedules that were going from Anchorage to McGrath and Unalakleet and on up to Nome. In those first years up at Nome, why Alaska Airlines was still a bush outfit. They hadn't gotten their first DC-3s yet. They got their first DC-3s in the fall of 1946, and from that point on why they went from the DC-3s into the equipment that they fly today. And so it was a pretty busy place to work at that time. I worked as a mechanic for two years up there and then I went to flying full time. I'd learned to fly back in Delaware in 1938 and I'd gotten a commercial license along the way. Most all of the flying was VFR (visual flight) in those days and pilots used to fly in some pretty tough weather up there in that country. There weren't any trees out there in that part of Alaska, so you get these whiteout conditions and you get high winds out there and blizzards and so forth. And you get coastal fog along the coast lines up there that made flying pretty difficult. So, as time went on, why things naturally improved, but there was a big turnover of pilots up there, for one reason or another, and so when an opportunity arose, why I went to flying. And I was flying bush up there a number of years, up until 1959, when I finally quit Alaska Airlines and came over to Fairbanks.

Jim: Were you flying the mail planes then, Bob?

Bob: Yeah, we were flying the mail planes into all of those villages over in western Alaska and on down to Bethel and along the Yukon. We'd go from Unalakleet over to Kaltag and Nulato twice a month. And in those days there wasn't landing fields as we know them today, in hardly any of the villages. A good bit of the operation was conducted on floats in the summertime, because you could land on the rivers all over in Alaska, and operations out of Kotzebue were the same way. There were very few airstrips up there that you could land on in the summertime. I flew out of Kotzebue for over a year, during that period, and we'd go as far north as Point Barrow with the mail. At that time, all the mail that went out to western Alaska and up to the villages, including Kotzebue and Barrow, came through Nome, where it had to be redistributed. It was flown up to Kotzebue and then the post office up there redistributed it to the villages up that way. Many times we had so much mail for Barrow that, in the summertime, we'd go up to Point Lay and land on the beach, or if we had floats we'd land on the lagoon. And a plane would come down from Barrow and pick up the mail and take it from Point Lay up to Wainwright and Barrow.

Jim: You said you were up there 14 years?

Bob: Yeah, I left there in the spring of 1959 and came over here to Fairbanks.

Jim: We have a call, Bob. Hi, welcome to Alaska Gold Trails. You're on the air with Bob Jacobs. Do you have a question for Bob?

Caller: Yeah, a question for Bob. Back in 1949, one of the first times I flew to Alaska, McKinley Airways was the name of the outfit. I was just wondering whatever happened to it? Was it absorbed, or what?

Bob: I don't know really what happened to it. Back in that period after the war, there were all kinds of surplus airplanes available in the states and in Alaska, and there were a lot of small outfits that started up on the strength of picking up cheap airplanes. And some survived and became airlines that we have up here today, but the majority of them fell by the wayside somewhere along the line.

Caller: Exactly. I was just curious if you knew what had become of that one. Thank you very much. Enjoying the program.

Jim: Bob, did you have some experiences that were a little bit out of the ordinary, or maybe some airplane problems during your flying time up on the Seward Peninsula, you would care to share with us?

Bob: Well, in those days, airplanes weren't as reliable as they are today. For example most of the airplanes that we were flying in those days had radial engines in them, and a lot of the airplanes that were operating up here at that time didn't have any kind of cowlings on them. And these big radial engines had these cylinders sticking out in the cold air, and a lot of times when it was cold, like it is here now, you'd have a temperature inversion, and maybe you'd take off from a place in Alaska where the temperatures were warm enough to operate this particular airplane OK, but you'd be going into an area where maybe the temperature was 40 or 50 below zero, or colder, and the top of this cold air would usually be somewhere between a thousand feet and three thousand feet, and the airplanes, the majority of them, carried a thermometer out in one of the wing struts there, and you could look out there and see the temperature change real quick when you drop down into that cold air. And a lot of times those old engines would freeze up as soon as they got down in the cold air, and the engine would quit. And so, you'd better be in a position where you could land someplace without too much trouble. Of course, we would put the airplanes on skis along about this time of the year, maybe a little later, depending on how much snow we had, and they'd be on skis until there wasn't enough snow left in the spring to fly any more. And then eventually they'd go on wheels or floats.

Jim: And you had perhaps some interesting experiences up there at Nome, with one of these aircraft? They also had a problem with the oil in some of these engines, didn't they?

Bob: A lot of these engines, the older type of engines, didn't have a pressurized oil system, in that the valves and so forth had oil pressure. The engines had to be checked every 20 hours. One of the things that had to be done was to pull all the push rods out of the engine, dip the ends of the push rods in a barrel of Marafax grease, and put them back. And the rocker boxes had Zerk fittings on the rocker arms, and you'd give them a couple of squirts with a grease gun, and put the rocker box covers back on. And so, for the first 10 hours you'd be flying along and you'd see little bits of grease come back off the engine and land on the windshield, and you'd sit there and watch for another piece to come back and hit the windshield, and so after about 10 hours, why the grease up in the top rocker boxes would run down the push rods inside the push rod housings, and the tops of the push rods would start to run dry. And when you'd pull the prop through, before you started the engine up, to make sure you got the oil cleared out of the cylinders, you could hear those push rods squeak, up in the top. And if you happened to pull one out, they would be kind of a red color, all the grease had run down to the bottom. So those engines weren't as reliable as engines that they had later. And those engines, if you were lucky you'd get 300 hours out of them, and then you had to pull the cylinders off and top-overhaul the engines. And with a little luck you could get another 300 hours out of them, and that was it, before they were major overhauled.

Jim: When you lost all the oil, what was it like?

Bob: Well, some of those engines had weaknesses. For example, the eight-cylinder Lycoming engines, the smallest one was 215 horsepower and the biggest one was 300 horsepower. They would burn out pistons occasionally, and when that happened, why you'd get a hole in the top of the piston, or it'd burn out down the side of the pistons, past the rings, and when that happened, every time the piston came up on the compression stroke, why that pressure would go down into the case. Now there was a breather on the case that would handle the normal pressure that was built up, but in this instance, the pressure was more than the engine could handle. So it would go out at the next weakest spot. And that weak place was always around the thrust bearing, up in the front of the engine. And it'd blow the seal out of there, and it'd start pumping the oil out, right through the thrust bearing. Now, if you had a single-engine airplane, with the engine right up in front of you, why all of a sudden, the windshield would be covered with oil. And oil would come back on the hot exhaust pipe, and it'd start to smoke.

Jim: Did you ever have that happen to you?

Bob: Oh yeah. I had that happen quite a few times. One thing we used to do is carry some rags around in the left-hand door pocket, and if something like that happened you could reach out the window and scrape a hole in the oil out there enough so you could see to get down. But when it happened, the engine was still running, but it didn't have any power. And it wasn't very long before the engine would run out of oil and then it would seize up and the prop would stop right out in front of you. So when that happened, why you'd better find a place to get down pretty quick.

Jim: You had that experience near Nome, didn't you?

Bob: Yeah, I had that experience quite a few times, and I was just lucky enough to be someplace where I could get down safely.

Jim: We've got a call, Bob. Hi. Welcome to Alaska Gold Trails. You're on the air with Bob Jacobs. Do you have a question or comment for Bob?

Caller: I was just going to ask Bob if he could remember Charlie Traeger.

Bob: I sure do. Charlie Traeger had an inn over there at Unalakleet when I first knew him, and when I went up to Nome there that first time in '44, why of course we stayed at Charlie Traeger's place there in Unalakleet, when we were working on that old Travelair. And I think it was about two years later, I was down at Unalakleet on the mail run and in those days, why it was at this time of year, when the days were short, why we'd spend the night in Unalakleet, and so we used to stay there at Charlie's place. And this particular time it was Charlie's 80th birthday, and there was another Alaska Airlines pilot in there from Anchorage, who was up flying a fur buyer around to the different villages, and Charlie had a cook there by the name of Ivanof, and he was up there cooking a big dinner for Charlie's 80th birthday. I don't think Charlie lived very long after that.

Caller: He died in '50. Was that Ivan Ivanof that was cooking?

Bob: Yeah, right.

Caller: That's Emily Ivanoff's father. In fact I met you in '49 at Charlie's in Unalakleet, so I've gotten to know you better since then, but that's the first time I met you was at Traeger's in '49.

Bob: Yeah, right.

Caller: Those were the good old days and I guess we'll never get done talking about them. I don't guess they'll come back, but we sure had a lot of good times in those days. Take care, Bob.

Jim: Bob, tell us a little bit about flying people and supplies into a couple of the tin mines up there on the Seward Peninsula.

Bob: There was one tin mine off the coast a little bit from Teller. Teller is 60 miles west of Nome, on the Bering Sea coast there. And this place was called Lost River. There was a hard rock mine up there, about five miles up the canyon from the beach, and of course the mine went back up into the hill there, and they brought the ore out of the mine on little railroad cars, and they had a facility built down the side of the hill that had all the shakers and the ball mills to grind up the ore. The ore would start up at the top of the hill and pass through all these pieces of machinery and wind up down at the bottom of the hill as a black ore. It looked like coal that had been all ground up. And the little pieces of tin were about the size of rice, and they'd put them in 50-gallon drums. A 50-gallon drum of that tin ore weighed about 1800 pounds, so it was a little hard to handle. So they started just filling a half a drum, and they'd put the cap back on and haul it off down to the beach, and later the next summer, one of the Alaska Steamship boats that was going back to Seattle empty would come in and pick the tin up off the beach and take it down to Seattle.

Jim: Wasn't there also a placer mine up there that used a gold dredge for tin mining? Where was that?

Bob: Up back of Tin City. Tin City is on the Bering Straits there. There's a military radar site there. In the early days, there was mining in the creek that comes right down next to the airstrip where the radar site is today. And about 15 miles northeast of there was a tin mine called Buck Creek, and that was a placer outfit. And back in the early days that had been mined with a dredge. The old dredge was still sitting there next to the airstrip, but it hadn't been run. When I was first in there was back in the late '40s some time, and the dredge probably hadn't been run for 30 years. In fact, when the dredge was run all the operation was done with horses. There weren't any Cats or anything at that time.

Jim: I understand that they later turned that into a dragline-type operation and that the families would camp out in tents up there. Is that right?

Bob: The operation was a placer outfit all right, and they were using a dragline to pull the ore in, and they had a grizzley there and various kinds of machinery to shake the ore down. Eventually, the tailings would go out on the conveyor belt to be dumped, and the ore would wind up going to a sluice box, because there was a lot of gold mixed in with the tin. And they would take enough gold out of there to pay most of their expenses, and what they got from their tin was extra.

Jim: They picked some of the big tin nuggets off the conveyor belt, didn't they?

Bob: Well, most of those people were from over at Williams Village, and the women and kids were living in tents over there in the summer. And they'd sit up on the conveyor belt and pick the tin nuggets off the belt. The mining company would pay them extra for that.

Jim: Bob, we've run to the end of the trail. I want to thank you for joining us here on Alaska Gold Trails and a most interesting interview.

Bob: My pleasure, Jim.

Neville Jacobs
with
Jim Madonna
October 26, 1989

Jim: This afternoon, folks, we have a guest who has recently made a fine contribution to the community of Fairbanks. Neville Jacobs, welcome to Alaska Gold Trails.

Neville: Well, thank you. It's a pleasure to be here, Jim.

Jim: Neville, give us a little bit of your background, regarding where you were born. I'm not going to ask you the year you were born. You made it clear before the beginning of the show that it was not a number that you were handing out frequently. So, where were you born?

Neville: I was born in San Francisco.

Jim: Give us a little background of your early years, Neville.

Neville: Well, you said that you were born in San Jose, and actually my mother was born there a few decades before your time. But she went on a trip to Canada in the '20s. My grandfather had a new Buick, I think, and so they were on their way (she and her mother, my grandmother, and family) were on their way north, and this car broke down—because I understand roads were somewhat less smooth than they are today, and the car broke down—and she walked into the little town of Dunsmuir and a man came along, as she was walking back, in his van, and she thought maybe he was a delivery man or something, but it turned out he was a local highway engineer. They were putting in the highway which is I-5 today. And so it turned out it was my dad, and that's how they met. And so then he courted her and wound up in San Francisco courting her some more and they got married, and then they eventually moved, after the depression time came along, they moved to southern California, and then I was born. Actually I was born in San Francisco and then they moved down to southern California. So I grew up in the Los Angeles area. And in 1949 we had a friend who came to Alaska right after the end of World War II and we had lost track of him—the friendship had become sort of vaporous—when all of a sudden a letter appeared and he said he was now head of real estate for Useral, and he was working closely with the territorial division of highways, and they needed a highway engineer with my dad's specialization, and would Daddy come up. That's how we came to Alaska.

Jim: I'll be darned. What year was that?

Neville: Well, that was in 1949.

Jim: In 1949. And you went where, to Fairbanks?

Neville: We went to Anchorage at that time. Dad was chief of operations and assistant district engineer for the Anchorage judicial division during territorial days.

Jim: And how old were you then, Neville?

Neville: I was in my teens.

Jim: I see. Had you finished high school?

Neville: Yes. I had gotten out of high school and actually I had gone to college a little bit in California.

Jim: And did you go to school here, or what did you do when you came to Anchorage? Were you just a homebody, or what?

Neville: No, I went to work. I was trying to remember—I hadn't thought about it for awhile. I actually went to work for KENI Radio, and I wrote advertisement—what do you call that ... continuity—I was continuity writer, and I wrote a radio show called Mukluk Telegraph, a news radio show.

Jim: You didn't tell me you knew all about these things, but you did tell me that you also put together a program interviewing the sourdoughs. And we want to talk about that a little bit. But first tell us a little bit more about what you did in Anchorage, before you came to Fairbanks.

Neville: Oh, I also started painting. I had become acquainted with Jeannie Laurence, and it was for some reason a great inspiration, and Sydney Laurence had died 10 or 12 years before that time. But I started painting. I had painted since I was a youngster in California. At one point, when I was a child, we had lived at Laguna Beach, and I'd studied art there. My grandmother was a painter, so after we came to Alaska the beauty of the land was a real inspiration and I started painting and I had my first one-person show in the early '50s in Anchorage. So I was painting and then I was also working and doing other things.

Jim: You painted all your life, but you also had a focus in terms of higher level education. What was that?

Neville: Well, I had been interested in anthropology. I didn't know a whole lot about what it was. I knew that it was about the study of peoples and I was just really profoundly interested in different cultures and the ways of different peoples and their belief systems, and I wanted to go on to school. So, eventually, I came on back up here to the University of Alaska.

Jim: Tell us about your experiences in education and anthropology and where you went and what you did.

Neville: Oh, that's such a big subject. Most recently I've been interested in graduate research, I think somebody called it. But I was in the Himalayas, in the Tibetan refugee communities, and I've also painted there. I've gone there both from anthropological and philosophical interests and as a painter. And I suppose going back, moving forward chronologically, in the early '50s my folks became interested in mining, and I had become involved with an Eskimo show—the Eskimo dance pageant—during the Fur Rendezvous, and made friends with some Eskimos there, so when we went to Nome the following summer, they invited me to go with them out to Little Diomede Island. This couple, Sammy and Mary Mogg—his father was a whaling captain, and if I ever wrote the books that I say I'm going to write, that would be an interesting story to write about that family—they invited me to go out to Diomede Island with them, and I was painting and making notes about my experiences with the people, the Eskimo culture and the fading of the old traditions. I found that fascinating. Eventually, I came on up to the University of Alaska here, and I finished a bachelor's degree during the time that Dr. Skarland was there.

Jim: Oh, is that right? Of Skarland Hall fame?

Neville: Yes. I knew Dr. Skarland, and Dr. Geist, of Geist Road fame. And then I went on to Hawaii into graduate work, and then I came back up here on a business trip and friends convinced me that I should really move back up here. Dr. Skarland had passed away, and they had a whole new graduate school formed, and I actually did finish my master's degree up here, although I had put a year in at the University of Hawaii in graduate studies there. I worked at the Bishop Museum there, and that was fascinating. I've had some nice experiences in connection with that aspect of my work experience.

Jim: Now, I understand you are doing postgraduate work.

Neville: Postgraduate. Somebody said, "Oh, you're doing postgraduate research." Since the late 1970s I've been interested and involved in the Tibetan refugee people. That is another subject that's far removed from gold mining, other than I might mention that people ask, "Why in the world?" They don't know what Tibet is. It was an independent nation prior to being taken over by China in the 1950s, and they say, "Why would China want to take over this high plateau, this barren land?" Well, the Tibetans didn't mine. They picked gold; actually, they placer mined. They extracted gold from surface areas where it was abundant, but they never mined Tibet, so it is a very highly enriched area, mineralogically. So that's one reason China would want it.

Jim: You said that you spent some time up at Nome and you went over to Little Diomede. What took you to Nome?

Neville: Well, my dad had become involved in a mining operation. And so my parents went up there for the summer of 1953. And in the meantime, the previous spring, I had become acquainted with these Eskimo friends, Sammy and Mary Mogg, and she and I had a very strong personal rapport, and ever after she referred to me as her white sister, and she was my Eskimo sister, and I have a funny story to tell about that. We were at a little potlatch one time and she introduced me to a friend as her sister—she didn't qualify it and say, "This is my white sister," and imply that it was strong friendship, she just said, "This is my sister." And the woman drew back and looked at us back and forth, and Mary said, "Same mother, different fathers." And the woman nodded. She said, "Yes, it happens that way sometimes."

Jim: How did you meet Mary? You said you met her in Anchorage?

Neville: Yes, I was pulling the curtain for the Eskimo dance pageant that was being sponsored by the Business and Professional Women's organization, during the Fur Rendezvous. That's where I became acquainted with the Eskimos, and then also, my parents and I were involved with a small photographic group. And it happened that there was a professional lecturer there, he was on the Cavalcade of America, and he heard that Sammy Mogg had a whole lot of movie film, 16mm movie film, of Eskimo life and walrus hunting out in the Bering Sea. So he wanted to see those movies. We had a 30-foot long living room, so we invited everybody over one evening, to look at these movies. And this lasted for hours. They reviewed thousands of feet of movie film. So Mary and I sat over in the corner chatting, and we just developed a friendship very rapidly, through the hours of watching these movies go by.

Jim: Did Cavalcade of America, ever use any of those movies?

Neville: I don't know. The man's name was Vincent Palmer, his wife's name was Lucy, and among the things that they did, he told me that they made a lot of underwater movies. And that's what they normally lectured about, but he wanted to make a movie of his Alaskan travels, and I know he acquired a lot of film that particular night. Whatever happened to it, I don't know.

Jim: He got the film, then. It didn't end up in the archives of one of the libraries?

Neville: No. He didn't buy all of the film that he reviewed, but I know he sat over in the corner with a little talky machine—it was a little tape recorder. And he was enumerating to this machine, as he watched these films, certain shots that he wanted to acquire dupes of from Sammy Mogg.

Jim: Well, that's a little information for somebody interested in perhaps archival type films that might have been developed.

Neville: Actually, I don't know what he ever did. Now, Sammy's films, which would have been wonderful films to have in the archives, they were lost. He had loaned them to a man at Kotzebue who had a trading post, and it burned.

Jim: Oh no.

Neville: Yeah. So a lot of his film was lost.

Jim: Oh, that's too bad. Neville, lets change gears here. Tell us about your summertime in Nome?

Neville: Of course, Nome is an appropriate place to talk about for someone who had a radio show about gold and gold mining. That's a real interesting town from the historical point of view. Well, we went up there with a mining venture, which eventually was not successful. In the meantime, as a result of my friendship with the Eskimo people in Anchorage, I was invited to go out to Diomede Island. And that's a long story and a great adventure. Incredible things happened. I did write it up and it was published in 1954-55, a three-issue, three-part serial. I titled it "Voyage on a Walrus Hide," and I think that's what they called it when they published it, in what was *Alaska Sportsman* magazine then. But something I didn't write up and put into that story, because at that time it was very hush hush, we had a passenger who turned out to be a Russian spy. And he took a rubber life raft out of his luggage, inflated it, and paddled over to Big Diomede, and that story has not ever been told publicly that I know of. It was quite an unexpected adventure.

Jim: Tell us a little bit more of the adventure of that particular walrus hunt. How long were you supposed to be out there on that hunt?

Neville: Well, some friends had chartered the boat. Sammy and Mary Mogg were going to go out for a visit to the family, and so some other photographers came along, and then they invited me to go too. It was to have been a seven-day trip, and we were gone almost a month.

Jim: Did you hunt a lot of walrus?

Neville: Yes, I have slides which I used to show frequently for groups, and I would call it a walrus hunting trip, you know, and somebody made the complaint, he says, "This isn't about a walrus hunt. It really isn't a hunting film. But we did hunt walrus, in the middle of the night when we were out crossing the Bering Strait, we were in a 35-foot umiak, which is an open boat made out of skin—walrus hide. And we were traveling in the ice pack, and always aware and alert to the presence of animals, because that was our meat supply. We took tinned goods—we took a lot of canned goods, of course—but the meat was hunted along the way, and we shot seal and got out on the ice pack—the floating ice—and would put the Coleman stove out and boil up a seal right there, and you know it's a very strong meat to a person not accustomed to that. And I discovered that it was somewhat more palatable if you chewed it with an onion. I taught myself to eat seal meat in the beginning.

Jim: Neville, let's see if we've got a caller here for you. Hi, you're on the air.

Caller: Jim, this is Bettye Fahrenkamp.

Jim: Hi, Bettye, how are you?

Caller: Well, right now I'm in a little bit of trouble. I got arrested, and I'm in this Jail-or-Bail program, over at the March of Dimes. And if you're not familiar with it, what you do is, somebody swears out a warrant for you, a real policeman comes and gets you, they put you in a jail over here at Bentley Mall, and you have a certain fine from the judge. My judge fined me $350, that I've got to raise through phone conversations. So, I, on the way over here in the police car, heard you on the air and I thought, "Oh, oh, I'll call Jim Madonna, and see if there are any of my friends that are listening that might want to help me get out of this Jail-or-Bail situation, with a contribution to the March of Dimes."

Jim: I hope everybody's listening to this program for you, Bettye, because we'd hate for you to sit in that jail overnight, kid.

Caller: And Jim, you might want to help me out, would you not?

Jim: Oh, love, you know I'd just be more than happy to donate a few coins your way.

Caller: OK, would you tell me what you would contribute.

Jim: You want me to do it now? What is the standard contribution?

Caller: Well, my fine's $350 and any and all of it that you want to donate would be welcome.

Jim: Well, look, with the number of friends that you have out in this community, I would be willing to bet that you'll have no trouble raising that $350. I'll go ten bucks.

Caller: Oh, thank you very much, Jim. The number they can call if they want to help out is 451-6489 or 451-6490. And I do need help, 'cause I need to get out of here and get to work.

Jim: We have to have you working for us, love. Get out of the can, OK?

Caller: I would like to. This private suite doesn't go well.

Jim: What do you think of that, Neville, this kid calling us up and asking for money?

Neville: Here I thought she was going to ask about...

Caller: Hey, Neville, you're not off the hook, either, honey.

Neville: Oh, no, I'm aware of that. I'm going to have to match Jim's ten dollars.

Caller: OK, Neville, what's your address?

Neville: 1126 6th Avenue. I don't know if I should put that over the air. But I was going to come down and put the $10 into the kitty right away this afternoon, to get you out of there.

Caller: Fantastic. I appreciate it.

Jim: Can you make another call out of there?

Caller: Yeah.

Jim: Well, I want you to call Oxford Assaying and Refining. You know who they are? Their number is 456-3967. And by the way, they have a special quote line, that's 452-7858, just in case, sitting in the can there, that you need the prices on gold, silver and platinum, you give their quote line a call, and that might be something to talk about while you're sitting there overnight.

Caller: I can't be here overnight. I've got stuff to do.

Jim: Now they may give you silver or gold, because they've got lots of silver and gold ingots over there.

Caller: Then we'd just have to sell it and get the money.

Jim: OK. They're located at 208 Wendell Street. You ask for Dee Church over there, I'm sure she might give you a little bit to help.

Caller: Oh, thank you very much, and don't forget, if I've got any friends out there, get me out of this can.

Jim: OK, love, nice talking to you.

Neville: Good luck, Bettye.

Jim: Hi, you're on the air.

Caller: Hello, Jim. This is one of your old students calling.

Jim: I know who it is exactly.

Caller: Don't say any more.

Jim: I won't say any more.

Caller: Jim, I need to know this afternoon, on potash and borax, what's the most likely mixture to use for melting gold in the production of a Dore' Bar?

Jim: Borax. You can use a mixture of borax and soda. The ratio depends on how much black sand you have accompanying your gold. A good person to call on that and get more definite mixes would be Tom Benjamin. He's associated right at the moment as a graduate student up at MIRL (Mineral Industry Research Laboratory). If I am reading you right, you're having trouble getting the melt to go. Talk to Tom and he'll give you the exact soda/borax mixture that is appropriate.

Caller: You know, you always told me it was 25/75, and I can never keep it straight.

Jim: Oh, borax would be 75, soda 25.

Caller: OK, that's all I needed to know, Jim. How's everything else going for you?

Jim: Well, Neville Jacobs and I are having a great conversation here. She's just about to fill us in on the 30-day trip that was supposed to be a 7-day trip walrus hunting up at Nome. So, thanks for the call, my friend.

Caller: OK, you bet, Jim. I'm glad I can always turn to you for a little advice. I really appreciate it.

Jim: No problem. The door's always open.

Caller: OK, Jim, thank you so much now.

Jim: Bye. Neville, tell us what happened. Where did you end up?

Neville: This trip went on and on. On our way back we were detained and queried by the OSI (Office of Special Investigations) and the FBI (Federal Bureau of Investogaton), and finally we left Diomede, made our way back to Cape Prince of Wales, and a storm came in at our heels, and we were holed up at Cape Prince of Wales for a week, and finally this raging high wind went down a little bit and we were staying in the schoolhouse, about 20 of us, from this little 35-foot boat, and the wind went down, then there came the drone of an airplane, and Sammy Mogg jumped up and he ran over to the window and he said, "There comes Bob Jacobs. There comes Bob Jacobs. Only Bob Jacobs can fly in this weather." So we all looked over, and everybody rushed down to the beach and they pulled the boats off the beach and the dogs and the barrels, and cleared the beach so the airplane could come in and land. And by this time quite a bit of time had gone by. So I scribbled a postcard to my parents at Nome, to let them know I was alive, I rushed down to the airplane, and I said to the pilot, "Here is the postcard, but I don't have a stamp. Would you please mail it for me?" And he was handing out bags of mail, and he looked down, and my parka hood went back and I had yellow hair, you know, and came forward, and he nearly fell out of the airplane. And that's the man I married.

Jim: You told us how he felt. How did you feel? Was there a little spark back and forth, going on?

Neville: Oh, well, it was like great flashes of electricity going, you know. Lightning struck and the ground trembled. It really, it was a very... I was breathless. I don't know, I never experienced this. He eventually left Alaska Airlines, where he was flying at that time, and started flying on the Arctic slope for what is today Mark Air. So he was flying in one day and I was out there, this was several years ago, but I was standing in the office with a friend and I said, "You know, it's been a lot of years, but I still get palpitations." It was love at first sight. I still get the pitter-pat. That's embarrassing.

Jim: I think it's romantic. I'm sure the audience is enjoying this very much.

Neville: Well, you know what we should be talking about. I'm going to change the subject. I'm going to be signing posters Saturday, for MUS, of the riverboat on the telephone book cover.

Jim: Yes, Neville, let's talk a little bit about your art work. You've been doing artwork since you were a young person. Do you have outlets or studios, or what do you do?

Neville: In Fairbanks, here, two galleries particularly, carry my work. My work is in various places, but especially at New Horizons Gallery, on Cushman, between 2nd and 3rd, and at House of Wood, between 6th and 7th and Lacey and Noble. So those two galleries in Fairbanks and an Anchorage Window Gallery carries my work. And I have two new prints out, released this spring, which are part of an Alaska historical series that I'm working on, and the telephone book cover, of the riverboat *Nenana*, is a part of that historical series. And the painting was wet when I discovered the contest. I was working on it when I saw the thing in the paper, and I rushed it into the telephone company for their competition.

Jim: Just in time. We have a call, Neville. Hi, welcome to Alaska Gold Trails, you're on the air with Neville Jacobs.

Caller: I was just wondering if Neville was going to be able to get us another nice picture for next year's phone book?

Neville: Well, what a lovely question. It is a competition, and there were twenty-some submissions for this year. I'm certainly going to work on it. You know, this particular painting came out very nicely, and it was especially appropriate. They had picked the *Nenana* for a national historical monument—a landmark.

Caller: Usually I've been complaining about the phone book covers, and this year I was left with nothing to complain about.

Jim: My wife has said the same thing. She says, "Boy, this phone book cover is just the best we've ever had."

Caller: I appreciated this one, and I thank her for producing that.

Neville: Well, I thank you very much, and if you will stop by Bentley Mall on Saturday afternoon, we'll say hello to you and you can take a look at the posters that they have run from MUS.

Jim: Is that where Bettye's at?

Neville: That's where Bettye's at, if she's still over there.

Jim: Well, if Bettye's still over there, you can take a small donation to her while you're over there.

Caller: She was speaking about Bob. I've known him a lot longer than she has. I've known him for 40 years.

Neville: I recognize the voice of our caller. He's another Bob.

Caller: OK, well, I'll see you Neville.

Neville: OK, thanks Bob.

Caller: Bye.

Jim: OK, now, tell us about the wet painting.

Neville: Well, I was working on it when I read about the competition. I called them. It was Monday or Tuesday. I said, "What is the deadline for this?" And they said, "Friday." So I had to finish the painting and I got it into the House of Wood that morning and they matted it and shrink-wrapped it and I took it over by four o'clock, which was the deadline. It was still a little damp under the mat. But it's a part of a series. The first one I released is a print of a Fairbanks waterfront - *Golden Days on the Waterways.* That was released in April from House of Wood, and that's a painting which depicts Fairbanks in the period of 1910, 1915. And you know, people came in and they looked at this painting showing all these riverboats tied abreast in front of the old Northern Commercial Company docks, and one man said, "Oh, that's not plausible. The river is not that big." He said, "This is not authentic." Well, in fact, what they don't know is that in the early days the present Chena River was like a branch of the Tanana. It was a channel of the Tanana. After the railroad came in, in 1921, they diked off the channel of the Tanana, which flowed together with the Chena upstream about 20 miles. They put a big dike up there and that created the Chena as it is today, and it became a clear-water stream. And then they filled in the banks where Samson Hardware is; they put all the rip-rap along in front because of floods, and they put it on the other side of the river in front of Barnette's Trading Post, which had become the Alaska Northern Commercial Company. So then they narrowed the river down, and eventually they built the permanent bridge. But every year that bridge would wash out, but these steamboats could tie abreast five or six boats, in front of where Nordstrom's is today. It's just a period of history in early Fairbanks which is fascinating. I thought we might be talking about riverboats. During my research and study I've been sketching them for many many years. Originally over at Whitehorse and then up at Dawson. They have two big posts on either side, in the front of the housing. And those two big posts—people don't know what those are, they think they're masts or something, but those are walking posts. It's something rather unique to riverboats. When they get into shallow water and they get onto a sandbar, they take those out and put them out on the front of the boat, mount the boat to them, and it's like hoists. And the sternwheel power drives the boat and it rises up on these walking sticks, and it lifts the bow of the boat so it can get free of and travel over a sandbar.

Jim: That's interesting. I think Jim Binkley called those grasshoppers or the process "grasshoppering." Where again do you display?

Neville: All of my prints are fine art prints, numbered limited editions, and they are at House of Wood and New Horizons Galleries. And then I did another one, it's a small little picture, of a train over Hurricane Gulch Bridge. But the poster put out by MUS, is an MUS production, GTE, and that's a poster, and that's available from MUS. And I'll be signing those Saturday afternoon, between 1:00 and 3:00 p.m. at Bentley Mall.

Jim: And you say you have paintings on display at various businesses around town.

Neville: Oh, I have a painting, over at Mt. McKinley Bank. I have paintings here and there around town. I think you can see it when you walk right down the street on third Avenue. Mt. McKinley Bank is on third there, between Lacey and Cushman, and if you walk by and you look in the window, I have a small picture of a cabin in the winter.

Jim: Do they have to look in the window? Can they go inside?

Neville: They can go inside, and of course anybody would want to go inside Mt. McKinley Bank.

Jim: Well, of course, and I'd like to make a point. They are one of the sponsors of Alaska Gold Trails, so if you go inside and you're looking at Neville's painting, say hello to the folks there. Neville, we've got a couple of minutes here. Let's sum it up real quick about your experiences painting.

Neville: Oh, we could do a half a dozen more shows.

Jim: I'm sure we could.

Neville: I was painting this summer on Denali Highway, and one time, years ago, I met this wonderful sculptor, fresh from—I think he'd come from New York. Anyway, he had done a sculpture and it was up on top of Chena Ridge Road. In the middle of winter I drove him up there to see if his sculpture was surviving, and his name was Alfred Skondovitch. Is that name familiar?

Jim: My goodness. Alfred, you have more talents than we knew about here.

Neville: I buy supplies from him, at McCauley Reprographics.

Jim: I didn't know that. Well, thank you so much for mentioning him here. So you met Alfred and that was when?

Neville: Oh gosh, that was back in the '50s one time. So, to sum up is a really hard thing to say, because Alaska is so diverse, and a wonderful country, and adventures here are endless.

Jim: And they have been and will continue to be, won't they, Neville.

Neville: I hope so.

Jim: I could sum it up real nice. I'm sure that the listening audience is very pleased to have had you on Alaska Gold Trails today, and I want to thank you very much for joining us.

Neville: It's a pleasure to be here, Jim Madonna.

Ray Lester
with
Jim Madonna
September 14, 1989

Jim: This afternoon, on our Alaska Gold Trails radio show our special guest is Ray Lester. Welcome to Alaska Gold Trails, Ray.

Ray: Thank you Jim.

Jim: Ray, give us a little background. Where were you born and when did you come to Alaska?

Ray: I was born in Seattle, Washington, in the late '50s.

Jim: Nothing specific just the late '50s. How old were you when you came to Alaska?

Ray: When I was four or five years old my parents and I moved up here from Seattle. We drove up to Anchorage. We lived there about three or four months. At that time, my dad had gotten a job which required transferring him back to California, near Oakland. We were there for awhile and didn't like it so we returned to Alaska. This time to the Fairbanks area for a few months. After that, my dad and uncle had decided to spend some time in the Brooks Range, so we headed there.

Jim: What part of the Brooks Range?

Ray: We were about 80 river miles north of Bettles, on the Alatna River.

Jim: What was the attraction on the Alatna?

Ray: I really don't know. It's something that I know my dad and uncle must have talked about for some time. They just wanted to spend a winter out there in the woods, so to speak.

Jim: Was there a home there? What was the story behind it?

Ray: No there wasn't.

Jim: You mean they just went up the Alatna River? What year was that again?

Ray: It was early '60s. In fact, there was just my dad, my uncle and myself to begin with. I was only about six years old at the time. There was a fourth member at that time, a friend of my dad and uncle who backed out about halfway through the trip. I don't know what happened. Something happened along the line he just didn't want to continue. Anyway, the three of us continued on our way and settled in an area about 80 miles or so north— I believe the village was Allakaket—and proceeded to build a cabin.

Jim: Did you help build the cabin, with your dad and uncle?

Ray: Tried the best I could.

Jim: How big was the cabin?

Ray: It was a one-room cabin, big enough to hold about eight people.

Jim: That must have been your dad, your family, and your uncle's family.

Ray: Right. It was a combination of two families.

Jim: You all lived in that one-room cabin? Did it get below zero there?

Ray: I would imagine pretty cold.

Jim: Things get kind of tight inside a one-room cabin for eight people, especially when it is freezing outside, don't they?

Ray: Yeah, they do. You have your problems.

Jim: Tell us, did you have a fireplace? Build an atmosphere for us, so we can get an idea of what life in this log cabin was like?

Ray: This is a log cabin, a very crude log cabin. As far as I can remember, we had a cookstove, and a kind of barrel-type stove for heat. Heat really wasn't a major problem.

Jim: What did your dad and uncle do up there. Did they prospect?

Ray: They did some prospecting in the spring and summer and they trapped throughout the winter.

Jim: Do you recall, at your young age, what kind of animals they trapped?

Ray: All I can remember is marten and wolf.

Jim: Marten and wolf, that's pretty good. Did they hunt moose and enter into the full frontier lifestyle?

Ray: Whenever we ran short of meat, all I can remember is living on moose and caribou.

Jim: I see. Did you do any fishing?

Ray: Yes, we did.

Jim: At four or five years old, were you a fisher person?

Ray: I tried my hand at it.

Jim: Did you ever have any interesting experiences that might be a tale of excitement to the listening audience, regarding any of your trips in and around that area?

Ray: I never had a problem with animals. I can remember one instance, we went fishing one morning in a creek that was near our cabin. During the day, we had a lot of rain, and there's a log over one creek where we would always cross. On the way back, the creek had flooded. Lo and behold, I slipped and fell in.

Jim: What happened? Did you get rolled down the creek?

Ray: No, luckily the jacket I was wearing somehow had gotten stuck in some of the branches of the fallen tree that we had used. At that point, my dad went down underwater looking for me. I can't remember how much time actually elapsed, but he did get me.

Jim: I see. So you were actually submerged.

Ray: I was submerged and tangled in the branches. That's about the last I remember.

Jim: If it wasn't for Dad coming back looking for you and grabbing you out of there, I might not have a guest today.

Ray: I was just fortunate that the tree had branches.

Jim: How long did you live out there in the wilderness area?

Ray: Let's see, we were there from probably mid-summer through winter, and I believe it was late spring that we came out. We were there for about 9 or 10 months, if I remember right.

Jim: That's quite a bit for a young man of that age to remember, I realize that. How did you get in? Did you go upstream or downstream?

Ray: We went upstream by boat. It was an old prop motor. In fact, I do remember breaking many many shear pins on the way up the river. When we came out it was early spring, because I remember we had a pilot come in and pick us up. He landed on the river.

Jim: Did you and your family have enough of the bush? Was that why they left?

Ray: No, I think it was something that was predetermined. It was just an adventure that my father and uncle had in mind. They wanted to try it out— it was something they wanted to do.

Jim: Your dad is kind of an adventurous-type fellow who likes to be outside, work outside and, if I'm not mistaken, he's currently a miner.

Ray: Yes, he is.

Jim: When you came back out, you were around six or seven and about ready to start school.

Ray: I was in the second grade at the time. In fact, I did have some schooling in the village of Allakaket before returning to Fairbanks.

Jim: What was school like in Allakaket? Was it different?

Ray: I can only tell you that it was a one-room schoolhouse with all the grades in one room.

Jim: That must have been an experience. When you got back to Fairbanks, where did you go to school?

Ray: I went to Denali School from the second through the fourth grade.

Jim: Give us a rundown, and then where?

Ray: In the fifth grade, I was at Nordale (Elementary). Sixth, I went to Joy (Elementary). Seventh and eighth was at the Old Main School. Ninth was at Ryan (Middle School), and I finished out tenth through twelfth at Lathrop (High School).

Jim: I see. And did you take some time off after high school?

Ray: I took one year off after high school. Of course, at the time the North Slope was going real well and there was always a chance of getting a job there.

Jim: Did you work there?

Ray: No I didn't. Things didn't pan out that way. About a year later, I enrolled at the University.

Jim: What did you major in at the University of Alaska, Ray?

Ray: I started off in the mining engineering program, and switched to geological engineering about midway through the second year.

Jim: That was in the School of Mineral Engineering?

Ray: Yes it was.

Jim: Well that's interesting to note. Did you obtain a degree?

Ray: Yes I did. I graduated as a geological engineer.

Jim: What year was that?

Ray: In 1981.

Jim: In 1981. I had an experience at the University of Alaska that was interesting. I came from a school in California up to the University of Alaska because that's where I intended to enroll for my master's degree, but I came up for field camp at the University at the beginning of the summer, and of course I enjoyed that. That experience provided the outdoor background that I needed to relate to when I took my formal, in-class preparations for my master's degree. It was exciting from that standpoint, but the following year, I was hired as the teaching assistant in that field camp. You deal with a lot of different aspects of geology and environment that you don't quite think about. A lot of people think, "Well you go out in the field and you do geologic mapping and it's pretty much routine, educational stuff," but in the state of Alaska, you have to put up with a lot of other things, like mosquitoes and rain.

Ray: You sure do.

Jim: And I know that in order to obtain your baccalaureate degree from the University of Alaska, it was required that a School of Mineral Engineering student take that field camp.

Ray: Yes it was.

Jim: You took your field camp course long after I had gone away. What kind of interesting experiences besides geologic mapping did you have, in terms of animals, weather and things of that nature?

Ray: We didn't really see any animals at any of the places. We spent about two weeks just east of Cantwell. For those two weeks it rained just about every day. In fact, the creek we were at was nearly flooding by the time our two weeks had expired.

Jim: So you had rain as your major problem?

Ray: Yes, it rained constantly.

Jim: I don't know if anybody has ever been out trying to do field mapping in the rain, but it gets pretty difficult.

Ray: Yes, it does. In fact, it can't hardly be done.

Jim: Were you living in tents? We had tents.

Ray: Yes.

Jim: You had to do all your write-ups in tents?

Ray: Everything was in tents.

Jim: That's interesting. Ray, we've got a caller here and let's see what they have to say. Hi, you're on the air.

Caller: Yes, Jim Madonna?

Jim: Yes.

Caller: Yeah, this is Larry Taylor. I was listening to your show there.

Jim: Hi Larry, how are you doing?

Caller: Just fine.

Jim: How's everything out at the Fortymile?

Caller: Just great, the water's a little low.

Jim: It is? Are people getting gold out there?

Caller: Yes they are.

Jim: Well, I'm glad to hear it.

Caller: Yeah, in fact Ray can attest to that. He was telling me earlier this week.

Jim: Oh, you've been in to visit Ray?

Caller: Yes I have, and was in there again today looking for him, and I heard him on your show.

Jim: Well, that's good. Hey, tell us where's "in there."

Caller: Into the Oxford Assaying and Refining Company right there on Wendell Street.

Jim: Okay, we're going to have Ray talk about that a little bit in just a few minutes.

Caller: Oh good!

Jim: You bet! What else is going on in the Fortymile?

Caller: Well, really the situation has kind of calmed down since we got settlements with the BLM and the Sierra Club. Really the dredges are going along real good. Some of the Cat miners have started up and are doing pretty good out there, but it's give and take.

Jim: Well we're glad to see that the mining is resuming and that everything has been settled. A lot of the problems have been cleared out of the way; everybody can live in harmony with one another.

Caller: Well, we've been hearing a lot of it on your show, because we listen to it all the way out there in the bush.

Jim: Well, you probably know I've had a number of flattering letters from the people out in the bush areas, and I want to thank everybody for dropping us a line and letting us know what's going on and I'm really pleased with the fact that you would take the time to phone and let us know what's going on in the bush. I appreciate, most of all, hearing that this radio station reaches that far. My goodness, how far is that, Larry?

Caller: About 200 air miles and 350 by road.

Jim: So we've got quite an arm there.

Caller: Well, you know, the main thing I called for, Jim, was I've been in town here several times and I've been out there several times, and I've never been able to stop long enough or to get to a phone at the right time when you guys were on the airways talking to everybody out here in the public about gold mining and the old times. I just wanted to let you know how much we appreciate you.

Jim: Well, my friend, I'll tell you, I really appreciate hearing that from you. If there're any suggestions you might have, drop me a line and I'll try to put them on the air for you.

Caller: Well, I'll tell you what, you put more people on like Ray.

Jim: Okay, my friend, thank you for the call.

Caller: I just thought I'd call to say thanks. Bye.

Jim: Thank you, Larry. Well, that's your fan club. How do you like that, Ray?

Ray: Real good.

Jim: Well, where were we? We were talking about field camp. You know, I had an experience that was kind of animal related. At the time of field camp, this was a couple of years ago. Actually, it was, my goodness let me think about this; it was about 20 years ago, I guess. I was a single parent at the time. I was in McKinley Park, leading the camp; it was permissible for me to bring my son along. This one day, we were required to go into an outback camp. We were hiking up one trail, one drainage system, and then we had to make a right turn into a small creek that drained into that larger river drainage. We were walking up through the thicket there and encountered a sow and two cubs. That was quite an experience for the two of us to confront the grizzly bear in that environment. As you know, it's not legal to carry firearms in the park, so we were unarmed. I can't express myself clearly enough as to the fear that ran through my body when I took a look at that sow and her two cubs. She and her cubs ran off, and here we are doing Alaska Gold Trails. Ray, we were talking about school and the University of Alaska. It's interesting to note that while you were studying for your degree I took a refresher class.

Ray: At the same time I was. That's right.

Jim: I was taking a refresher class in ore deposits. Tom Smith was teaching it.

Ray: Right.

Jim: My, but that was a few years ago. We really had a lot of fun in that class.

Ray: Yes it was—a lot of work though.

Jim: Yeah, a lot of work. What do you think about your education at the University of Alaska School of Mineral Engineering? You think you did pretty well there?

Ray: I think it was a real good education.

Jim: You know this School of Mineral Engineering has gone through several cycles when people have attempted to reorganize it and do away with it as an individual school and blend it with other programs. It was interesting to know that one student said to me one time, "Well, how would you feel if you graduated from the School of Mineral Engineering and went out to get a job and you told them you graduated from a particular college and they said, 'Oh yeah, we remember that school, that's the one they did away with.' That wouldn't reflect well on your education, would it?

Ray: No it sure wouldn't.

Jim: So he was out there beating the bushes for support for the School of Mineral Engineering to maintain its autonomy and integrity within the University of Alaska. That was interesting to me to note that the students were putting that much energy into it. Anyway, let's go on, just for a brief moment, to the kind of work you finally ended up in when you graduated from college? What was the first job you had?

Ray: Well, the year after I graduated I started work at Oxford Assaying and Refining back in the spring of 1982.

Jim: 1982. When did Oxford Assaying and Refining originate?

Ray: It opened a Fairbanks office here I believe in the fall of 1980.

Jim: 1980. You said Fairbanks office. Does it have another office?

Ray: Yes we do. We have one in Anchorage that opened, I believe, about six months prior to the Fairbanks office.

Jim: I see. And you do basically the same thing. Do you do assaying?

Ray: Yes. Oxford does both smelting, assaying and refining of precious metals.

Jim: I see, and where do you do the smelting and assaying?

Ray: Presently everything is done in our Anchorage office.

Jim: Do they do the refining there as well?

Ray: No, the refining is done through our parent company, which is Oxford Metal Recovery, which is based in New York.

Jim: I see. And that's closer to the trading area?

Ray: Very close.

Jim: Do you trade in terms of 400-ounce Good Delivery bars?

Ray: Yes we do. In fact, well it's a combination of some bars and some of what they call shots.

Jim: Tell us a little about your experience when you walked into Oxford Assaying and Refining and asked for a job. Did your education help get that job?

Ray: Yes it did. However, I noticed that others who had applied for the job had similar backgrounds.

Jim: You went to work for them in 1982. You have been with them quite a few years, and we just had testimony that a lot of people appreciate your efforts. That was nice that Larry gave us that call and that bit of support. Tell us a little bit about what would happen if I walked in with a poke full of gold. Let's say I had a hundred ounces of gold. Do people walk in with that much gold?

Ray: Yes, they sure do. Sometimes more.

Jim: They do? More, like a thousand ounces?

Ray: Sometimes.

Jim: A thousand ounces of gold? If gold is $500 an ounce, that means it would be worth $500,000. Isn't that amazing, a half a million dollars, one plunk on the counter. Do you get big nuggets?

Ray: A few.

Jim: Do you ever get or see anything like a five-or ten-ounce nugget?

Ray: I've only seen one that was about 11 ounces. A miner brought it in to show us what he had found.

Jim: There are certain areas of the state that have big nuggets while others had just fine gold.

Ray: Yes, that's the way it runs.

Jim: Just because an area only has fine gold, doesn't mean that it isn't a productive area.

Ray: No, in fact, it used to be a real common statement with the miners that it's fine gold that pays the bill, the nuggets are just nice to have.

Jim: Let's say that a miner brought in a hundred ounces of gold. Would you run through the procedure of what you would do with that gold, how you would determine what the gold was worth, and how the miner would get paid?

Ray: The first decision the individual would have to make is the terms he would like for the gold. We offer a couple of different refining schedules and time lengths that pay a varying percentage. From that point, the gold is sent to our smelter, where it is smelted. After that, it is assayed. The next step beyond that would be the actual refining of the gold, whether it would be put into shot form or to become part of a good delivery bar.

Jim: Once they have it assayed, they are paid on their assay?

Ray: Right. Payment is based on the amount of fine gold that is actually recovered from that placer.

Jim: When a miner brings the gold in, there is sometimes the black sands or it might be wet or it might have some iron oxide encrustations on it. How does that fit into the scale of evaluating the gold?

Ray: Basically there is always going to be some dirt with gold even though some black sands may not necessarily be present. We have some gold that has minute hidden impurities where the gold is encrusted by something else. So there is no outward visual presence. Black sands, any oxides, sulphides and so forth are removed at the smelting stage. The batch is fluxed and melted to separate impurities from the gold itself.

Jim: Okay, and so that gives us the shrinkage. Once the gold has been fluxed and poured into a miner's bar, it is then evaluated. Is that correct?

Ray: Right, at that stage, drillings are taken out of the bar. Those drill cuttings are then assayed. From that stage, the balance of the bar is taken directly to the refinery.

Jim: What other major elements occur with the gold?

Ray: Silver.

Jim: Mostly silver. So if you have 80 percent gold and what, about 18 percent silver?

Ray: You can have right around 18 percent silver, the other two percent can be a combination of base metals.

Jim: We are running out of time, Ray, one last question: Do you like living here in Alaska?

Ray: Yes, I do. It is home.

Jim: Thank you for joining us on Alaska Gold Trails; it's been a pleasure having you. And, by the way, Ray, we like it that you live in Alaska too.

Leah Madonna
Interviewed for Jim Madonna
by
Lowell Purcell
June 29, 1989

Lowell: Well good afternoon and welcome to Alaska Gold Trails. No this is not Jim Madonna; I'm Lowell Purcell here sitting in for Jim. However, we have a very special guest here in the studio—Leah Madonna. So this hour, it's going to be everything you ever wanted to know about Jim Madonna. Leah, welcome to the show. You're an old hand at this, right?

Leah: Well, not that much of an old hand at it, Lowell.

Lowell: I've got to ask you, and it's probably a question that Jim doesn't ask you because he probably knows the answer. Where did you and Jim meet?

Leah: Would you believe that we met in a Mining Extension course; I happened to be a student interested in rocks, minerals and prospecting.

Lowell: Was this at the University of Alaska?

Leah: Yes, University of Alaska Fairbanks.

Lowell: What first brought you to Fairbanks?

Leah: Well I came up here many, many years ago. At that time, I was a military housewife, and I've been here ever since—about 30 years.

Lowell: Is that right? You got me, I think, by a year. You came up in the late '50s, right?

Leah: Correct.

Lowell: I got here in 1960. You know, Leah, we were reminiscing out there in the office here prior to the newscast, and you brought up something that I had totally forgotten. About 25 years ago, we were both in the local archery club together.

Leah: Correct.

Lowell: I wonder if the Golden North Bowhunters Association is still going?

Leah: I believe it is Lowell, I haven't shot a bow in many years, but I believe they are a very active club.

Lowell: I was not that good myself. I used what they called a low-weight bow. I spent thousands of dollars on lost arrows.

Leah: That was a common problem that we shared. I used to lose both aluminum and fiberglass arrows.

Lowell: It doesn't matter what kind they were. We figured if you could put some kind of tracer bullet in them so that you could see where they went, that might be the way to go, but they never figured out how to do that. But we are here to talk about mining today. You and I were also talking about the fact that although we were both here during the '67 flood, we pretty well killed that issue here in the last couple of days on Bill's (Walley) and my show, but let's talk about Mining Extension. There are some women in mining up here, and you're one of them.

Leah: Yes, there's an organization called Alaska Women in Mining, which consists of both lady miners, miners' wives and women who work in the industry, and those who are simply interested in the mining industry.

Lowell: So does this local group get together very often? Are there scheduled meetings?

Leah: Generally, they have a monthly meeting, fall through winter and spring. They're not too active in the summer with meetings, because everybody's out working at the mines.

Lowell: How many members do you have locally? Any idea?

Leah: I'm not sure what it is at the present time. I would guess that it is probably 40—50 members. It was the Fairbanks group that started the organization, and then later started an Anchorage branch. So we're pretty proud of that.

Lowell: What's the purpose of the group?

Leah: To promote mining, to educate the public regarding mining, to offer scholarships for young people who are interested in the industry, and also to do community-service type projects. The community has certainly given to the mining industry, and we'd like to give something back.

Lowell: Does Alaska Women in Mining, either the Anchorage or the Fairbanks organization, go down to Juneau and lobby for mining issues?

Leah: No, we are more of a service and a public relations organization. We leave the politics to others as a rule.

Lowell: Okay, if you have a question for Leah, give us a call at 479-8255, that's 479-TALK. Now I know over the years here, you've taken a lot of courses at the University of Alaska in the Mining Extension program. What might those courses consist of, and what did they do for you, Leah?

Leah: Well, I started taking the Mining Extension courses in, well beginning in 1970. As a matter of fact, even before Jim was teaching, I took courses from another professors—Willow Burrand. My purpose initially in taking them was to learn how to locate gold. Also, I was interested in rocks and minerals. If people are interested in getting out in the field in Alaska, it's an excellent course, because it covers so much that helps the student understand what they see in this country.

Lowell: Alright, you folks should know, because you can't see Leah, that she has a gorgeous hairdo. Now I'm going to have you mess it up by putting on the earphones, because I think we have a phone call for you Leah. Hi you're on the phone with Leah. Do you have a question or a comment?

Caller: Yeah Lowell, I have a question. Has there been any Japanese interests in the mining industry of Alaska? And let me follow this up with a rumor I heard that there's some Japanese or Korean business group that's thinking of building a private road from somewhere northwest of Fairbanks into the Seward Peninsula and charging tolls. I'll hang up and get your answer.

Lowell: Alright, thank you for your call, 479-8255. Leah?

Leah: I have not heard that particular rumor, although it could be true. I'm sure there is a lot of interest in hard-rock mining by foreign companies.

Lowell: Does that bother you a little bit—foreign interests coming in?

Leah: I know that has been controversial lately. It doesn't bother me, because generally, the companies that come in are dealing with local companies who for years have had claims and done their assessment work on them, but they don't have the financial backing to start a large operation. Putting these mines into production is very beneficial to our locals as well as the outside interests, and the mining industry as a whole.

Lowell: Leah, we were talking about the Mining Extension service and that you have been attending courses there. Correct me if I'm wrong, but you are the owner of Alaskan Prospectors.

Leah: That's correct.

Lowell: Were you a miner before you owned the shop—before you met Jim—or not?

Leah: No, I had an interest in rocks and minerals and the formations I viewed in Alaska, like around the Healy coal district, just a genuine interest. I was a little concerned at first that perhaps signing up for Mining Extension courses that I might be the only woman there. I thought perhaps it was just for miners, and I found out that wasn't necessarily true.

Lowell: Do you actively mine?

Leah: No, I recreationally prospect occasionally. I love to find the minerals and trace them up to the vein system. Through the courses, I have learned how to do that type of thing.

Lowell: Any gold nuggets?

Leah: No, I have to be truthful. I have never yet found that elusive gold nugget, and I'm still hoping, as any good prospector would, that one of these days I will.

Lowell: We were talking the other day. In fact, it was part of a contest that I held on the radio which was basically, "What was the largest nugget ever found in Alaska?" Of course it was the one in Nome at 107 ounces, 2 pennyweight. I couldn't believe the size of this nugget. It was like eight inches long and four inches wide. We figured out, that at the current gold prices in today's market, it would sell for about $39,000 plus. That was what this one gold nugget was worth. That's not bad, I guess. Don't all miners dream of making that big hit or finding that big nugget? Isn't that part of the excitement of it?

Leah: Oh I think it would certainly be exciting, but if you stop and think about the placer miner, for the most part, the nuggets are rare and it is exceptional to find something that large. Not all creeks would have something like that. They really count on the gold dust. When we see it in the pan we think that it isn't very much gold, but that's what they are extracting with the big equipment that pays the bills, buys the groceries and diesel and all of the materials that they need. This is what helps support the economy of this town.

Lowell: Let me ask you a question, because I really don't get a chance to hear Jim. This may sound a little naive, but are there any areas left in Alaska where the "Big Strike" might happen? I mean, where are companies looking right now?

Leah: Well I think in hardrock. Many of our local exploration companies are looking at the hardrock sources throughout the state. Areas that in the past were not economical to mine because we didn't perhaps have all the technology we have today.

Lowell: Alright Leah, we've got a couple of calls for you. Let's go back to your phone calls at 479-8255. Hi, you're on the air with Leah. Do you have a question or a comment?

Caller: Yeah, Leah?

Leah: Yes?

Caller: Leah, Dave here, a couple of quick questions and I'll hang up and listen. In your operations have you come upon fossils of any type, and what is the proper procedure when a miner discovers bones or fossils? Do they have to report it?

Leah: That's a good question. In my prospecting, I have run across fossils in the Rainbow Mountain region off of the Richardson Highway, but I don't believe that was the type you were speaking of. I think you're talking more of the mastodon-type fossils we find in the Fairbanks region. There is a requirement, but it is important to have accurate facts; you may want to check with BLM, Bureau of Land Management and certainly you could find out from the University of Alaska School of Mineral Engineering or the UAF Museum. I am certain they have the documents regarding requirements there.

Lowell: Let's go to another phone call for Leah. You're on the air.

Caller: I have a concern about some of the activities in the Lower 48 where very large foreign corporations are coming in and reprocessing tailings, and going over ground that was not profitable before, and are using cyanide to melt down the particles of gold and then gathering them in containers of some type, which leak into the ground and into the groundwater. Have you heard of any such activity up here or any possibility of any such activity?

Leah: I was fortunate for two or three years now to accompany Jim when he was giving conference presentations outside of Alaska, in particular in Nevada. I visited some heap-leach mining sites. With the containment ponds, liners, and overflow cells, these particular mines had absolutely no problem either through cyanide containment or overflow. They are monitored carefully by both the federal and state agencies at required company well sites for contamination. To answer your question, I haven't heard of any cyanide leaking into the groundwater up here.

Lowell: Heap leach was the term that you used. Can you describe that for us, what is it?

Leah: My description will be a little bit crude. The material is excavated then crushed to a proper particle size. It is then put onto an impenetrable rubber pad. Sprinkler pipes are run over the material. A cyanide solution is pumped through these pipes. It sprays like a very light sprinkler system across the ore; the heap-leach solution dissolves the precious metals as it percolates through the pile of ore and reaches the impermeable pad. These pregnant solutions run into pipes leading to tanks where they are stored for processing in the plant. As I said, that is a sketch, as I saw it. Jim could explain it better, but everything was very clean, and very safe. I visited two very large operations, as well as one one-man operation. They had not had problems. In the case of one of them, they had been using that process for many years.

Lowell: Leah, I would assume that there is some of it going on in California too, or is California now too populated?

Leah: I know that there are several. There is one in the vicinity of Sonora, California and the people of Sonora, in fact, were quite happy to have this particular mine in operation again. It has been operating for several years, and there have not been problems there to the best of my knowledge.

Lowell: Now probably the reason they were well received was because of the job opportunities and the money the mine brought into the community?

Leah: Job opportunities, right. To keep people employed in their local area, and certainly, if it can be done successfully in California, where they would be under the scrutiny of not only all of the federal and state agencies, but several strong environmental groups, similar environmentally sensitive mining operations could be developed elsewhere.

Lowell: Okay, we have a caller on the line for you Leah. Our guest is Leah Madonna. This is Jim Madonna's wife. Jim is out of state this week so Leah consented to join us on the program. Thank you for waiting. You're on the air with Leah. Do you have a question or comment?

Caller: Leah, in the Goodnews Bay area, that was platinum wasn't it, pretty much, in that area?

Leah: Yes it was.

Caller: I was just wondering. I went to a symposium at the University about seven or eight years ago, and they were talking about some of the problems they had with high clay content, which the fines used to stick to. I was just wondering if they ever came up with a way to process those fines more efficiently?

Leah: Well again, that's a little out of my line of expertise. I do know that clay is a problem in many areas of Alaska, and of course, they do have many systems that they are using in placer mining today, from high pressure washing through trommels to concentrating tables and wheels. Some people run half-inch material through desliming cyclones before running it through jig systems. It is especially important for large rocks to be very thoroughly cleaned, because clay clings to them and small gold or platinum particles cling to, or are picked up by, the clay as the clay-coated rock rolls through the sluice.

Caller: At that same symposium a fellow made a presentation on cribbing and putting shafts straight down to bedrock and hydraulicking underground. Do you know if he ever did anything with that?

Leah: I think that was Hugh Fate. I would like to say that when a miner or prospector has a problem, they can make an appointment with Jim or any of the professors at the University of Alaska School of Mineral Engineering, and they will work with you on resolving mining-related problems such as the clay problem you spoke of. They can also bring you up-to-date on what is happening with underground hydraulicking.

Caller: Okay, thank you very much.

Lowell: Thank you very much for the call. Hi. You're on with Leah Madonna. Do you have a question or a comment?

Caller: I have a question for her. Did she happen to see the 20/20 program Friday night about cyanide heap leaching in Nevada?

Leah: Yes I did. As a matter of fact, I was a little disappointed that both sides of the picture were not presented.

Caller: Well, I think that both sides of the picture were presented. They had the mining president present his case, and they had a resident who's well was poisoned with cyanide present his side of the story.

Leah: It was a very interesting program, and certainly people should be concerned about any kind of contaminante going into their system. If the host would have stuck with that particular issue perhaps we could have drawn some valuable information regarding what is being done to prevent this type of thing from happening in the future. The host was using subjective reasoning to capture the emotions of the audience rather than objective reasoning that would have provided documented facts and attracted the intellect of the audience. I will address one point that is typical of the host's flood of subjective reasoning. The host made the comment that, "Well, gold is only used for jewelry, right?" The lady she was talking to said "That's it," I have written several research papers on the uses of gold and during that time I ran across a wonderful videocassette at the University of Alaska Fairbanks Rasmuson Library on the uses of gold. It describes far more valuable uses of gold than jewelry and coins. It shows that gold is indispensable in our modern-day lives.

Caller: That's a very small inaccuracy; that was only a very small part of the overall program. The basis of the program was a look at the fact that at these huge open-pit mines in Nevada there is no reclamation that is required, there is very little in the way of pollution control required, and there are no royalties paid to the U.S. government for the right to take the gold out of federal land, which all of us own.

Leah: We can come back to just how "very small" that inaccuracy was in just a minute. This is a controversial subject that perhaps I shouldn't get into, but let me attempt to address each one of your concerns. As far as royalties are concerned, the 1872 Mining Law indicates that a person must seek to open a mine on his mining claim. The objective of this law was to add to the economy of the country. Mining companies, just as other businesses, pay both federal and state taxes on their profit. Some would say, "Yeah, but they never show a profit." That may or may not be true. However, the businesses and employees in the community, state and country where they trade make a profit and they do pay taxes. So it is simple: no mine, no employees, no economical contribution, no taxes to the government—both federal and state. We can talk about this all day. The fact is that when you sit down and think about it from an intellectual point of view rather than an emotional position, the United States benefits financially from the mining that goes on in our country that we all own, and when we think about it one way or another we all prosper. Now let's take a look at that statement, "There is very little in the way of pollution control required." There are three federal agencies—the Bureau of Land Management, the Army Corps of Engineers and the Environmental Protection Agency—in addition to the associated state agencies, that regulate pollution control. I am certain that if you contacted these agencies in Nevada and elsewhere they could supply you with mine pollution regulations sufficient to take care of your reading requirements for a year. I have binders full of requirements to mine here in the state of Alaska. What was that other one? I jotted them down here—oh, yes reclamation. I will not spend a lot of time on this subject—it isn't necessary. To open a mine like those open-pit mines in Nevada requires a Plan of Operation which includes the reclamation intended at the end of mining. This Plan of Operation is closely scrutinized by the appropriate government agencies before mining is allowed to commence. Then the mining company is required to put up a tremendous bond, up front, prior to doing the mining. I wonder if these were the types of omissions the host didn't choose to cover. Now to that "very small inaccuracy" about the uses of gold. In the past couple of decades gold has moved from its position as strictly a precious metal used in coinage and jewelry to an industrial metal. Today gold has applications in medicine, architecture, space travel and most important to modern education, the computer. Gold is inert and therefore does not corrode, therefore it is a perfect long-lasting conductor in electronic circuitry. It is used in spacecraft where safety is most needed, in satellites, in hospital equipment, and closer to home, in the computer. Gold is a modern metal with modern applications. Let me finish with this last statement. Just like auto accidents, plane crashes and rockets blowing up on the launchpad, accidents happen in the mining industry. We are not going to quit driving, flying in airplanes or sending ships into space. Similarly, if a mine, through some unfortunate accident, leaks cyanide into an individual's well, we are not going to shut down all the mines in the United States. From what I have seen government agencies do in the past, it can be suggested that they will assess the situation and draft regulations that will prevent such a thing from happening again. I am as much an environmentalist as the next American, but I am not foolish enough to think that the United States could do without mining. I would like to close my comments with this. I too have strong feelings when I hear about cyanide leaking into the water table and ultimately into someone's well. However, I want objective reporting that answers questions not attempt to stimulate my emotions. I can make up my own mind after I review the evidence.

Lowell: Alright, thank you for the call. We have a lot of calls for Leah this afternoon. Hi, you're on the air with Leah Madonna. Did you wait? No. Hi you're on the air with Leah Madonna. Lost that one too. You're on the air.

Caller: This is no disrespect to your guest, but if the questions get too hot and heavy for your proported experts, Lowell, perhaps you should get some new experts.

Lowell: Well, he hung up. I'll ask the question anyway, where have you been? I don't think that Leah, in her defense, ever said she was an expert, but I don't think Jim or anyone else could have answered that one any better. Leah, we were talking, at the start of the program, about the Mining Extension program at the university.

Leah: Well, what I wanted to point out, Lowell, was that the Mining Extension program has a lot to offer people, male or female, of almost any age, who are not necessarily interested in mining but wish to learn more about their natural surroundings. Perhaps they are interested in rock and mineral collecting, or just knowing more when they go out in the field, say fishing or hunting. It is a program where a woman doesn't have to feel uncomfortable. She can go freely and enjoy and learn. That's a good place to ask about environmental concerns. If anything, these programs through the University are interested in environmentally sensitive mining.

Lowell: Okay, let's go back to your phone calls at 479-8255, that's 479-TALK

Caller: Hello, am I on the air?

Lowell: Yes, you are.

Caller: Hello Leah, this is Rachelle Elliot. I missed the last 15 minutes, but I just took the Rock and Mineral Identification class this spring, and I want to continue. I feel that I might repeat a little of what you have already done. Where do I go from here? I want to take more classes. I'm a woman, naturally, a little bit nervous. I'm not a gold miner—purely fun, recreational. I'm interested in geology. What did you do? How did you do it? What courses did you take? Did you take it over years and years?

Leah: Well, I took some of the courses several different times, but of course, in the last few years, Jim has developed a mining technology program, both a one-year and a two-year program, so that you have courses in rocks and minerals, basic prospecting, geochemical prospecting and many others. In addition, he started and led two mining tours to Australia, which included a lot of ladies.

Caller: I'm glad you brought that up. When are you going to do the next one?

Leah: Well, I don't know. Of course, that's up to the University and Mining Extension, but it was interesting. We had a BLM (Bureau of Land Management) lady who worked in the Anchorage offices, and we had a Fish and Game biologist who worked there, as well as a Bureau of Mines geologist, and we also had local Fairbanksans who were simply interested in learning more about the mining industry, seeing how it was done in another country. Of course, it wasn't all play. We had a lot of fun, but we visited all types of mines and saw our share of animals, including kanga-roos. In addition, we had to write reports, and it was the first time that Mining Extension students were involved in the Placer Mining Confer-ence that spring, to present a paper and poster. Something interesting about that course too, there were some who could not go to Australia, but in conjunction with our part of the course, which was called Mining and Mill-ing, the students who stayed in the Fairbanks area had homework and projects to do, so that when we all got back together we presented the poster sessions at the Placer Mining Conference. Since that time there have been some who have given their first formal presentation and have been published.

Caller: I attended part of the Placer Mining Conference this spring too. I got to go down to the Valdez Creek Gold Mine, and I went to a couple of sessions, but I'd be very interested in that Australian trip. I'd be ready for it by the time it's offered again.

Lowell: How different is mining in Australia from here? Do they use the same techniques? Were you able to gather any new ideas?

Leah: Well, where we have a lot of cold and a lot of water, in Australia, the opposite is true. In many areas, it is dry and very little water. They cer-tainly have environmental concerns there, but Australia is a tremendously large country and its population is growing and they've been mining for many many years. The interesting thing is that the people seem to grow up there recognizing that mining is important not just financially but to build-ing their country. It starts with mining and goes through the process to the fabrication of products they use everyday.

Lowell: Is our caller still on the line?

Caller: Yes I am. I just wanted to make one comment. I found when I took the Rock and Mineral Identification course, I was interested in geol-ogy. I think that course and the weekend course about the history of gold mining, with the associated field trip, would be wonderful for any-body who lives in Fairbanks that's interested in our history and what's happened here. Thank you.

Lowell: Alright, thank you very much for your call. Our guest this week on Alaska Gold Trails is Leah Madonna. I'm Lowell Purcell sitting in for Jim Madonna, and we're taking your phone calls at 479-8255. Leah, we were talking earlier and you mentioned that the courses offered by the Mining Extension service are non-credit courses. So basically, a person has got to really want to do this, right?

Leah: That's right. These are public service courses that are open to people from all walks of life—male or female. If you're essentially interested in mining or prospecting from a recreational point of view, or just learning more about these things in nature, it's something that you'll probably find interesting. That's the way I got into it. I'm not a miner. I have never been a miner. I have no intention of being one, but I am interested in collecting rocks and minerals and studying the terrain I'm looking at. Out of 30 students, maybe one or two would eventually wish to become a geologist or enter a related field. It just opens up your eyes to many different fields that would lie in either teaching or the study of earth science.

Lowell: When I was a kid I had an interest in rocks for a couple of years. Did you as a little kid have a little rock collection going, like a lot of us did?

Leah: Yes, I did for awhile, Lowell, and then I got away from it. It was only when I came to Alaska and started seeing these beautiful mountains and scenery that I got back into it. I wasn't thinking of mining, I just wanted to know more about how these things happen. I didn't understand what I was seeing because I'm from flatland. I'm from Florida, and this was all new to me.

Lowell: Okay, would you say it rekindled an old interest that led to a desire for a deeper understanding rather than just the rock collection?

Leah: That's right. I wanted to know more about it. Like I said, Mining Extension—the name doesn't really cover all of what you get out of the courses. Jim starts his courses with the beginning of time and comes forward. You learn about volcanoes, different rock types—igneous, metamorphic, sedimentary—as well as the minerals.

Lowell: You mentioned the Australia trip. Is there anything planned this year or next year regarding an Australian trip available to people from Fairbanks?

Leah: That's probably a question that would be answered by Jim Madonna at Mining Extension.

Lowell: So you would recommend again as we wrap up this afternoon's edition of Alaska Gold Trails that if someone has an interest in Mining Extension courses that they contact the Mining Extension Service at the University of Alaska Fairbanks and go from there.

Leah: That is correct.

Lowell: Leah, thank you for being with us.

John Miscovich
with
Jim Madonna
March 25, 1988

Jim: Welcome to Alaska Gold Trails, ladies and gentlemen. Today, our guest is Johnny Miscovich from Flat, Alaska. How are you doing today, Johnny, and thanks for being on Alaska Gold Trails with us.

John: Well good afternoon, Jim. I'm glad to be back in Fairbanks, and always feel at home here since I graduated from high school here in 1936. Fairbanks has sure grown since then. It's nice to meet the old-timers that are still around.

Jim: Johnny, tell us a little bit about your background. Were you born in Alaska?

John: Yes, I was born over at Flat. And when I mention Flat to a lot of people today they just laugh, but when I say eight miles east of Iditarod, why they know exactly where I'm from. I'm one of seven children of the Peter Miscovich family of Flat, and I've lived there all my life, going on 71 years now.

Jim: Tell us a little bit about Flat in the early days, Johnny. And by the way, how did Flat originate?

John: Well, Flat originated when the Iditarod stampede took place. And the Iditarod stampede was the third largest in the state of Alaska. It was Fairbanks, Nome, and then Iditarod. And Flat,being eight miles from the river terminal point at Iditarod, became the central area for servicing all the mines in the area of Flat, which go out 15—16 miles from Flat to the south and to the north and east, and so Flat got its name from Flat Creek, which comes into Otter Creek right at the town of Flat. It's not flat, by any means, because it's surrounded by fairly high mountains, and it's just a valley that's about 20 miles long, running into the Iditarod River, and about a mile wide.

Jim: I think Flat had a pretty large population in the early days, didn't it?

John: Yes, the area around Flat had a population of—and there's conflicting reports but I think—around five or six thousand would be a good number to use, because they were migrating in and out as the stampede took place. So there wasn't a fixed population there because they were coming and going.

Jim: You know, I heard that it was on Christmas Day 1908 that they made the discovery up there on the Iditarod. Was that accurate?

John: Well yes, the discovery of gold was on the Discovery Claim, which is about three miles east of the town of Flat, by John Beaton, on Christmas

Day 1908. He was very fortunate to be able to pan some gravel that was exposed along Otter Creek, which runs through the valley, and he found this rich pay—him and a fellow by the name of Frank Dikeman, who was his partner.

Jim: Johnny, tell us a little bit more about Flat and being raised in the Flat area in the early days.

John: Well, Flat in the early days was a community of, as I said, during the early stampede several thousand people, and then it dwindled down to a few hundred when World War I came along because it took a lot of the men out of Flat, and when the war was over it never did revive like it was before the war, and then when the tractor and bulldozer came into being in 1934, my father shipped the first Caterpillar tractor (dozer) into Flat, and that started the movement on to more tractors, and mining revived again because of the machinery and the price of gold going up to $35 an ounce. Then of course, World War II came along and that shut Flat down again. But during the early years Flat was a very active community. It had all the facilities of a city. Iditarod was incorporated. It had three newspapers, it had a bank and several stores. There was I think about 15 or 16 saloons operating, and the dog teams were bringing the mail in from Seward and Anchorage, and then later from Nenana down to McGrath and then over to Flat. So we enjoyed life during those early days. And I moved out of Flat for the first time, having to go to high school here in Fairbanks, in 1931, and that was the first time that I was able to see a moving picture show.

Jim: Is that right, they didn't have anything like that in Flat?

John: No, they had a lot of things moving, but they didn't have a moving picture show.

Jim: What was Fairbanks like when you came in to go to school?

John: Well, when I came out of Flat the first time, my brother George and I were flown to Fairbanks in a Fairchild 71; we landed up by the Buzby Ranch, which is now Ladd Field, and when I saw Fairbanks, built along the winding Chena slough, my gosh, I thought, what a large place I'm gonna move to.

Jim: Tell us, was there pavement on the streets at that time, Johnny?

John: No, there wasn't. Fairbanks was a pretty dusty place during the dry weather. There was Weeks Field, of course, operating here in Fairbanks as the airport. And the railroad, of course, was a big event, going to and from Seward, and of course the trail to Valdez was open. Fairbanks was a real fine community and I enjoyed those early years a great deal.

Jim: Were they dredging here in the Fairbanks area when you came into the high school, John?

John: Yes, the FE Company had already started and they were dredging at Chatanika.

I remember going out there for the first time to see the big dredge with a fellow by the name of Leonard Weltzin—his father was working on the dredge and that was quite an exciting trip to see those big monsters churning away.

Jim: Did you ever have an opportunity to work on any of the dredges?

John: No, I never did work in the Fairbanks area, because we would go back to Flat every spring, and when school was out, and sometimes before school was out, Noel Wien would fly us back to Flat, and we would take off from Fairbanks, making the 400 miles non-stop because there weren't any airports in between. McGrath had a small airport that was usually flooded in the spring, so Noel would look at the weather to the southwest, and when he felt he could go and come back, why, we would take off.

Jim: I see. You attended school here for four years, is that right, John?

John: That is correct.

Jim: Was that at Main School? Was that the structure that was here, or was there another school at that time?

John: Well, when we came up here it was a big wooden schoolhouse and I think there were about 125 students in the Fairbanks high school, and that building burnt down during the course of my high school here and we thought high school was going to be over for a while, but then we were put in the Eagles' Hall and in the Presbyterian Church, and we carried on somehow.

Jim: Just how did that school burn down?

John: Well, I really don't remember the particulars on that, but I think it was in the basement where they had the boilers for the heating plant.

Jim: During that period of time a lot of the structures in and around Fairbanks, say from 1930 up until the '50s had a problem with fires, as I recall.

John: Well, they did, because they were burning wood and coal, of course, and stovepipe fires were quite common, and of course the fire service was limited at that time. They had a good fire department but there were problems during the 60—70 below weather like we had during those years in the winter months.

Jim: Johnny, tell us what you did following your experiences at high school here in Fairbanks. Tell us what kind of activities you entered into out there at Flat.

John: Well, when I left high school here in Fairbanks, my father and mother had been at Flat for 25 years and pickings were pretty slim until he got the first tractor and bulldozer, and that year he had a very good cleanup, so he decided he would make a trip to the big outside again. He hadn't been out there since 1910 when he came to Alaska with my mother and my older brother George. It was during the Christmas break at school, and my father wrote me a letter telling how exciting it was going to be to see big Seattle after all these years, and it made me get itchy feet too. The weather was about 50 below in Fairbanks, and I didn't like the school too well anyway, so I got on the train and went down to Seward and got on Alaska Steamship and joined my father and mother and brother in Seattle.

Jim: Well, that was a great trip. Tell us about that Alaska Steamship. Was that a steamship company that was running back and forth between Seward and Seattle, is that it?

John: Well, yes. The Alaska Steamship Company and the trips on those boats were probably the most memorable days that I can remember, because we had six or seven days together with a bunch of people we knew, and we would stop at all the ports, 'cause they would be loading fish and unloading supplies, and we really had a great time, except possibly for the rough trip across the gulf when everybody was feeding the fish.

Jim: Is that what you call it, John, feeding the fish? OK, tell us about your experiences and what the Outside looked like to you during that first experience.

John: Well, for a young boy, as I was, going to Seattle for the first time and looking at all those tall buildings and then going up the elevator to the top of the Smith Tower and looking down at all the buildings, it was quite an experience. And of course, the clanking streetcars—it was during the holiday season, there were thousands of people on the streets, and believe me it's quite a shocking experience for someone coming out of Flat.

Jim: So it was a social shock. John, following that period of time, did you enter into mining?

John: Well, I was in mining, along with my father and the family at Flat and the older brother. When the tractor of course did such a good job, my father wanted more machinery and we started looking at backhoes. So we had a lot of hard bedrock to dig at Flat, and my father felt a backhoe would do a better job than a dragline, which everybody was shipping in at that time. So we shipped the first yard-and-a-half P&H backhoe from Harnischfeger Industries Inc. in Milwaukee to Flat, and that was the only backhoe, really, in the northwest states, and the only one in Alaska.

Jim: Did it prove to be more efficient than the dragline, for your applications?

John: Yes, the backhoe increased our production further and we began to take out a lot more money and there were a lot of other properties in Alaska that prospectors had gold nuggets in their pockets from, and my father always felt, "Well, he made it in Alaska, he'll spend it in Alaska." so we then branched out in the Manley Hot Springs area on Amelia Creek. We were in the Circle District on Butte Creek, right off of Birch Creek. And then we later moved into Fairbanks Creek, in partnership with the Sathers. And we were up in the Goodpaster District with John Hajdukovich. And then we also went down into the Goodnews Bay area on Watermoose Creek. Plus going into the Ruby area on Poorman and Flat Creek. So we really were quite an extended family operation.

Jim: Now, you mentioned early in the show, John, that you had a number of brothers and sisters. Were they also heavily involved in mining in Alaska?

John: Yes, they were. The Miscovich family at Flat was a family operation for many years, before we moved out of there, and in 1940 there were four boys and three girls in the family. We formed what was called Pete Miscovich and Sons, which the four brothers and father were involved in, and we operated as a partnership for many years under that name. We later bought a dredging company at Flat, a three-and-a-half-cubic-foot dredge, which we ran for a number of years, and so we were well extended in the state of Alaska in the gold mining business.

Jim: Tell us a little more about Otter Dredging Company. That three-and-a-half-foot bucket—how much gravel would a bucket, line dredge like that, with a three-and-a-half foot bucket, process in a single day, or a 24-hour period, John, can you give us an idea?

John: Well, that was a wooden-hull construction, shipped to Flat from Nome, where it had gone in on a property that failed, and there was a promoter, by the name of George Riley, who shipped it into Flat and took over the claims on Flat that the drift miners had. And by the way, George Riley was shot at Flat by a crew member that he had. The fellow that shot him was hung in Fairbanks here behind the old wooden courthouse that they had, and that was a good lesson for promoters, of course. It was a tragedy, but it was certainly one that stopped promoting. And so he put the dredge in at Flat, and after he was shot in 1918 the dredge went into limbo. The dredge could handle about 2500 cubic yards in 24 hours, and could take about 18 feet below the water level, and it was quite an efficient plant. It did quite well during those years.

Jim: Johnny, give us a little background on this Miscogiant that I've heard so much about over the years. I have to bring a little personal experience into this. I have been attending gold mining conferences in Alaska ever since they began and this is the conference that's occurring right now, which is the 10th Annual Conference on Alaska Placer Mining, and that's where I first met Johnny Miscovich a number of years ago, when he gave his presentation on the Miscogiant, and I still remember the major portion of that presentation. As somebody else said, "You can always tell the effectiveness of a talk—it's value is based on how much the listener can tell his wife about it the next morning at breakfast." And I'll tell you, Johnny, I can still remember some of the points that you made about the Miscogiant. And I'm going to let you tell us about your experiences and how it came about that you developed the Miscogiant.

John: Well, Jim, that is a very long story, but I'll shorten it up within the time frame that we have. In Alaska, before the advent of the tractor and bull-dozer and all the other heavy equipment that you see today, all mining and material was moved with water, and it was called a hydraulic giant, and it was a very cumbersome, very heavy and hard-to-operate tool. And so, as a boy, working the monitor at Flat, during my early years, 10 hours a day, I always felt there ought to be a better way. My father was a very innovative man. He came from Yugoslavia, without an education, but educated himself here in the United States. And so, having probably rubbed off a little of what he had, I began to think about improving what is called the hydraulic giant. Now when I started, back before the war, in 1939, there were many people in the Fairbanks area, old timers, who had jobs as hydraulic monitor operators, and when I was talking about developing a fully automatic water-controlled giant, they looked at me, and would look at each other and walk away, and that was the response I got in those early years. However, when I went into the Army for four years or a little better, and when I got back out I immediately started improving the design of the hydraulic giant, because we took on a property down in the Ruby area that had about 60 feet of overburden. And it was necessary to cut our costs down, reduce our crew, in order to make a profit. It was necessary to do something in order to stay in business. So I went to the States, and I was in contact with some very good drafting engineers out there, and we started working on what became known as the Intelligiant, which got its name from a giant with intelligence. Now, this was a fully automatic pre-set pattern control, which has now gained international fame, and from there, of course, it's a very long and interesting story where it became involved in fire fighting, the missile program, the Vietnam War, and many many other industrial applications that I can't even begin to tell you about.

Jim: So it started out as a gold mining device and ended up having application in a wider field. Now, they're currently on the market, isn't that correct, John?

John: That is correct. I had patents on the Intelligiants for 17 years, and they expired in 1969. So after they expired, of course, the patent became public domain, and now every fire company in the United States and in Europe, England, over in China, Japan, Russia, they're all building the same design and using it in their mining operations, and the use is on the increase— tremendous increase.

Jim: Johnny, tell us a little bit more about your experiences. I understand that you're now mining once again out in the Flat area, is that correct?

John: That is correct, Jim. The placers of Otter Valley have been pretty well mined out, but at the head of the placer deposit, there's a deposit known as the Golden Horn, and it's a lode structure. I bought the Golden Horn from Bob Lyman in 1969 and have been developing it as a hardrock and residual-lode property, and it looks very encouraging. The Doyon native corporation has selected four townships in the area, and we're in the northeast township. So we're hoping that this work that I'm doing is going to lead into becoming one of the large, if not the largest open-pit mining operations in the state of Alaska. We have a lot of very important minerals there besides gold and silver, and that is what we need more of here in Alaska so that we can employ people and develop a little income for the state treasury, which is badly needed at this time.

Jim: Johnny, there's an activity going on in Fairbanks this week called the 10th Annual Conference on Alaska Placer Mining. You recently gave a paper at that conference, covering the Golden Horn, is that correct?

John: That is correct. I presented this paper as a follow-up on what Tom Bundtzen of the DGGS (Division of Geological and Geophysical Surveys) has been writing about, as well as other people who have been in the area, and so I will continue doing that so I can keep an update on what I'm doing over there at Flat, and I'll be going back in there about April the 20th.

Jim: John, we have a call. Hi, welcome to Alaska Gold Trails, you're on the air with Johnny Miscovich.

Caller: I've certainly enjoyed the program today. It's been real interesting. And he just reminded me of something. I've lost track of some old friends of mine, Carl Lundfelt or rather his son Buzz. Could you shed any light on that?

John: Yes, Carl passed away in Anchorage some years ago, and I believe Buzz is in the Anchorage area.

Caller: Buzz is in the Anchorage area? Well, wonderful. I'm glad to hear that and I sure do appreciate it. Thank you.

Jim: Well, we were discussing the placer conference here, and just one quick question. What do you think of the conference this year? Do you think it is doing what it is intended to do, and that is provide a little something for everybody?

John: Well, I've certainly enjoyed the conference. I flew up from Los Angeles to attend it, day before yesterday, and I hope that this conference will pass a message to Governor Cowper that he should take a greater interest in the problem that the miner has and get his staff and his legislators and the people in Juneau on track there to see if we can't help them out a little bit more.

Jim: Johnny, we've got another call. Hello, welcome to Alaska Gold Trails. You're on the air. Do you have a question for Johnny?

Caller: Hello, Uncle John, this is your nephew Andy, and I just called up to say hello. It's been nice hearing you on the radio there.

Jim: Thanks for the call, Andy. Sorry we are running out of time. You're going to hear about the placer mining conference on the front page of the Daily News-Miner today, and an article by Fred Pratt, and I just want to thank Johnny Miscovich for being our guest today on Alaska Gold Trails. Johnny, thanks so much for coming on.

John: Thank you, Jim. It's been a pleasure.

Maurice 'Ozzie' Oswald
with
Jim Madonna
Anchorage, Alaska
October 9, 1988

Jim: On our traveling interview segment we are in Anchorage, Alaska, with Maurice (Ozzie) Oswald and we are looking forward to hearing how Maurice happened to come to Alaska and his experiences throughout his life here. Currently, Maurice lives in Anchorage, Alaska. Maurice, give us some of your background. Where were you born, and what was the lifestyle like where you were raised?

Maurice: Thank you for the nice introduction, Jim. I was born and raised in western Washington and grew up in the Depression years on a farm in that area. I always had an intrigue for Alaska. My grandfather was a stampeder and came over the Chilkoot Pass in '98 and came to Dawson. So I grew up with stories of Alaska and the Klondike. It was a natural thing that when I got out of high school that I would be planning to come to Alaska. So I did.

Jim: Did your grandfather have some stories that he told you?

Maurice: Yeah, he had some stories but unfortunately he passed away when I was very small. I can barely remember him, so most of his stories that I got were handed-down stories.

Jim: Did he make any big discoveries in the Klondike or did he just work the mines?

Maurice: No, he was just one of the masses that arrived after the claims were pretty well staked. He did come back with a little gold but not a significant amount.

Jim: Where did you go to school?

Maurice: I went to a small college named Grace Harbor College in Aberdeen, Washington.

Jim: Did you get a degree there?

Maurice: Yeah, I got an associate degree in science and civil engineering there.

Jim: Did you go on to more advanced schooling?

Maurice: Yes, in Alaska.

Jim: Did you graduate from the University of Alaska?

Maurice: No I didn't graduate here, but I've taken a lot of courses.

Jim: You then became a surveyor. Do you have some kind of professional engineer's or surveyor's certificate?

Maurice: Yes, I'm a registered professional land surveyor in the state of Alaska and an appointment as the U.S. mineral surveyor through the (U.S.) Interior Department.

Jim: What year did you come to Alaska?

Maurice: I came to Alaska in 1949, the year I got out of high school. I went to work for the FE Company (Fairbanks Exploration Company) in Fairbanks.

Jim: I didn't know that. How interesting. Tell us about it.

Maurice: Started out as a laborer and found myself on a surveying crew, and that's how I got started in surveying.

Jim: You started as a laborer? Did you drive thaw points?

Maurice: No, I was mostly clearing brush and laying pipe. I worked on what they called a bull-line crew laying hydraulic pipe out in Dome Creek, actually. Worked for Jim Williams, who was the camp foreman at that time and became a life-long personal friend. I guess he saw some possibilities because he told me he was going to get me something better. The next thing I knew, he had me on a survey crew. I worked out of town and worked for Don Cook and Pat O'Neill and that's how I got started surveying and in the engineering field.

Jim: I interviewed Don Cook probably three or four months ago and he told us quite a lot about the FE Company. I also interviewed Doug Colp and he was telling me, if you didn't pack your load, they packed you out. Is that correct?

Maurice: I think that was pretty much true. They ran a pretty tight ship. They made everybody tow the line.

Jim: Now did you have the surveying background prior to coming to Fairbanks?

Maurice: No, I was just out of high school at that point.

Jim: Was it the position with the FE Company and the surveying crew that you were on that sparked your interest in surveying?

Maurice: Yes, it really was. Of course mining, I had a ready-made interest, probably through my grandfather, but then working for the company there I had an increased interest. Then, that winter, when I was working, I went to night school at the University. I took some courses. One of them was from Earl Beistline so that's how I got to know Earl. I actually had intended to go ahead and further my education in mining engineering, but it seemed about that time was a real flat period in mining. It didn't look like it had much of a bright future for the next few years, so I broke off into civil engineering.

Jim: This mining business is kind of cyclic in Alaska isn't it?

Maurice: It certainly has been.

Jim: Not only the price of the commodity, but also the time it takes to initiate a mining operation here. There was something I wanted to ask regarding the University of Alaska. Did you find that there was a lot of energy in those days in regards to the professors associating with the mining industries and recruiting students into the School of Mines?

Maurice: The University at that time was a very small school. I think that there were only about 200 students. Of course, Earl was very interactive with the students and the mine tours and things of that type, but other than that, I don't recall that was the case. If you wanted to go, fine. If you didn't, well up around here nobody really cared.

Jim: How long did you work for the FE Company?

Maurice: I worked for them for that full year into the winter of 1949-50. We ran out of work in the winter. I had some friends in Anchorage. I came down here and ended up going to work for the Bureau of Land Management on a survey crew. That was sort of the next event of my career was working for BLM for the summers and I was going back to school in the winters. I worked all over Alaska for BLM in the summers, all over Southeast—Ketchikan, Wrangell, Petersburg, Juneau, Admiralty Island, all over the Kenai Peninsula—Homer and Seldovia, and then we worked up into the Interior from Susitna Valley, up to Tok Junction. You name it and we were there.

Jim: Why were you surveying this land?

Maurice: We were surveying homesteads and homesites, trade manufacturing sites and some new section-type rectangular networks, a bit of everything. I was mostly on a crew doing homesteads, the remote site parcel surveys. A lot of fly-in type things. It was fascinating, I was young and loved the outdoors. It was an intriguing experience.

Jim: You must have had not only the enjoyment of the outdoors, but the reward of meeting a lot of the old-timers that were in these areas.

Maurice: Yes, we did that too, and saw a lot of neat country. It was just a fun thing.

Jim: During your experiences, did you ever have any encounters that might be of exceptional interest—a bear encounter, a moose encounter? Everybody's had something.

Maurice: Yeah, everybody's had some. I didn't really have anything that significant. I scared myself with a bear down out of Homer. I was like the postman; on my day off, I had to go for a walk. On Sundays we took off, so I climbed up into the hills and was walking around looking at the country, taking pictures. Coming back down to the camp, I was going through the tall native grass. I was down in it about head high. I was walking on a game trail, watching were I was walking because the grass was overgrown on the trail pretty much. I looked up ahead of me, oh maybe ten feet, or eight feet or something. There was a bear standing up on his hind legs looking down at me in the grass. I looked up at it. I guess we scared each other because it ran off and he gave me a good case of shaky legs there for a little bit, but it was about as a close as I wanted to get.

Jim: I see. I've had some similar cases where I woke up in the morning and climbed out of the tent and had a couple of bears, a sow and a couple of cubs, outside. The excitement there, unless you've experienced it, you'll never know. You talk about your shaky legs. A person has to go through that to recognize exactly what shaky legs are all about. It's absolutely...you don't have anything left to move any longer.

Maurice: Yeah, that's right.

Jim: Might as well just sit down and take a breather. You've surveyed all over the state of Alaska. Like you said, these were in your younger days with the Bureau of Land Management. Did you ever have any survey-ing experiences on ore deposits or things of that nature that might have been particularly interesting?

Maurice: Not at that time. Primarily, it was land surveys, things that the BLM would be involved in so I really didn't get back into mining claim surveys until later. I had a little stint with the Army. I was in the Army during the Korean conflict. When I got back from there then I came back to Alaska and again worked for BLM for a year and had a family started. I just kind of thought maybe it was a good time not to be wandering all over the country anymore.

Jim: Now that you mentioned your family, when did you get married?

Maurice: In 1954.

Jim: How many children do you have?

Maurice: Five children.

Jim: Five children. Well you got busy didn't you?

Maurice: Yeah, and that was part of it. We all came to Alaska. One of them was born when I was in the Army. The oldest daughter and the rest of them were all born here in Alaska, near Anchorage.

Jim: What are their names?

Maurice: The oldest one's Connie, then Elaine, and then Maury, and Laurie and Russell's my youngest.

Jim: How old's Russell?

Maurice: Russell is 27. He's a senior at the University this year up at Fairbanks, in civil engineering.

Jim: Wonderful! Do you have any grandchildren?

Maurice: Yes, five grandchildren—one girl and the rest boys, about to have one more. They're all out of state. We don't see them very often, but I expect we'll have a couple of them back in a year and a half or so.

Jim: The Oswalds are carrying on the line.

Maurice: It seems like it.

Jim: When you got out of the Army did you come to work with BLM?

Maurice: Yes I did. I came back and worked in the Tok area. They assigned me the project of surveying new rectangular work there in the Tok junction vicinity. I spent the summer there, then in Anchorage during that winter writing up the notes. When I got that done, I got an offer from the city of Anchorage to work in their engineering department. I worked there for a year. Then I worked construction.

Jim: Were you surveying in construction?

Maurice: Surveying and engineering, some bid estimates, a variety of things, with the city of Anchorage. Then I took a job with the territory of Alaska under the Department of Lands. Actually, Phil Holdsworth was in charge of the department.

Jim: Yes, I know Phil. In fact I just interviewed him this morning. He was chairman.

Maurice: Yes, It was run by a board at that time. He was chairman of the board. I worked here in Anchorage and we kind of set up that department at the time of statehood. I was there as the chief of surveying.

Jim: When did you go to work for the territory, what year was that?

Maurice: It was in December of 1958.

Jim: Why, that was just a year before statehood.

Maurice: Yes. There was a director of, what they called, the Department of Lands and his name was Everett Brown, but Phil was chairman of the Land Board. So I got to know Phil pretty well at that time and we were able to implement a number of the programs and things in anticipation of statehood. At that time, there was the Mental Health Trust, which granted the territory a million acres. That was really why I was hired, to start doing some things on development on that million acres. That worked right on into statehood, a lot of things on oil and gas, land disposal, land subdivisions, developments, access roads and things of that type. So I worked there until about 1962. We kind of got caught up and it seemed to be slowing down. I sort of lost interest, so Lou Dickens and I went into the engineering and surveying business—at first just surveying. A year or two later, Lou got his engineer's license, so we were engineering and survey-ing. So we had the company we called Dickens and Oswald and Associates at that time. Later, we took on new partners and new initials, W and L, Walsh and Lee. Ken Walsh joined the firm and then we merged with Alaska Test Lab and Harry Lee joined the firm and then it was DOWL Engineers we called it. We were the D and the O.

Jim: So that is how DOWL Engineering got it's start. Well you then began surveying claims during patent application.

Maurice: Yes, that's right. I got an appointment, I think, in '60, or thereabouts, from the Department of the Interior. I took an exam and got the appoint-ment as a U.S. mineral surveyor. So that kind of played a role in my going into business. It was another service we offered—mineral surveys. Of course at that time, there wasn't that much demand. There was some min-ing going on in the state but it was pretty basic. Everyone that was mining was close to the cuff. There wasn't much money because the price of gold was only $35 an ounce. I think the big thing was that I was available and I talked to a lot of people. The miners were interested in patenting and they'd spend a lot of time with me, especially in the winter, talking about it—ask questions. We'd go through the procedures—how much it would cost, how much time it would take and things of that type. They all remembered that, and in the later years when the price of gold came up and when the miners had their time limit cut off after the (Alaska) Native Claims Settlement Act. They had a five-year program to begin their patent process or else be sub-ject to selection by the native corporations. They remembered that, so they came to me. That was when my mineral surveying business really picked up, back in the late '70s.

Jim: Tell us, what exactly is the track from the miner's initial stages of apply-ing to finally being given patent to his claims? What was your role in that?

Maurice: Well as a mineral surveyor, I had to watch my role very carefully because I am treated as an employee by the Department of the Interior, and it's very specific on what my limitations are in the appointment. I cannot do anything to help the miner even make an application for his patent sur-vey or anything to help him in his actual patenting process, other than doing the mineral survey, which is primarily a combination of a boundary and a legal survey that creates his boundaries, monuments and corners. I locate all of his improvements and write up a long report showing the values of the workings that he's done and verify that he has mineable ground subject to the type of mining that he's doing—things of that type, which are spe-cific rules in the mineral survey appointment.

Jim: Do you actually evaluate his ground?

Maurice: Yes. Not the in-ground reserves; I evaluate the ground to show the working—how much money is actually spent in development of the claims. To be eligible for patent, a miner has to have at least $500 worth of work expended in mine development for each claim. That can be all on one claim if he has a group—you can associate that to others. I have to verify that.

Jim: Do you actually determine whether or not he has met the Prudent Man Rule(show sufficient mineralization to justify developing a mine)?

Maurice: No. The mineral surveyor doesn't really have to know anything about geology or mining. His role is more of as a surveyor and technician, to make sure that the miner complies with the law in size dimensions of the claims and that he's done enough development to be eligible. The man that handled my appointment with the Bureau of Land Management, when I got it, advised me, the less you know about mining the better off you are. In other words, keep your nose out of the miner's business and just do what you're sent out to do. So I've always tried to be very careful with that.

Jim: The amount of work you did as a mineral surveyor probably escalated during the late 1970s when we had our mini-gold rush to Alaska. Did it fade off in the '80s?

Maurice: It sort of peaked there about in '76 into '78 and it's really been pretty consistent ever since up until this year (1988).

Jim: It is just now starting to fade.

Maurice: But already I seem to have a number of jobs again for next year. I had a backlog of surveys for awhile with the (Alaska) Native Claims (Settlement) Act. I probably had, oh, 150 or so different surveys on order, where people were working me in as they could afford it or were ready for it in one way or another. I kind of handled those on an annual basis—whoever wanted them, well I would do them, and those who didn't want them, well we'd just leave them in the file. Now BLM has gradually canceled out some of those that haven't been surveyed. I think that the interesting thing is that about four or five years ago I started getting new ones. I have the old ones that were phasing out and then I started picking up new ones that people were applying for, and that's kind of carried on. I didn't do any work, or not very much work, this year, because of my health. I had surgery last year, and I just kind of wanted to back off and do some things different for me this year, and enjoy the summer other than doing mineral surveys.

Jim: While you're on that subject—enjoying your life—we've talked a lot about how you've grown in Alaska, and what you did in terms of employment, but we haven't discussed anything about what you did in terms of enjoyment. Like the postman, you didn't have to always go for a walk, what other kinds of things do you do? You appear to be quite an outdoorsman.

Maurice: Yes, I've always enjoyed the outdoors and still do. I have a lot of good outdoor activities—fishing and hunting. We've had a cabin on the lake in the Matanuska Valley we enjoyed a lot in the years past when the family was small and growing up. We used to spend a lot of time there.

Jim: Did you build that cabin?

Maurice: I built it, yes. In fact, it was one of those nice sites on a little lake. The only trouble, it didn't have any access. So I had to drag lumber in there in the middle of winter and skid it across the lake, hand-cut everything. So it's kind of a small cabin, but it's been fun. Gradually we got the road built; now it's kind of in the middle of a subdivision. It's been subdivided around us, so it's no longer remote. As you know, I retired from DOWL Engineers the end of 1986. My wife and I bought some property on the Kenai River. We built ourselves a new house down there, and we enjoy staying down there as much as we can, fishing, boating and company—we have a lot of company. That's been an off-time activity here when I'm not doing mineral surveys, I'm usually down there enjoying the Kenai. I've also done a lot of hunting—one trip to Africa on a safari.

Jim: What an adventure that must have been.

Maurice: And I do shooting. I'm a trap shooter and have traveled all over the United States doing competitive shooting with that sport and had a lot of fun, lot of good times.

Jim: You were competitive; have you won?

Maurice: Yes, I've had some good wins.

Jim: I didn't know any of this.

Maurice: Yeah, I have been competitive and fortunate.

Jim: You're not giving yourself enough credit. Fortunate is one thing; seemingly you have had a lot of good days because of your skill.

Maurice: Yes, once in awhile, but once in awhile you get lucky.

Jim: Do you get to know all of the trapshooters from around the different clubs and who the good ones are?

Maurice: Oh yes!

Jim: So you know who the competition is. That's exciting. But more exciting is that they know who you are.

Maurice: Well yes, pretty much.

Jim: What other kind of outdoor activities have you had? You spent some time in the Interior of Alaska, in your early days. Have you spent any time there more recently other than surveying claims?

Maurice: Oh, I go back to the Interior quite often. I guess the most significant thing was when I was in business back in the middle '60s. I had a contract, we had a contract with the Department of Transportation to do the surveying and mapping for all the highway programs in the Fairbanks District. So, I got to know College Road, Steese Highway, University Avenue, Airport Way and many of those very intimately. We had to do complete surveying and mapping in recovering the subdivision corners and tying them all into the road networks. That was an ongoing two-year project. In 1964 and '65 I was up there a lot. I get back there regularly to do mineral surveys and other related jobs.

Jim: You, of course, saw Fairbanks as a fledgling town when the only street paved was Second Avenue and perhaps a little bit of Cushman (Street) up to Gaffney (Road).

Maurice: Yeah, that's what I remember. The old metal bridge over the Chena Slough that made a lot of noise when people drove over it with their chains on in the winter.

Jim: It was quite a town. What was the atmosphere like when you first entered Fairbanks?

Maurice: I think Fairbanks was a close town. It was probably a little harder to break into—a lot of really neat people, but they were kind of close-knit. The first winter that I was there, I guess I was fortunate, I played basketball in an independent league team. It seemed like it opened a lot of doors to me. I got to know a lot of people. It was a popular pastime in Fairbanks. People came out and saw the games and got to know the players. I got to meet a lot of nice people. Some of them I still have fond memories of and see once in awhile. I think those days are gone; we've lost that element.

Jim: And here we've grown to what, 50,000 people now? So, it isn't quite as close-knit as it was in those days.

Maurice: That's right. I think that there were about 6,000 people in town at that time.

Jim: What else can you tell us about your life in the initial stages here? We saw that you didn't think you had anything interesting. Now I find out that you're a trapshooter. You came to Fairbanks and worked for the FE Company. I mean, all of these things happened to just pop out from what was originally going to be a rather uneventful life. You hunt, you fish, you have a cabin on a lake. People look at that kind of lifestyle that you've led, and while you don't think it is quite so exciting, other people say, "My goodness, look what that man has done." I mean, how many guys have faced a grizzly bear in the wilds of Alaska? Very few people, especially in the lower states, have ever experienced anything like that.

Maurice: No, that's right. Especially in the lower states. I probably had my strangest bear encounter when I wasn't surveying. Lew Dickens and I used to fly down to Pilot Point to hunt ducks and geese every fall. We used to pick and clean our birds as we got them. At that time, we could have a three-day limit. We could get so many birds, and bring back a three-day limit in possession. I don't remember what that was, but it was around 20 geese or something we could get. We had been there for several days, and had gotten our limits of geese, and were on the verge of getting our limits in ducks. We had them all picked and cleaned, and so we would hang them from the struts of the float plane to drain and cool out. One morning, we got up, and we didn't have any birds left on our airplane. There was a sand dune right up in back of our camp where we had our tent set up; we crawled up there, and looked out in the dunes and here were nine brown bear.

Jim: Oh my!

Maurice: It was three mothers with twins and the twins were probably a year old. They were not small bear by any means, but they'd come in that night when we were sleeping and cleaned out our birds. Just wiped us out. We were fortunate that they didn't damage the plane. They didn't do anything. As I recall, there was a big muddy bear print on the side of the plane in one place, but it didn't damage it. So, we were lucky.

Jim: You were lucky not to have an encounter personally with the bears, and just lost the ducks. Since we have you started, tell us a little about some of the other places you have visited in Alaska.

Maurice: Well, I suppose in what you're interested in, the mineral surveys have been very significant to me. I've gotten to travel a lot. I've been to Nome, Lost River, Greens Creek, Cache Creek, Petersville, on the Kenai, just about everywhere that there's a mine or mining, I've been there doing mineral surveys. I've surveyed about a thousand mining claims over the last 10 or 12 years. I've gotten to be well known. I have a lot of good mining friends in the field. I guess as I got to going around the country more and more, doing mineral surveys, people started recognizing me as "the" mineral surveyor. At one time, I was the only one in the state. After we started getting more and more demand, BLM offered the test again and made some more appointments, so now there are a number of mineral surveyors, but still the miners looked to me as "the" mineral surveyor because they were used to dealing with me. It used to be kind of funny that I'd call someone up at Nome or something to make a room reservation, rent a car, get some equipment or something set up and I'd tell them who I was, and I'd hear silence on the phone, and I'd say, "I'm the mineral surveyor." "Oh yeah, you're Ozzie," and I'd say, "Yeah, I'm Ozzie." So, it kind of opened the door. So when I retired from DOWL...well we talked about my coming back and doing mineral surveys through them for BLM, and it just seemed like it was going to be complicated. It seemed like it was better if I just started another little company to do mineral surveys. So, what are you going to call your company? It just seemed like it was going to be, The Mineral Surveyor. So now I'm The Mineral Surveyor.

Jim: Do you have a certain amount of satisfaction when you go in and survey an area and see it come into production and become a successful mine?

Maurice: Yes. Not only that, but I get my rewards from the miners. They'll call me up and tell me, "I got my patent today." I'll see people at the conference here, and they'll say, "Boy, I'm sure glad that I got that patent thing going and listened to you when we started this. It helped me out so much." It really makes me feel good.

Jim: You have given a couple of papers at my request at various conferences. Your presentations are always well received. You will never know how much I appreciated the effort. You were always there when I needed you to give a paper. Of course, when I prepare a conference, I attempt to give it a flow pattern direction, with each paper linking with the next to give a full body of information. When I asked you to come and give a paper, it was because you always gave valuable information that was an important element in the entire flow of things. I noticed one time you said, "Gee, I think people get tired of me." You and Doug Colp—I kept calling on you a couple of times in just a very short period of time, but the flow was right and everything coupled together so nicely when the whole program was presented. I enjoyed working with you, Ozzie.

Maurice: Well thank you, Jim. I really enjoyed talking about mining claims. You know, it's been one of my most interesting topics. I not only give you the spiel, you know, I serve on the board of advisors over at the community college at the University of Alaska Anchorage. They have a survey technology department over there, and I have to give the same spiel to those classes every year. So I speak about mining claims to a lot of people. A couple of times, I have given papers to the surveying and mapping convention here in Alaska about mineral surveys, mining and mining activities. It's a favorite topic. I just enjoy it.

Jim: Well, I think we're very fortunate to have had you come into the country when you did and fill that important niche, not only from BLM's point of view but to ultimately move into the mining industry. I appreciate you joining me and giving this interview sharing some of your experiences, not only with me, but with those who will read it in the future.

Maurice: Thank you Jim. I have enjoyed this.

Tim Sander
with
Jim Madonna
Fairbanks, Alaska
October 24, 2001

Jim: Our nomadic microphone is coming to the end of the trail. Today it has stayed in Fairbanks, Alaska, where we have only traveled across town. It is October 24th, 2001, and we are here with a man who has been my close friend for over 20 years. Tim Sander, welcome to Alaska Gold Trails. You have had a very interesting life and we want to hear all about it. Let's start at the beginning. Where were you born, Tim?

Tim: I have looked forward to this interview, Jim. Thank you for the nice introduction. Now I have to live up to it. I was born in Ashland, Oregon, on September 12, 1915.

Jim: How long did you stay in Ashland?

Tim: I was told that my dad moved us up to Tillamook when I was about two and a half years old. I grew up in Tillamook, where they make the cheese.

Jim: Did you go to grade school there?

Tim: Yes, and I went to two years of high school there.

Jim: What did you do after your two years of high school?

Tim: I went to the seminary. I went to study to become a Catholic priest. There were priests who taught in the seminary in the parish in Tillamook. They made an impression on me, and that's where I wanted to go to school.

Jim: Were you a Catholic at that time?

Tim: Yes.

Jim: Before that time, were there any exciting adventures that you went through as a young boy or a young man in high school that you can relate to us— fishing, hunting, hiking, getting in trouble, throwing a skunk down the outhouse hole—whatever you did?

Tim: Well, let's see. My dad rented two different places, successively, in Tillamook. We stayed in each place about a year or so. Then he bought a place up the Wilson River. That's where I grew up. It was a beautiful place near the river; right at the foot of a hill, out in the country seven miles out of town on a road that was difficult to drive.

Jim: What was it, a farm or a ranch?

Tim: It was a 60-acre dairy farm. Some of the land was not...well, it was swampy. So he cleared it off, and made it all so it would grow grass—pasture. I learned from him how to fish. He was a great fisherman. He knew the name of every fish in the river. Whenever my mother needed something to eat for breakfast, he would go down to the river and catch one. They'd still be flopping in the pan. Hunting: I would go out with him, ducks, mostly ducks and that kind of thing. Trapping: right on the river there, he trapped mink and otter and raccoons. I learned a lot of good outdoor skills and activities from my father. He was handy at doing things. He came from Missouri, and he grew up as kind of a self-made person.

Jim: Where did he meet your mother?

Tim: I don't know the exact years or when it happened, but they met in Tillamook, as far as I know, and then he went back to Ashland because he was interested in greenhouses. He grew flowers, but it affected his health, being inside all of the time, so he had to get out. He gave up the greenhouses and went into a small farming operation down in Ashland. Then he moved the family to Tillamook so that my brothers and sisters and I could get a Catholic education.

Jim: Was he pleased when you decided to seek education at the seminary?

Tim: Yes, but I hope I didn't do it for that reason.

Jim: Well, it was a secondary value, wasn't it?

Tim: Yeah.

Jim: Before you went to the seminary, were there any events in high school you might like to elaborate on? Were there any kid pranks you pulled?

Tim: Well, I set fire to the grass and trees on that hill where we lived.

Jim: Oh, you did?

Tim: I lit a match, and it went up in flames—I mean it burnt all the vegetation all the way up the hill.

Jim: It did? Good thinking. What were you doing with the match? Where were you?

Tim: I was coming home from school. I was walking home from where the bus left us off. I was cold, and I thought, "Hey, I'll have some fun here and get warm?" I lit the match, touched it to the grass, and it took off. Burnt the whole damn hill down.

Jim: You mean it burnt all the dry grass and trees off that hill? Did you get warm. I'll bet you got your butt warmed after that stunt.

Tim: Yeah, it burnt it all, but nobody knew I did it.

Jim: And nobody knows to this day that it was you?

Tim: I don't think so.

Jim: Well they do now! I'm not going to omit this story. Are there any other little things you would like to confess to us at this time, Tim Sander?

Tim: I shot a seagull, and in those days, that was forbidden.

Jim: It was? Tell us about it.

Tim: Yeah, another kid and I used to go hunting and fishing together. We were out in the boat, on the river by our place, and I got carried away with shooting from the hip with my .22, and there was a seagull flying overhead.

Jim: A rifle?

Tim: Yeah, .22 rifle, and I aimed it from the hip, pulled the trigger, "I got him!" He flopped down right in front of us, and I was scared silly.

Jim: Were you?

Tim: Yeah, because it was a $50 fine back then. However, nobody caught up with me.

Jim: Is there anything you ever did that anyone ever caught up with you on? Did you steal a car? Did you borrow a car? Did you ever drive a car?

Tim: Well, yeah.

Jim: I mean when you were a kid.

Tim: I drove a car when I had to. Okay, we were kicked off the public school bus, down there. They used to haul kids to the Catholic school. Then in the '20s, the school district wouldn't haul us anymore, so I had to learn to drive.

Jim: Now how old were you in...you were born in 1915. If it was 1929, you were only 14. My gosh, that car must've been an ancient thing.

Tim: Well it was a Ford or something.

Jim: It was a Ford. It was a Model-T Ford?

Tim: Model-T, yeah.

Jim: You drove it to school?

Tim: Yeah, I learned how to drive. In fact, I already knew how. I was driving in the fields. So I got the license. I could only go on a certain route. I drove and I had brothers and sisters that went along with me. So we stopped at the cheese factory on the way in, I left off the milk and I parked the car at school. On the way back, we would pick up the whey for the pigs, and drive home. So I learned to drive at 14.

Jim: Well, I'll be darned. That was pretty good wasn't it?

Tim: I thought it was.

Jim: That was an interesting story. You got any more like that one? I can just visualize you driving your brothers and sisters to school—how many brothers and sisters did you have?

Tim: I'm the oldest of 11.

Jim: Small family! I didn't visualize quite that many in the car. Are you sure it wasn't a truck? How many were boys and how many girls?

Tim: Seven boys and four girls, and we lived out in the country—nobody to bother us; the nearest neighbor was a half a mile up the road.

Jim: How many students were in your high school?

Tim: Maybe 50—60 I don't know.

Jim: Pretty big for that time.

Tim: The public school was a lot bigger, but that's all that we had in the Catholic school.

Jim: Eleven kids. Did you and your brothers and sisters ever get into any trouble?

Tim: I don't recall anything.

Jim: You didn't burn down the barn, run over the cow or hang the cat?

Tim: No, I don't think we did any of that. We were too busy.

Jim: Kidding aside, I'll bet all of the kids worked hard on the farm?

Tim: Yeah, we milked cows.

Jim: Did you hand-milk the cows?

Tim: Hand-milked them, you betcha. It was only after I left the seminary that Dad got the electricity out there. Otherwise, it was lanterns and all of that stuff.

Jim: Okay, so it was a real pioneer-type living.

Tim: Oh yeah. In fact, my dad was a real pioneer-type guy. He'd make things to fit the situation or the need. He did a lot of raising vegetables and stuff, and he'd bring them in to the market, get credit and buy groceries. In fact, through groceries he paid the hospital for delivering us individually.

Jim: He paid the doctor off in produce—that brings back memories.

Tim: Let's see, '29, that was the big Depression—living conditions were tough.

Jim: But being on the farm like that, you kids must've done pretty well, because you had all of the produce. Did you raise any meat as well, for the family?

Tim: Yeah, we had hogs, chickens and cows, eggs, all of that stuff—good stuff.

Jim: Did you have a root cellar?

Tim: Yeah, coming from Missouri, my dad knew how to do all of that. What else is there? I remember in those days too—that's when I began getting interested in airplanes—they would have air races from Portland over to Tillamook.

Jim: Those must be those two-passenger bi-wings like Ben Eielson's *Jennie* hanging out at the (Fairbanks) Airport.

Tim: Yeah, like that, although they were probably a little more advanced than that one. They arranged to have air races from Portland over to Tillamook, about 75 miles straight over, and there was an airport at the fairgrounds, which they use for taking-off and landing. I'd get up on the hill and I'd hear them coming, and I'd wait for them, and just loved watching them fly by.

Jim: Did you dream of flying?

Tim: Oh, yeah. That's when I really got interested.

Jim: When was the first time you went up in a small airplane?

Tim: Oh, it was way after that.

Jim: Okay, let's save that for the chronological development of your life. You seem to have grown up totally in a farm environment. Is there anything else about the farm that was particularly interesting? Did you have ferocious animals hanging around?

Tim: No, but we did have some deer hanging around the place, but no bear or anything like that.

Jim: What nationality was your father?

Tim: Both my father and mother were born in this country. My father's parents came from Germany, and my mother's came from Switzerland.

Jim: European people, Germanic. What exactly made you decide to go to the seminary? Was there somebody that influenced you?

Tim: Well, the high school was taught by nuns. The nuns were great at talking the kids into becoming nuns or priests. They were sincere about it. I don't think they'd do it today the way they did it then, and I wouldn't even respond to it if they did, but it was a sure way to get to Heaven if you became a priest. That was the message. I figured I was such an evil kid that I needed something extra to get there.

Jim You were a hell-raiser?

Tim: Yup, hell-raiser, right.

Jim: In fact, you were such a hell-raiser that you decided you needed something extra to get to Heaven. Is there something you aren't telling us here?

Tim: Well, let's put it this way, I thought I needed something extra to get there. I thought, "Well, that's a pretty good way." Then, I had an uncle who was a priest—my dad's brother. He was a neat guy. So that was an attraction. I'd known some priests who had come to the parish, and they were pretty nice people, so I thought, "Okay, I'll try it."

Jim: In trying it, that meant you went to the seminary to study. Okay, just a brief glimpse of what you did in the seminary. What was the atmosphere like in the seminary? First, the day you walked in, what was it like?

Tim: The day my dad drove me up to the seminary, which was about 100 miles from Tillamook, and the day I stepped out of the car, some of the guys were there. They said, "Where are you from?" I said, "Tillamook." "Oh, Cheese." That's the name that stuck with me.

Jim: They called you Cheese?

Tim: They called me Cheese.

Jim: They all called you Cheese. Well that doesn't sound very seminarish to me.

Tim: No, it wasn't, but it was a lot of fun. Life was regular school, like high school or college, like any other place.

Jim: But it was a boy's school. Not even any nuns?

Tim: Well, they cooked in the kitchen, some of them, and we used to go down there and buy pies because they made good pies.

Jim: But you were not supposed to visit with any women, is that it?

Tim: No, that wasn't it exactly. We couldn't visit with them—like the high school girls, for example. They had a high school for girls down the hill. We couldn't associate with them too much. It was limited. Of course, some of the people did...in the woods. I didn't.

Jim: Oh, I see—where there is a will there is a way. Okay, I understand. Did you complete your four years of high school at the seminary?

Tim: Well, the first two in Tillamook, and then the second two at the seminary.

Jim: Then you went into college?

Tim: Then I went into college courses, but it was the same kind of routine. There was school studies, then we had meals together. They had readings during the meals and we had religious services every day.

Jim: With the exception of Sunday, start from when you woke up. When did you wake up? What time? Seven o'clock?

Tim: It was earlier, probably around six.

Jim: And what would you do then?

Tim: Get up and wash, then immediately go down to morning prayer, and then breakfast.

Jim: How long was morning prayer?

Tim: Twenty minutes or so.

Jim: And then breakfast for 30 minutes to an hour?

Tim: About that. Then get ready for classes, and the rest of the day was classes, until lunch, then classes again in the afternoon.

Jim: These were academic non-religious classes.

Tim: Yes. There was only one religious class in there. Otherwise it was all regular academic stuff. It was a classical education, in college at least; I studied Latin and Greek and German. That kind of stuff.

Jim: Yeah, you never got that good at Italian, I'll tell you that.

Tim: I know that.

Jim: And the Latin is a little bit wobbly too, I'll say that.

Tim: I taught Greek for 12 years.

Jim: Well. I know from experience your Italian needs some polishing. Well, that's another story isn't it? We'll get to it. What did you do after school?

Tim: After school then we would have a ball game.

Jim: When was that, three o'clock?

Tim: Three-thirty, four, somewhere, 'round there we would have our ball games. Then at six o'clock we would eat, have a meeting, a little recreation, and night prayer, then we would go to bed.

Jim: At six o'clock you would eat for about an hour?

Tim: Yeah. A little recreation after that.

Jim: Then you would pray? A little recreation then some prayer. How much prayer?

Tim: A half hour maybe, at the most.

Jim: I didn't see anywhere, other than the prayer and one course, where there was any other religion. Was there anything we missed?

Tim: We went to Mass every day. That was in the morning before breakfast. It was part of the daily activities—not just on Sundays.

Jim: How long was the religious educational portion of your daily activity?

Tim: In high school and college, maybe an hour a day.

Jim: How long did you go to college?

Tim: Four years.

Jim: Four years of college, and you had a bachelor's degree in religion?

Tim: Right. It was a bachelor of science degree.

Jim: When you completed your education...by the way I realize this is in an environment where you are supposed to be studying God, and being very religious and dedicated, but you did say that some of the boys and some of the girls got together. When you get a bunch of young boys together, they are going to pull something off, aren't they?

Tim: Let me see. Once a month, we were allowed to go downtown, and we went to Worley's Drugstore. All the girls were there, and we would sit there and talk with them and drink sodas. I suppose there were times when the boys would have a little beer on the side, but not down there or with the girls.

Jim: But certainly you didn't partake of any beer on the side.

Tim: Well, I remember once—I think it was in my third year. A bunch of the guys had some beer and wine and we went down under a tree and we drank.

Jim: Good or bad?

Tim: Horrible!

Jim: You got sick and said, "Never again!"

Tim: No, no, no, not that radical. Just at that time, I didn't feel good. I was always blessed, because I would get sick to my stomach if I drank too much.

Jim: By this time you were in college. You were 19—20 years old. Were you fully aware of what you had to give up to become a priest?

Tim: Well, we were told. It was in the head, but not in the gut.

Jim: You lost me.

Tim: Okay, we were told, and as time went on the responsibility was more and more emphasized.

Jim: It was more a responsibility than a requirement?

Tim: Well, it was both. We were aware that we couldn't get married. We could not be in any kind of a relationship with a female.

Jim: Okay, that was one. What else couldn't you do? Aside from the ten commandments—let's not get into that.

Tim: Well, let's see—had to be obedient, to do what we were told.

Jim: By whom?

Tim: By the superior, whoever it was. If it was the bishop, okay. If I was going to join the monastery, it would be the abbot. That was part of it. Basically, that's what everybody faced.

Jim: What about material things?

Tim: Okay, I'll get into that when I get into the monastery.

Jim: Okay, right now we are in college, which is not the monastery. Right or wrong?

Tim: Right. We could go home in the summer, work, and all of that stuff.

Jim: You were just in college? You were testing yourself to see if you wanted to become a priest?

Tim: Yes. Now, at the end of the second year of college, then, I had to make a decision of whether I wanted to continue on and become what they call a diocese priest who goes out and works in a parish, or if I wanted to join the monastery—big decision. A friend of mine, who I grew up with and spent some time with in Tillamook, was going to join the monastery. He was in the seminary at that time. He came to the seminary and the first year of college, so we were there together, and he was trying to influence me to join the monastery, and he finally won out. Again, part of this decision was, I guess, a little bit more insurance about getting to Heaven.

Jim: You were worried?

Tim: I was worried!

Jim: You must've had some hidden problems that you had to deal with. Did you have an emotional demon that you were working on?

Tim: I could have had, deep inside.

Jim: Did you know what it was, or did you just feel that you weren't worthy to go to heaven at that time?

Tim: Well, I wasn't worthy because I was such a renegade.

Jim: You set the field on fire, so you considered yourself a renegade. Was there something worse than setting the field on fire?

Tim: Yeah, but I wouldn't talk about it.

Jim: I see. Those are the kind of things many young boys do.

Tim: Exactly, and we were told that we would go straight to Hell if we did that!

Jim: Well of course, that's right.

Tim: See, that was the kind of thing that was driving me. There were not grounds—it was not rational—valid grounds—for ever becoming a priest, for that reason, or to join the monastery. I can see that today, a little late.

Jim: Well, of course. You were in your early 20s and you wanted to be saved. You didn't want to go to Hell.

Tim: That's right.

Jim: Where do you think you're going right now? Is it marginal? Do you think your going to make it?

Tim: Yeah, I feel at peace with God. I do. I'm not worried.

Jim: Can I make a personal comment here? I'm not worried about you making it either.

Tim: We'll meet.

Jim: You know, I think that's in your mind. Like you said, you don't have to go to the monastery to be a good man. You just keep trying.

Tim: Exactly. That's right. You keep trying.

Jim: Okay, you were influenced to go to the monastery, and you went.

Tim: At the end of the second year of college we asked for permission to join the monastery. There were seven of us. They didn't all go through with it, but we entered. That's called a novitiate (the period of being a religious novice). I spent a year trying this monastic life out—to see if it was something that I really wanted. It's rough. They test you in all kinds of ways— to see if I fit into the program, if I can stand the life and if I want the life, am I willing, and if I'm acceptable to them—all of those questions. At the end of that year, the monks vote on you.

Jim: On the seven of you, or individually?

Tim: Every one of us individually.

Jim: How many of the seven made it?

Tim: There were five that made it. Two dropped out.

Jim: And you were one of those five. Are you glad that you were in the monastery rather than out in a diocese or some other lifestyle?

Tim: Probably, yes, as I look back on it.

Jim: That was a good place for you at your age?

Tim: I think so, yeah. It probably saved my butt.

Jim: How long were you in the monastery?

Tim: Well, since that day.

Jim: You're still in the monastery?

Tim: Well, I don't live there, but I'm a monk.

Jim: You're a monk? You mean I've been palling around with a monk? A Catholic monk? My God, and all the things I've been saying. No wonder everyone refers to us as unlikely pals. We should write a book; we could call it *The Agnostic and the Monk*. No, *The Monk and the Agnostic*. Tell me something. How does this work? You went to a monastery. You could have gone out to a church as a priest, couldn't you?

Tim: Well, I could have gone out under a bishop, or stayed in the same place, in the seminary. After the first two years of college, then came two years of philosophy in the seminary and I had to go through that with the other guys. The monks had to do that right along with the other people who were not monks in the same seminary. After that, we had four years of theology—church history, ethics, dogma, all that kind of stuff.

Jim: You have eight years of college basically—the equivalent of a Ph.D. in theology.

Tim: Darn near it. They didn't give it to us, but it was the equivalent.

Jim: Do you have a master's degree?

Tim: Well, I do now.

Jim: Is it in theology?

Tim: Well, since I was there they have set up a different arrangement. You have to get a master's in divinity. I didn't have that. I got two master's degrees after I left.

Jim: In divinity?

Tim: No, one was in education. The other was in psychology. I went to the University of Oregon for the master's of education. Then to Pepperdine for the psychology

Jim: I'll be darned. Pretty impressive, Tim.

Tim: Oh, I learned a lot.

Jim: Before we get too deep into that let's get back to the seminary. Now, let me get this straight. You went to four years of college.

Tim: Right. Graduated from college. I was in the monastery at that time, when I graduated from college.

Jim: Okay, you were in the seminary for the first two years of college?

Tim: Yes.

Jim: And the second two years, you were in the monastery?

Tim: With a year for novitiate thrown in there after the second year of college.

Jim: Okay, but the third year, which was the novitiate year, was the same as your third year of college.

Tim: No, no, we didn't go to school.

Jim: Oh, five years then. Okay, two years of college at the seminary. Then you went to the monastery for one year of novitiate, and then two more years at the monastery for your college education for a bachelor's degree in science.

Tim: Right.

Jim Anything funny go on there that you observed?

Tim: Well, they were all human you know. I'll tell you something you can include, I don't care. There was an old brother up there. This was a story I was told by one of the monks. Years before this, they used to raise grapes on the side of the hill up there. The monastery is on top of a hill in the middle of the valley. So they had these grapes, and they were sour! But, they made wine out of them, and this old brother—I guess he worked in the dairy, and he was having a hard time this particular night and he wasn't doing his job, and they found him. He'd drunk a little too much. So, the priest that was in charge said, "Brother, what's the problem here?" He replied, "Oh...I've been drinking some of that monastery pith." He was right, I've tasted the stuff; it's horrible.

Jim: Yeah, but the way he was slurring his words, it sounds like it did the job.

Tim: Yeah, it sure did it for him. On weekends, Saturday especially, we'd go out and help the brothers in the orchard or whatever the job was that had to be done. They had a big fire in 1926. One of the buildings on the hill burnt down, so they rebuilt the whole thing, but we had to remove these old rocks from the foundation—real heavy stuff. We broke a hell of a lot of rocks up on that hill. That wasn't my favorite job.

Jim: Any other stories?

Tim: That's all that I can think of at the moment.

Jim: You graduated, got your degree, what was the next step?

Tim: Well, then, four more years of theology.

Jim: Right there at the monastery?

Tim: Right. After the third year of theology, then we were ordained priests. Then we finished the fourth year after ordination.

Jim: Why did you become a priest after the third year? What was the fourth year all about?

Tim: It was the completion of the theological courses. The guys who weren't in the monastery, who were doing the same courses, would go right on through the four years. We were allowed to be ordained after the third year, but we couldn't go out and exercise or get our faculties, to hear confessions, preach and do all of that until the end of the fourth year.

Jim: It wasn't until the fourth year that you had all of the skills and background to perform as a priest. Did you hear confessions?

Tim: After the fourth year, yes. I was scared spitless.

Jim: Why?

Tim: I was worried that I would do something wrong. I'm no longer scared like that. I mean, we treat each other as human beings.

Jim: Did you ever hear a confession that shocked you?

Tim: In a way yes, but not that bad.

Jim: Did anybody ever say that they committed murder?

Tim: I don't think so. I don't remember that.

Jim: I wonder if I could make a confession that would surprise you.

Tim: Probably, I don't doubt that you could. In fact, if anybody could, I know you could.

Jim: Never mind!

Tim: You know, after I was ordained, that was May 22, 1941. I went over to Tillamook for a mass there with a parish, and there was always a big celebration for that. On the way over, we passed by a river and they had a guy up on the bank. He was lying down. He had just fallen in the river. He'd drowned. I'm supposed to know what to do. It's an emergency.

Jim: You didn't know what to do.

Tim: Well, I gave him sort of conditional absolution, but I didn't know what else to do.

Jim: Did you have the collar on?

Tim: Yeah.

Jim: Do you think anyone around knew the difference?

Tim: They probably knew I was a priest, but that's it. In fact, I asked if this guy was a Catholic and no one seemed to know, so I did what I could do and went.

Jim: As fast as you could?

Tim: Yeah.

Jim: Wait a minute. This fellow is lying dead on the riverbank, and you gave him conditional absolution?

Tim: If you were alive and you're Catholic, "I absolve you." That's how it was done in those days.

Jim: So if he was a Catholic, you absolved him. If he wasn't?

Tim: I don't know.

Jim: Let's get back to the monastery.

Tim: So I finished my final year, fourth year. Then the abbot, at the time, wanted to send me to a new monastery that was being founded by Mount Angel in British Columbia. So, he sent me. I had to go—I didn't have any choice. I said "Well, I'll go, but when I get the chance to come back, I'm coming back." So he said, "Well that's all right. You have that liberty." So I, along with two other fellows who were in my class, went up there. This was during war time, and this was in Canada. I didn't feel too comfortable being there. It was a whole different way of living for me. I used to go out to help out in the parish over in Vancouver Island and Victoria, places like that where they needed help on weekends. I taught in the seminary there by the way. It was mostly high school courses.

Jim: You taught high school students?

Tim: Yes and some of the first two years of college. Whatever they needed, that's what I taught.

Jim: How long were you there?

Tim: Thirteen and a half years and one week.

Jim: You seem to know the time frame very exactly, thirteen-and-a-half years and one week.

Tim: I'll never forget it.

Jim: You liked it so much, or you didn't like it?

Tim: I did not like it, no!

Jim: Can I print that?

Tim: Well, let's put it a different way. I found it very difficult.

Jim: If it were me I would say, " It probably wasn't the best years of my life."

Tim: I'd say that, yeah.

Jim: What did you do following that time? How did you get out of it?

Tim: I wrote to Rome and said, "I can't stand this any longer. I need to get out. They won't help me." So Rome answered and they gave them orders to let me go.

Jim: Honest to God? You are a renegade. Where did they let you go to?

Tim: Back to Mount Angel where the monastery was.

Jim: The monastery was at Mount Angel. What was the new monastery called in British Columbia.

Tim: Westminster Priory. Then it became Westminster Abbey.

Jim: Were you happy when you went back to Mount Angel?

Tim: Yeah.

Jim: How long were you there?

Tim: Until I came to Alaska, on August 26, 1970.

Jim: Where did you go? Fairbanks?

Tim: Yes, I came to Fairbanks. I've been in Fairbanks ever since.

Jim: You've been in Fairbanks 31 happy years.

Tim: Absolutely. Right-on.

Jim: What did you do in Fairbanks?

Tim: I came up to work at Monroe High School, teaching and doing post-high school counseling. I helped kids get ready for college or whatever training they needed for work after high school.

Jim: Is that all you did? Did you just teach high school or did you do some other outside activities?

Tim: Oh, I'd help in parishes occasionally.

Jim: Did you give sermons?

Tim: Yeah, when I went out to help. In fact, it was not too long after I got up here that I started to go up to Murphy Dome and help out. At first it was once a week. Then it got to be twice a week for mass and talking with the guys. So I did that for about 12 years. I was doing counseling with the kids over there at the high school and became aware that I needed more training to deal with the many questions they had. So I got some advice up at the University. I set it up to go down to Los Angeles to the American Institute of Family Relations to learn marriage and family counseling. So I spent the school year of 1974 to 1975 going to school there.

Jim: Nine months?

Tim: No, it was 12 months. At the same time, I was part-time chaplain at St. Francis Hospital just outside of Los Angeles—Lynwood. It was a good year. I learned a lot about myself, and a lot of other things, about life, during that educational experience. I came back up here after I got my master's there, and found out that the kids didn't need any more counseling or any more help. At least that's what it seemed like. It was not too long after that Fairbanks Counseling and Adoption opened up, and the bishop asked me if I would join the staff there. I said, "Okay." One thing I want to mention is that in high school I got an aviation class started, both ground school and flight training. We had use of a Cessna 172 from a local operator. So I got a number of kids through. They got their license. That was one of the more enjoyable experiences.

Jim: Tim, before we get into flying, and believe me we are going to get into it, let's finish up with when you went to work for Fairbanks Counseling and Adoption. I understand it was a Catholic family agency. What kind of service did they offer and how long did you work there? Or do you still work there?

Tim: At Fairbanks Counseling and Adoption they do counseling for marriages, adoptions, pregnancies, unwed mothers and several other programs. I worked there for 12 or 13 years. After I left, I started my own marriage counseling service.

Jim: I am unclear if when you started your own it was linked to the Catholic Church or was just a business venture on your own.

Tim: It was a business venture of my own to help supplement my living.

Jim: What did you do for the Catholic Church at that time?

Tim: After I finished with Murphy Dome, then St. Raphael's parish up here was started, and I was asked by the bishop to do weekend work there. So I did that for about 13 years.

Jim: You never had a church of your own?

Tim: No, not in the strict sense.

Jim: You never wanted one?

Tim: Never.

Jim: Did you enjoy working with the churches when the permanent priest was away?

Tim: Oh, that was okay. It was just fill-in stuff, which is what I do now, a little bit.

Jim: That's all you did, isn't it?

Tim: No, no, no. I was the regular, what they call sacramental minister at St. Raphael's for 13 years.

Jim: Oh, you were. That was your church.

Tim: Yes, in that sense. There was somebody who was called pastoral administrator, who took care of running the parish. I didn't want any part of that, but I did like my part of it. That was nice.

Jim: How did you dress when you were in front of a congregation?

Tim: Okay, there was an alb, which was a white garment, and over that was the chasuble and the vestments.

Jim: Okay, what was a chasuble—what did it look like?

Tim: It kind of draped around...

Jim: Is it like a scarf?

Tim: Oh, bigger, like some of these Mexican serapes. It kind of went down in front, and down the back. That's kind of what it was.

Jim: Okay, and what were the other items that you wore?

Tim: The alb.

Jim: The white gown?

Tim: The vestment.

Jim: The vestment, and I thought there were three.

Tim: The chasuble—that thing that goes down the front and down the back.

Jim: Just let me get this straight. What's the gown called?

Tim: The white one?

Jim: Yes.

Tim: The alb.

Jim: Then what goes over the alb?

Tim: The chasuble.

Jim: The chasuble, where's the vestment?

Tim: That is the vestment.

Jim: The Chasuble? Sounds like an Abbot and Costello show!

Tim: Yeah, vestment is a generic term

Jim: Oh, okay. Did you have a hat on?

Tim: No.

Jim: No hat.

Tim: That's only for bishops.

Jim: That's only for bishops. Did you have a rosary?

Tim: No.

Jim: No rosary. That's it. You stood up there, and what did you do?

Tim: Conducted the prayers, and led the prayers, read the scriptures, and gave a homily on the readings.

Jim: What's a homily?

Tim: It's a sort of explanation of the scripture, and then the application of our daily life with that in mind. How we can use that to help improve our daily lives.

Jim: I see. You did that for 13 years?

Tim: Yes.

Jim: You liked it?

Tim: I liked that kind of thing, but I was getting to be 80, and I decided that was enough and I retired.

Jim: Did you just get ahold of the Pope and tell him, "I am retiring"?

Tim: Well, I just wrote a letter to the bishop and said I was retiring. Period!

Jim I'm 80 years old. I'm retiring. That was six years ago. What have you done for the past six years?

Tim: I've done what I want when I wanted to.

Jim: Okay, but you continued to run your little business?

Tim: Right, a little bit of private practice, right? I still keep my license up in that.

Jim: And you continue to take part in religious ceremonies where you're needed by the church?

Tim: Yeah, where they need the help, I'm willing to help.

Jim: So, you'll go in and take over when the priest of the church is away, and that has been your religious activity over the past six years?

Tim: That's right.

Jim: Now, let's get down to the nitty-gritty of things. When did you learn to fly?

Tim: Now we're talking. My first flight was in Springfield, Oregon, on April 3rd, 1958. I soloed in May of 1958 and I got my license December 3, 1958. I was the 1,500th student to complete the training at the Springfield school.

Jim: And what kind of plane did you fly?

Tim: A single-engine 65-horsepower Aeronca Champ.

Jim: Single engine?

Tim: Single engine.

Jim: Two-passenger?

Tim: Two-passenger, tandem seating.

Jim: Tell us about your flying career.

Tim: Well, okay. I took my vacation time, which was two weeks, went down to Eugene and worked at it every day— week of flying. I soloed at that time.

Jim: In two weeks!?

Tim: Yeah, something like that.

Jim: Wow, magnificent! It took me two years.

Tim: Well, I can't remember—I got it in my log book. I also have yours in my log book. I did it in a hurry. I think it was 10 or 11 hours after, I soloed. Then I had to go from Mount Angel to Springfield to do this, and I went down on weekends. I got it set up so I could go down there to help out at the parishes on the weekend. It worked out good.

Jim: I see, a little manipulative labor.

Tim: That's what it turned out to be. That's what I've been doing all of my flying life.

Jim: Are there a lot of priests who fly?

Tim: No, not that many.

Jim: How about in Alaska?

Tim: There are more in Alaska, yeah, but down there, there are not that many. I worked on through. I got money from various sources. In fact, if I needed money I just asked somebody. They gave me $50 or $100 or whatever, and they helped me through. It only cost me about $500 to get my license, because rental and instruction were cheap in those days. So then they had a big celebration at Skyways when I got my license. I didn't know about it, but they called me and they wanted to do something nice. So I went down there, and they had the F.A.A (Federal Aviation Administration), in and they had the television, and the whole works out there.

Jim: Was all this ceremony because you were a priest?

Tim: They say that it was because I was the 1,500th student to go through their training.

Jim: Oh, I see. Tell us about it.

Tim: There was an FAA guy who gave me my check ride. He was a neat fellow. He helped me through, and I was smart enough I guess...you know, when you took your check ride you probably had to divert to a different location for your cross-country and all of that. I did all of that, and I was successful in getting the right answer. It worked out fine. Then we came back and landed at Portland International, and I wasn't too sure about that. So he sort of helped me through it. That worked out fine too. There was one experience I had in training that scared the crap out of me. We were practicing stalls, and the instructor said, "Now when you are stalled, you should have that yoke all the way back in your gut." So this particular day I was out practicing stalls, and I didn't get it all the way back, so next time I figured I'd get you. So I did, and that sucker started— my impression was that it started to go backwards. I don't know what they call that, but it was not funny. I got it out, and I was scared spitless, and I headed straight back to the airport. I could hardly walk.

Jim: Knees were shakin'?

Tim: Yeah. Oh, here's one. On my first long cross-country. I had to go from Troutdale to Centralia/Chehalis right in the same airport that was up toward Seattle, and then gas up and go down to Eugene, gas up, then go back to Troutdale. Well, I'd been trying to make this thing time after time, about a half dozen times. I had to get somebody to take my class at the high school and to have an airplane available, and good weather, and find transportation into Portland. Well, it worked—finally. I got there, and then this Cessna 140 they had for me, the radio was out, so that didn't work, but I went anyhow. They said go ahead. So I filed a flight plan, and on the way up the weather was not that great. I followed the highway, got up there to Chehalis, and had them refuel the airplane. I taxied down to the runway, and just about that time I felt the airplane wings start going up and down, from side to side.

Jim: What do you mean the wings were going up and down. Explain that, I'm confused.

Tim: Well, I was sitting there and the left wing went down and the right one went up. Then the right wing went down and the left one went up. A fellow had hold of the wing and was shaking it up and down. It was the guy who sold me the gas. He said, "Hold her, hold her boy. You have water in your gas." Just then, the engine quit. So he towed the airplane back to the hanger, drained the carburetor and drained the fuel out of the tanks. I'd been flying on the left tank. That's where there would've been water because the right tank was full. Somebody had broken into his hanger the night before, drained all the gas out of this little truck with the tank on it, and put water back in, and that's what I got in my tank. I mean that's a federal offense.

Jim: Of course.

Tim: Anyway, I've got that in my log book. So I didn't know what to do. He'd spent quite a bit of time getting the water out, and the weather wasn't that great. So I closed the flight plan by phone, and didn't think that I needed to call Troutdale, because I figured I'd get back there at the time I was supposed to anyhow. I went straight back from Chehalis to Troutdale. They were so worried that they were thinking of getting the Civil Air Patrol out there, because they thought I was lost. I wasn't worried, but I never forgot the way that fellow who sold me the gas reacted. He was really mad and concerned for my safety.

Jim: He was probably scared too, because if you'd crashed, he'd probably have been liable, for not checking his fuel. Tell us, how did your flying go from there?

Tim: I got the loan of several airplanes. There was a friend down there in Springfield who knew I liked to fly, and he had some credit at this flying school, and he said, "Use it up." So I used that up and soloed and did some more flying, but after I soloed, then I was borrowing airplanes, and other things until I got my time in. Finally somebody gave me an airplane. I couldn't keep it because monks can't have things, so I got my brother to take it, and I could use it—that worked. So I used that a lot. I built up a lot of time. It was a tandem Taylorcraft, which was the old version—neat airplane. My brother sold this to another fellow, and this other fellow wanted to get a different airplane. So he sold that and got a Pacer. It was a tail-dragger.

Jim: This other fellow allowed you to use the Pacer.

Tim: Well, it was a condition. I had equal rights to it.

Jim: Did you get a commercial license?

Tim: Yes, I got my commercial before I left down there, before I came to Alaska.

Jim: Did you have to have an instrument rating before you got your commercial.

Tim: No I didn't have to in those days.

Jim: Oh, you didn't? When you got your commercial that meant you could teach flying?

Tim: No, I just had a commercial rating and could get paid for flying.

Jim: Did you ever fly and get paid for it?

Tim: No, The only time I did is when I instructed out here at Phillips Field. That's the only time.

Jim: With the Flying Club?

Tim: No, it was Ed Bachner's and Glenn Wyatt's—the two of them had that operation there on old Phillips Field. So I instructed for them for awhile.

Jim: When did you get your instructor's license?

Tim: It was after I was up here, and I went down and worked on it during the summer. I'd go down there for vacation. I'd work on it down there at Klamath Falls. In fact, I was substituting for an Air Force chaplain down there at Klamath Falls at Kingsley Air Force Base, and that's where I did a lot of the work. I had a good instructor.

Jim: What year was that?

Tim: About '71 or '72

Jim: Didn't you get an instrument rating?

Tim: Oh yes, but I got that years later, in 1982.

Jim: Have you had a lot of students?

Tim: A fair number; I have given about 1,200 hours of instruction now.

Jim: Have you ever had any near-disasters in an airplane, other than the water in the tank?

Tim: There were two times I got caught in the clouds. One time was almost. I turned around because the clouds ahead looked worse than the ones I just come out of, and I was with somebody, and he said, "You better turn around again because it's worse behind." But we went on and we made it. On one trip down to Portland I had a couple of people with me and I did get into the clouds. I was lucky to get out. It was a Cessna 180, and I won't get into the details of that one. It scared the crap out of me.

Jim: Can I print that?

Tim: I don't care.

Jim: How many students do you think you've had that went on and got their licenses?

Tim: Oh, a lot of them, but I don't know the number.

Jim: I was one of those students.

Tim: Yeah, I can look it up in the logbook. I've got a record of everything.

Jim: You've been giving me biennial review for that past 20 years.

Tim: That's right.

Jim: I'll bet there is one story you don't have in your log book. Can I tell it?

Tim: Go ahead.

Jim: I've always been a person who's never been afraid to use a little bit of profanity from time to time—mild profanity, of course.

Tim: Expressive language.

Jim: Yes, I've been known to be expressive. I called you up because someone had said you were a good instructor. I was, at that time, a member of Arctic Flying Club here in Fairbanks, Alaska, and I had soloed with another instructor a couple of years earlier. In my opinion, he soloed me too early and it scared me, so I quit flying. Now, I didn't know what you looked like, but you said you would meet me at the airplane at such and such a time. So, I saw you drive up, and I said to myself, "My God, he's a mean-looking guy." You got out of the car and we introduced ourselves then we went around and did all of the pre-flight external examination to the airplane, and as I said, I had already soloed years before, and it scared me. I didn't care how mean you looked; I looked you in the eye and said, "We will fly and we will train. When it's time to solo, I'll tell you when I feel that I'm comfortable with soloing. You will not tell me. That is final." You may recall this, and that we agreed on this issue after I explained it. You had some books and some papers in your hand. I saw them and didn't pay much attention. There was some kind of leather-bound book and a bunch of loose papers, and you had the manual for the Cessna 150. We got into the airplane and we took off, and you said, "Let's go do some maneuvers." As I remember it there was some turbulence that day. So we went out to the buttes, and you said, "Take it up to 3,500 feet." And we did maneuvers. We were doing turns, 90-degree turns, 180-degree turns. Then you wanted me to do some stalls, and I got the airplane in a stall, and it shuddered and it shook and fell out of the sky and the wind was blowing us around, and it scared me, so I said, "Jesus Christ!" in a big, loud voice. Then we did another one and I said, "Oh, shit!" So then, we got back to the airstrip, landed the plane, somehow and we didn't die. In between that time and our next scheduled lesson, somebody told me you were a priest. So I looked at that leather bound book you had with you each flight, and when we were up in the sky, I was feeling real bad that I used all of that profanity when I was scared. I said, "I just learned you were a Catholic priest." And you said, "Yes", and I said, "Well hell, if I'd known I was with God's right-hand man, I wouldn't have been so worried. What's that book right there?" You said, "It's a Bible." And I said, "What do you do, get up here with me and pray that you live through this?" And you said, "Yeah."

Tim: You made it, didn't you?

Jim: Yeah. That was my introduction to Tim Sander and really learning how to fly airplanes, and I've been scared ever since.

Tim: That is why you're still alive—you're cautious.

Jim: That's been a lot of years of flying. So what did we do Tim? We learned to fly. We had a good time together. We even flew a helicopter together. You probably like flying the Cessna 206 better than the helicopter.

Tim: Yeah, that drives me crazy, all of those things that you have to do at once.

Jim: The thing is that we'd never fly it enough to stay current, with the helicopter. You've got to be on it all the time to be a good helicopter pilot, much more so than a fixed-wing. And we're more apt to have time in a fixed-wing than a helicopter.

Tim: That's for sure.

Jim: We've put a lot of hours in over the years, haven't we. Then, the big event of our life—we went down to Idaho Falls and picked up a brand-new Aviat Husky and flew it back.

Tim: That was a nice trip.

Jim: You're right, that was a good trip.

Tim: It was snowing. I remember that.

Jim: It was windy. I remember when we took off. I think we traveled about 10 feet and that thing was airborne, because we were heading into a strong headwind. Boom! It popped right off of the ground.

Tim: It's a good airplane.

Jim: We came up through the Canadian trench—spectacular!

Tim: Yeah, I'm not sure what the name of that first trench we went up, but it was a long one. We got as far as Prince George and then the other trench.

Jim: Okay, that was the Canadian trench. I don't know what the Prince George route was, but we came up through the mountains. It was an exciting and an educational trip for me. You taught me a lot about flying on that trip. That was a good cross-country. You allowed me to do all of the flying.

Tim: That was good, and you did pretty well for not being checked-off as a tail-dragger pilot.

Jim: Well, let's see, we've done a lot of things together. You've traveled. Tell me about your traveling, other than ferrying airplanes back and forth to different parts of the United States, which you've done quite a bit of.

Tim: Yes, I've done some of that.

Jim: How about foreign-country travel. You went to Australia.

Tim: I went to Australia and New Zealand. I spent a month over there.

Jim: How did you like Australia? That's where I got my Ph.D.

Tim: Wonderful, I want to go back there. I want to go to the Interior and go to the southern and western coasts. I hope to do that someday. I've been to Europe a number of times.

Jim: You go to Germany every once in awhile, don't you?

Tim: Yeah, a family thing. Dad's relatives are over there, and those have been good visits. Usually on trips like that people over there set up kind of a 10-day tour of different parts of Germany. That's been very helpful. I've been very impressed by it, especially the destruction during the war, and the recovery.

Jim: Are there still some remnants of the war visible over there?

Tim: Yeah, and the way people live their lives is different

Jim: Socially different than the United States?

Tim: Yeah, I look at it that way. There's one thing that I've found. The relatives over there are not nearly as close as over here. They don't get together that much, although they live close enough.

Jim: Where else have you gone?

Tim: Let's see. England—I've been there, and France, Austria and where? Switzerland—my mother's family came from over there. I went over there with my sister and my brother once a number of years ago. We visited all of those people.

Jim: Were they close? Closer than the Germans?

Tim: I thought so.

Jim: But still not as close at the people in the United States?

Tim: No.

Jim: No. Anyplace else?

Tim: Been to Mexico.

Jim: What did you do in Mexico?

Tim: Oh I visited down there when Mount Angel made a new foundation. They sent people down there to start a new monastery near Cuernavaca. So I went down there about three or four years ago and visited with them—it was interesting.

Jim: Was that an enjoyable trip?

Tim: Very.

Jim: You didn't have any responsibility down there? You were just down there as an observer?

Tim: Yeah, I knew some of the guys down in the monastery there, so I went down there, and one of them took me out to see the poor people. They really have poverty down there.

Jim: Tell us about your most recent travel. Did you ever go see the Pope?

Tim: You and I went on a trip to Italy. First we went to Rome on a tour—a cattle drive—and then to...well we went to St. Peter's, but I've been there before. I'm not that impressed.

Jim: Is that in Rome?

Tim: Yeah. And then before we went to Florence we took a side trip down to Naples and Pompeii—that was really interesting.

Jim: I have to agree with you, that was one the most interesting of the guided tours. For those who aren't familiar with it, years ago when the volcano, Vesuvius, erupted it sent out a cloud of ash and rock that covered Pompeii. What is interesting about it today is recent excavations and how the scientists have interpreted the people who owned the different dwellings. There were two features that were especially interesting. First of all, the streets were built with big rectangular rocks about three feet wide by six feet long, all fitted tightly together down the center of the street, and on each side were some smooth, narrow channels. The way this was interpreted, the horses that drew the chariots would trot along the top of the rocks while the wheels of the chariots would role along in the grooves.

Tim: Yeah, that was remarkable.

Jim: The other was the house of ill-repute. Inside the building there were rooms or cubicles and over each door there was a picture carved in the rock of what each of the ladies was best at—their specialty. That was interesting.

Tim: Yes it was, but the most memorable part of that trip was the bus ride down. Can I tell that story?

Jim: If you must.

Tim: For the people that don't know, Jim runs in footraces. I was there when he set the world record. Anyway, we were in Rome and had gotten up early that morning, had breakfast, and Jim of course likes his coffee in the morning. We got on the bus for the two-hour bus ride down the highway to Naples. They had one stop scheduled about an hour and a half down the road. Well, about a half hour into the trip, Jim has to go to the restroom, and of course our couch was the only one of the five that didn't have a restroom.

About an hour into the trip, things were getting critical. By an hour and fifteen minutes Jim was crossing his legs a lot and kind of gritting his teeth. I finally went up and asked the tour guide when the stop was scheduled, because if it wasn't very soon there was one passenger back there that needed a restroom so bad that he was ready to get out, let the bus go, and walk the rest of the way to Pompeii. She said if he could hold out ten more minutes we would be there. By the time we pulled into the rest stop Jim was gritting his teeth, his legs were crossed, and he was stiff as a board and there were tears in his eyes. I guess they were tears, maybe he was just full. Anyway, as you might guess we were in a caravan of five buses and the other four had arrived before us, so when we got off the bus there was a long line leading to the men's restroom. About 200 yards away there were some thick bushes and trees alongside a farmer's field. That is when I saw Jim break the world's record as he ran towards those bushes—I never saw a man run so fast. As a matter of fact the farmer was out plowing in that field. When Jim got back he said, "That farmer won't have to irrigate for a year."

Jim: Good, Tim. I won't omit this story, but keep in mind that I got one coming. Before the interview is over we will be even. Where did we go from there?

Tim: We went to Florence, where we went up on the hill to see that statue of *David* by Michelangelo.

Jim: We viewed two distinct different kinds of sculptural art. What were those? Michellangelo's and Bernini.

Tim: Bernini? I think so, but I am not sure. I do remember one was passive— just sitting there— and the other was active—doing something.

Jim: Personally, I saw so much art there, it started to all run together. What best described Italy to me was one word—Old. If it wasn't 4,000 years old, it was too new.

Tim: Yup, that's right, even out in the country. Then we went to Venice, and saw St. Mark's piazza, Basillica or whatever it was.

Jim: That was interesting, but the most interesting visit was the church you took me to when we went to mass, with the seats on each side of the isle where the monks sat.

Tim: Choir stalls. And then those people who were buried in the floor.

Jim: Yeah, that was kind of an interesting touch. Where did we go from Venice? Refresh my memory. What did we do after Venice?

Tim: Well we tried to hold our noses as we walked along the canals, then rented a car and went to northern Italy, to the foothills of the Appennines and fresh air.

Jim: What kind of car was it?

Tim: A little Fiat. Jim did the driving, and I did the drinking.

Jim: Yes, I was the designated driver, because I don't drink.

Tim: That was a great two weeks.

Jim: Since you told the story about me on the bus can I tell one on you?

Tim: Let's hear it, then I will tell you if you can print it.

Jim: In Italy they drive pretty fast, and getting out of Venice was an experience, because I was not familiar with an autostrada which is nothing but a big divided highway (four lanes in each direction) with toll booths at each entry. Well, the morning we rented the car we drove about 20 miles on the autostrada then turned off on a secondary country road, which was much easier. We remained on the country roads for the next few days, visiting wineries and having picnics with cheese, bread, salami, wine and sodas. I do remember this, that everyday about three o'clock Tim would like to have a glass of wine—a big glass. Well anyway, we decided to go to another town a fair ways away. So we got onto the autostrada and we were traveling along at about 140 kilometers an hour, zig zagging in and around the other cars. Somehow one of us had set our suitcase on top of our bag of food and cracked all the plastic cups. Tim knew this; I didn't. Anyway I was really concentrating on my driving—anything could happen at the speed we were going. All of a sudden I hear this pop. I glanced over at Tim and he had uncorked a wine bottle and had it tipped back, guzzling away. When he came up for air, I said, "I hope it wasn't my driving that caused you to do that." By then he was taking another big swallow from the jug. When he lowered it and caught his breath he said, "Yeah it is. It is three o'clock and you're driving like a maniac. You fit right in over here."

Tim: I liked that little town where we stayed—Cembra—wine country.

Jim: That was fun, wasn't it? Yeah, the Cembra Valley, the big wine valley. We went to Easter services there.

Tim: I really enjoyed that little town. That was nice.

Jim: We went to Fanano next. That was the whole purpose for the trip. We spent several days there.

Tim: And we met Felix Pedro's (discoverer of gold in Fairbanks) descendants. Had a nice visit with them.

Jim: Dairy farmers. You should've fit right in there.

Tim: Yeah, not only met the dairy farmers, but the fellow we met there at the restaurant in the hotel where we were staying.

Jim: Yes, that was Massimo, and the big guy was with the government. He was with the city mayor's office. Let's see if I can recount this: We went to see the shrine they put up on behalf of Felix Pedro; we then went to his burial spot, his tomb.

Tim: His tomb, yes. After that we went down in the valley and visited the house where he was born, and grew up.

Jim: And ultimately to the Spring of the Golden Waters.

Tim: Yup, down in the gully. We got pictures of everything.

Jim: And that's when I got sick.

Tim: Was it from the water?

Jim: No, I think it was from the food. And then we went to...La Cima for a couple of days, then you got sick.

Tim: I got sick.

Jim: But then you got well.

Tim: I got well in a hurry.

Jim: Yeah, you got well in a hurry and I was still sick. Then we went to Assisi, and then from Assisi, we went back to Rome, and caught the plane, and I paid the highest price I ever paid for a hotel room in my entire life. What did I pay, $250 for one night?

Tim: Is that what it was?

Jim: $275 I think.

Tim: Good gravy!

Jim: I didn't care. I was about to puke my guts out.

Tim: Do you remember what we saw there in the airport with the soldiers walking around—one was carrying a machine gun, and the other two had rifles. That's what is going on in our airports right now. Scary.

Jim: I didn't think we would ever see that.

Tim: I didn't either.

Jim: Do you have anything else you would like to add to this. What do you plan to do in the future? Do you own an airplane?

Tim: I have an airplane—thank God.

Jim: Can you own an airplane?

Tim: No.

Jim: So someone else must own an airplane.

Tim: You own the airplane.

Jim: A 172 is that what I own?

Tim: Yeah.

Jim: What color is it?

Tim: It's white with maroon stripes.

Jim: Oh, I own a white and maroon Cessna172 with stripes, and do you fly it often? You can fly it any time your want, right?

Tim: Yeah, I fly it anytime I want. Right. Thank you for your kindness.

Jim: Oh, anytime, just go ahead and fly it. Second part of the question: What are your plans for the future?.

Tim: I plan to stay here. One of my big things is working with Beginning Experience which is a support program for the divorced, separated or widowed, where there is a loss of a relationship—a serious loss of a relationship—and that's one of the big reasons I'm here right now. I want to stay with this program as long as I can. When I can't fly any more, I'll have to think about it.

Jim: You'll have to let me do the flying.

Tim: Yup.

Jim: Just bring the wine.

Tim: Right.

Jim: Tell us about Beginning Experience. You travel a fair bit to conferences.

Tim: Yes. I just got back from Nashville, which had the American Association for Marital and Family Therapy.

Jim: I see, and you go to these conferences what, maybe a couple of times a year?

Tim: At least once a year, because I have to get educational units to renew my marriage-and-family license.

Jim: Do you go out and see your family from time to time?

Tim: Oh yeah, I get down there about two, three times a year.

Jim: Do you plan to live out your life in Alaska?

Tim: I hope to, yes.

Jim: Do you feel that your life is not in the past, but all of your current activities are fulfilling to you?

Tim: Very much, yes.

Jim: You're happy?

Tim: I am.

Jim: You're content?

Tim: I'm content.

Jim: And you're at peace with God?

Tim: Yes, couldn't be happier.

Jim: Tim I've known you for over 20 years and it has been one of the best friendships I could have ever hope to have. Some of my other friends say, "Those are a couple of the most mismatched friends I have ever seen." I guess they just don't understand. Thank you for the interview, Tim.

Tim: Like I said, I couldn't be happier with the way things are. I agree with you it has been a good friendship—must be; it has lasted 20 years.

Mary Shields
with
Jim Madonna
November 16, 1986

Jim: Good afternoon, ladies and gentlemen. This is Alaska Gold Trails and I am your host, Jim Madonna. Our guest today is Mary Shields. Welcome to Alaska Gold Trails, Mary.

Mary: Thank you Jim. It's nice to be here.

Jim: First I want to tell our audience that Mary Shields has had an interesting life. Earlier, I asked her if she was famous. She said she wasn't. But many of us know she has quite a good reputation regarding dog mushing in the state of Alaska. Mary give us a little background—where you came from, when you were born, and how you happened to come to Alaska.

Mary: Well, I was born in 1944 in Wisconsin, and I came to Alaska in 1965. I came as a Campfire Girl counselor to work in day camps around the state for the summer, and I really liked the place. I had one more year of school back at the University of Wisconsin. I went back there, finished up, and returned the next summer and worked again for the Campfire Girls. The last place we had day camp was Fairbanks, Alaska, and I'm still here.

Jim: Let me catch this call, Mary, and we'll be right back. Hi, you're on the air.

Caller: Hi, I wanted to call and say hello to Mary. Mary, I just wanted to let you know that I had relatives here this summer. They were quite taken with you, when they were on the Riverboat Discovery tour. I thought it was great that they got to meet a person like you. I hope that you reconsider and continue running the (Yukon) Quest.

Mary: Thank you. That voice sounds familiar, but I can't tell who you are. It is really fun working for the Riverboat (Discovery) in the summer, and meeting all those people. Jim and I were just talking about that this noon; to find a job where you can share something you really love with people is a unique opportunity and I feel fortunate to have that opportunity.

Caller: Okay.

Jim: Thank you for the call, sir. Mary, in what kind of environment did you grow up, in the city or rural?

Mary: I was a city girl in Waukesha, Wisconsin, which is about 20 miles outside of Milwaukee. There was a little country between Waukesha and Milwaukee when I lived there. I was home to visit my mom last fall, and it is just all suburbs all the way now. Waukesha was a fairly big city then.

Jim: You were probably involved in outdoor activities all of your life. What did you have in a city to attract you?

Mary: In the city, I just did city things. On weekends, I would go out hiking in the country a little bit. My uncles had a dairy farm up near Wisconsin Dells, and we'd go there for a few weeks in the summer. When I went to the University of Wisconsin, I got involved with the Hoofers Club which was an outdoor club, and I became a sailor. The University is right on Lake Mendota. I really enjoyed sailing there.

Jim: We were talking a little earlier about when you were part of the Hoofers Club, and you saw your first dog team.

Mary: It was late in the winter, and I was just sitting on the bank of the lake hoping the ice would melt early, and lo and behold, the dog team came across the lake. Actually, it was a fellow from Alaska who was down there either as a graduate student or a professor or something. He had brought his dog team with him, and he was running them out on the lake. I've met him. He lives up in Bettles. I met him once when I was traveling on a trip out there in the springtime.

Jim: Did that start you thinking about dog mushing or was it just something that happened?

Mary: No, at that point, it didn't make much of an impression on me. I was just earning money for college working in camps in the summer, and I had applied to lots of camps. The Alaska job was the farthest away from Wisconsin, and they paid my transportation, so it just made sense to come up here, but I really didn't know anything about Alaska when I came.

Jim: Now the way I understand it, you were up here two years in a row. Is that correct?

Mary: Right, two summers. After the second summer, I stayed here permanently.

Jim: You ended up in Fairbanks?

Mary: Right.

Jim: Can you give us a little information about the lifestyle you selected when you first came to Fairbanks. What year was that?

Mary: That would have been 1966. I just had the wages I had earned as a Campfire Girl counselor which was a couple hundred dollars, I think. Day camp was out at Mrs. Brice's property off of Chena Hot Springs Road. Some of the local Campfire people, Leslie Salisbury and Lee Salisbury, had a little guest cabin they let me stay in for the first couple of weeks. I walked around the neighborhood, and Joe Lawler had a little wannigan where he let me live the first winter. They had nine children, so in trade for baby-sitting, I had a free place to live while I went to the University of Alaska that first winter.

Jim: In what area of education did you study?

Mary: I had been an English major in Wisconsin, although not a very serious student.

Jim: Did you graduate?

Mary: Yes, I got a degree in English there. I went into biology here. Well, while I went to college at the University, I decided I could be back in Waukesha if I was going to be so close to a big city. I wanted to see what the wilderness was all about. The conductor on the Alaska Railroad told me about a little cabin about halfway between Anchorage and Fairbanks that was abandoned and I moved in there for the winter and learned quite a few new things. In October some friends, Mike and Sally Jones from Fairbanks, came down to visit me. They saw me dragging in firewood and pails of water, and they suggested a few sled dogs would help with the chores, and it just so happened that they had dogs they weren't really using. They had lived up in Ambler, and had some dogs they'd brought back with them. Their lifestyle had changed, and the dogs were just chained up most of the time. So, they went back to Fairbanks, and the next southbound train stopped and out came these three furry dogs and a pile of Purina Dog Food, an old, broken-down sled, and taped to the sled was a note that said, "There's nothing to it. Just put the dogs in front of the sled." That's basically all there is to it and I've been enjoying dogs ever since.

Jim: That sounds like friends who were trying to help you out, and knew how.

Mary: They were very dear friends. I had to give the dogs back at the end of the summer because they were their dogs. It gave me the bug.

Jim: What did you do?

Mary: Well the next year I moved back to the Fairbanks area, and I remember walking down Yankovich Road everyday on the way to the University the year before and hearing all of these dogs bark. I thought, "Anyone who has a whole bunch of dogs in their yard might use a little help." I went up and knocked on the door, and it was Roger Burggraf's home actually, and he had a big kennel of dogs. I asked him if he needed any help with his dogs, and he said well yes, he'd let me try one dog. It happened to be his prized dog named Nacky who had won a lot of dog show awards. He told me I could take that one dog out for a trial run, and when I got down to Ballaine Lake, she'd want to go right and I shouldn't let her. I had to make her go left and come home. We did that and sure enough, she wanted to go right. She was a big dog, but I went out and yanked her around, and made sure she went where I told her to and brought her home. I think that was a test for me more than the dog. Roger was seeing if I would come home with his dogs in good shape. Then, the rest of the winter, he would let me come over there and run his dogs, which was really a generous thing for him to do.

Jim: You were hooked by then, weren't you?

Mary: I was hooked good! Then, I started picking up a few of my own dogs. Actually I had one dog at the time from the year before.

Jim: And what year was this then?

Mary: Around 1970. I get the years a little mixed up.

Jim: Well, when did you meet John.

Mary: That same year, 1970.

Jim: When you first saw John, tell us a little bit about that. Did you have a leap of the heart?

Mary: Well hopefully John isn't listening or he'll be quite embarrassed. Yes, the first time I saw him, I knew he was the one for me, and that's how I felt this morning too. He's a very special person.

Jim: Is that right? So then you and John are both deeply interested in dog mushing?

Mary: Well, when we first met back then, I remember borrowing Roger's dogs, and John and I would go off on picnics with them. He was working up at the University. We both got our own dogs, and began doing quite a bit of traveling with them. In the last few years, John has not been as interested in dogs as I am. He's a real perfectionist, and if the dogs aren't perfect, he'd get agitated. He enjoys skiing more than getting around with dogs. In the last two years, he hasn't been running them much at all.

Jim: Tell us about your experience dogsledding.

Mary: Well I had heard about this Iditarod Trail the year before. I'd never gone very far before with my dogs. In Christmas of '73—'74, John and I went on a trip by dogsled from Fairbanks over to Tanana to visit some friends. We really liked getting out and seeing new country. I heard of this race that was "a thousand miles of broken trail." A thousand miles of broken trail sounded real inviting. So I called up Anchorage and signed up for the race. The voice on the other end of the phone sounded real suspicious. I don't think they believed I would really show up at the starting line. I only owned six dogs. I had to buy a couple more, because I needed eight to start the race. So I rounded up two more, and arrived there with my eight dogs, and off we went.

Jim: For those of us who are not familiar with a dog team, Mary, describe the dogs' positions ahead of the sled.

Mary: Well when you have an even number of dogs on your team, you usually have a double lead just because it doesn't string them out so far away from the sled. My one leader was half black Labrador, half husky. His name was Cabbage. I owned that dog for the sixteen and a half years of his life. He was a real special dog. His mother was Ceyanna. She was one of those original three dogs I had borrowed from Mike and Sally and they let me use her again. My two other dogs, Ambler and Kobuk were just mixed-breed huskies.

Jim: Were they just behind the leaders?

Mary: The dogs just behind the lead dog we call swing dogs because they help swing the team around corners. The rest are just team dogs, except the two dogs directly in front of the sled are called wheel dogs. They really have to know their business. When you get on a trail with tight corners, they have to pull really hard to get the sled out around the trees so you don't bang into the trees. Usually you put your largest, strongest dogs in the back where you need some pulling power.

Jim: We have a call, Mary. Hi, you're on the air.

Caller: Yes, I'd like to talk to Mary.

Mary: Hello.

Caller: Mary, this is Cam. You haven't told them about your pet owl and also putting your English degree to use by writing books? I'll hang up and listen.

Mary: Oh hi Cam. First of all, the owl. The last year I was at Wisconsin, I was up in the biology library there. Some child had taken a baby great-horned owl out of a nest and their parents had finally tired of having it around the house and had taken it into the biology department and they were looking for someone to raise it. So I volunteered. When I came to Alaska, I had the owl and it would ride around on my shoulder. I remember I went on the Equinox Marathon that first fall. I guess I got the nickname the Owl Lady or something. People still come up and ask me about the owl. That was the year I was living at Lawler's. I took him around to the school that fall. When it got snow on the ground, I was feeding it mostly chicken. We'd catch mice in the field and get it to learn to jump on mice and catch its own food. Finally, I turned it loose, and for a couple of years I think it was the same owl that hung around that area. People that were out would notice an owl that would sit and let them walk right underneath it and look at them and stuff, so he survived for a few years anyway. Then I don't know what happened to him. About the writing, I started writing some magazine articles in the mid-70s and then I started writing books in the early '80s.

Jim: Tell us the first book you put out, Mary.

Mary: _Sled Dog Trails_ came out in 1984. It kind of tells about the trips we took, the Iditarod and being out in the wilderness with dogs. I guess I used dogs as a means to say something I felt was important. The book was trying to tell people to find something in life that is really precious to them and go out and do it. For me, it happens to be dog sledding. I'm not saying it should be dog sledding for anyone else. It's important to spend these days we have in life doing something that we really, truly love.

Jim: Did you put out a second book, Mary?

Mary: Yes, _Small Wonders, Year-Round Alaska_ is a natural history book. We have a cabin about 30 miles west of Fairbanks where we spend quite a bit of the time. We've kept journals out there. The book describes the changes in the seasons and the plants and the animals—just the basic lifestyle we had there.

Jim: I'll bet that's an interesting account. Are these available in the bookstores around Fairbanks, Mary?

Mary: The Book Cache, the University of Alaska BookStore, Art Works and some of the gift shops in town have them.

Jim: We were talking about the Iditarod and the fact that you showed up at the starting line with eight dogs. Do you want to give us a summary or an account of how that trip went and your experiences?

Mary: The starting line was certainly the scariest part, just having all those people hollering and cheering. Neither my dogs nor I had been in front of a big crowd like that. So that was pretty scary. I remember the first four or five miles or ten miles goes through downtown Anchorage or suburbs of Anchorage. I remember a bunch of people standing along a fence there, and some fellow hollered at me in kind of a real nasty voice. He said, "You better turn around now. You're never going to make it all the way to Nome." I don't know who he was, but I sure thank him for that encouragement. Boy, if there were ever moments when I wondered what I was doing out there, I just remembered what he said. I knew I was going to make it all the way to Nome.

Jim: Did you have stops along the way?

Mary: Racing was much different than it is now. Nobody really knew what we were doing. We just learned an awful lot in the last 16 years of racing. The pace was much slower. It took me 28 days to get there, and I finished 21st or 22nd out of 49 teams.

Jim: You finished with a good show, too!

Mary: Well, I was just happy to get to the finish line.

Jim: Let's take this call, Mary. Hi, you're on the air.

Caller: Were you the first lady to run the Iditarod?

Mary: Oh, there were two women in the race that year, Lolly Medley and myself.

Caller: Speaking for yourself, dog mushing out there, in the middle of no-where, do you have a conscious contact with a higher power? Do you find dog mushers more of a spiritual breed of Alaskan?

Mary: I really can't speak spiritually for other people. I find great strength in being out in the wilderness and feeling a part of the natural world out there. I think dog mushers do share a common love for being out in the country, and for dogs. But today there are dog mushers from all walks of life—university professors, trappers, racers, biologists—and we're a real varied group of people now.

Caller: I find the sleds that I see on tops of trucks now a lot different than they used to be. They are changing aren't they?

Mary: Yes, they're getting lighter, and they're taking advantage of some of the more modern materials—aluminum, plastic. There was a sled in the (Yukon) Quest last year, I believe, made out of titanium. Of course the rules in the Quest say you have to finish with the same sled you begin with. That 13-pound titanium sled broke halfway through, and the guy couldn't put it back together, and he had to drop out of the race. I take a nice wooden basket sled, and if it breaks, I chop down a willow and lash it together and keep on going. I've used the same wooden sled in all three Quests I've been on and run long trips every year in between. They're unbeatable.

Caller: Thank you.

Mary: You're welcome.

Jim: Mary, run through the Iditarod, and the more typical stops that you made and what you did during the stops, and how you cared for your dogs.

Mary: Well, we stopped all the time, actually.

Jim: Were there some preferred stops by all the mushers?

Mary: We had quite a few of the same checkpoints they still have today. At that time, we went over Ptarmigan Pass instead of Rainy Pass. That year we had a bad storm, and the teams had to turn back, and we had to spend 24 hours at the Rainy Pass Lodge waiting to get across and over the pass. The trail that year went down the Yukon to Kaltag then over the portage to Unalakleet. I was fortunate to stay with Edgar Kalland in Kaltag, one of the original serum carriers from the original Iditarod run in 1925. That was a real high point for me.

Jim: Oh my! How many mushers started the race?

Mary: Forty-nine teams started the race that year.

Jim: And how many completed?

Mary: Oh, I think there were just six or seven behind me that year. There weren't too many more behind. A lot of them had dropped out.

Jim: Did the other lady finish?

Mary: Yup, Lolly Medley was right behind me, about a half an hour or so. We didn't really travel together. We kind of leapfrogged each other along. We had different styles of running our dogs. She came in and did a real good job.

Jim: We have a call, Mary. Welcome to Alaska Gold Trails, you're on the air.

Caller: Yes, Mary, I apologize for calling back. I'll ask two quick questions, and then hang up and listen. The difference between sprint racing and long-distance racing. Do you see a common bond in dog mushers in that, or are they more of two separate breeds of people? The other thing is in the difference in the dogs in sprint racing and long-distance racing.

Mary: Okay, the first question, I think the people certainly share a common bond in that they love their dogs and they like being out on the trail. From there on, from what I see, they're pretty different styles of racing. I've never been in a sprint race. It looks like they go around in circles and just go as fast as they can, and that doesn't appeal to me. I know there's a lot more to it. I respect the people that are dedicating themselves to sprint racing. The distance racing has a lot more factors other than just speed. They have weather and camping and trail conditions and gear and they're out there for two weeks so it's a much different approach rather than just going out for a couple of hours on the weekend. I think which one you choose really decides your lifestyle. Some people can sprint race and still hold down pretty full-time jobs. The distance racers pretty much have to dedicate their winter to training those dogs because they have to get 1,500—2,000 miles on lots of dogs before a long-distance race, then select a team of 12 for the Quest or 15 to 20 for the Iditarod. It may be more time-consuming. I don't know that much about the sprint racers. I know they're out there training dogs every day, too. I think maybe the time is a greater demand for the long-distance racers unless you have a lot of helpers who can help train your dogs.

Jim: Good question. Thank you for the call. Mary, tell us what you have in the future. What your plans are in terms of mushing and other outdoor activities.

Mary: Well, I'm enjoying running my dogs everyday. I have eleven dogs right now, six of the eleven are eight or nine years old. They're getting to be old-timers. They've taken real good care of me, so I'm going to hang onto them. We'll just go a little slower. I don't plan on racing in anything this year. Maybe I would try some little race, but nothing big. I guess one thing that I would like to do in the future is make that trip over to Siberia with the dogs. The way they're talking now it is going to be kind of an invitational that will take probably the most competitive teams from the Iditarod and the Quest to represent the United States. I don't think I'll be included in that, but if some year it's open to other kinds of mushers like myself, I'd sure love to see that country from the back of a dogsled.

Jim: We'd like to see you in on that too, Mary. You've done a lot of work with mushing, and have a great deal of interest in dog racing. Do you have any last-minute, roundup comments you'd like to make?

Mary: Well another thing, I'm also working on a new book. I'm trying to collect stories from other mushers about their exceptional dogs. I think the mushers have gotten enough glory. I'd like to give the dogs a little of the glory, and I know there have been some amazing things that sled dogs have done for people.

Jim: Mary, unfortunately we have run out of time. We could listen to you for hours. Sorry the time seemed so short. I want to thank you for joining us on Alaska Gold Trails today.

Mary: Thank you, Jim.

Tom Snapp
with
Jim Madonna
March 11, 1988

Jim: Welcome to Alaska Gold Trails, ladies and gentlemen. Our special guest today is Tom Snapp. Thank you for coming on the show today, Tom,

Tom: Thank you, Jim.

Jim: Tom, when did you come to Alaska and what made you decide to come?

Tom: Well, I came to Alaska in 1960 to visit my sister who was living here.

Jim: And did you just spontaneously get on a plane and fly up here in 1960?

Tom: No, not really. I was going to graduate school in journalism at the University of Missouri and I had a whole summer that I was going to have to go somewhere and I had been going back home to Virginia for a long time, so I wanted to go somewhere different, and my sister had invited me to come for some time and visit her, but I had sort of negative connotations about Alaska, and well, at that time a plane ticket ... I've forgotten how much it was, but I thought that's quite a lot of money for a plane ticket, so I didn't come. And so, right about the end of my semester she sent me a round-trip ticket and she said I could come for one week, or two weeks, or all summer. So I thought, well, I can't beat that. If I didn't like it, I could always hit the next Pan Am flight and fly out. So I came and I was pleasantly surprised because it was quite different from what I'd imagined it to be, and instead of not liking it I liked it very much, so I stayed all these number of years.

Jim: And what did you do when you came?

Tom: Well, I stayed with my sister. Because I was in journalism, I was wanting to get to talk to people, but it was in June and people were real busy and I'd go out trying to talk to people and they'd seem to not have too much time to talk like we do in a leisurely way back in Virginia. So, I told my sister, well, I'm going to have to get some kind of a job. And I applied at the employment office. Well, first I applied, I think, at the Daily News-Miner and they didn't have any openings, and then I applied at the employment office and they wanted to send me to Clear, where they were building the Clear BMEW (Ballistic Missile Early Warning) site then, and when I started investigating I was going to have to work real long hours, like 58 hours a week, so I didn't go there. Finally, we saw an ad in the paper for enumerators for the city directory, and that was right up my alley, because I was just itching to go in and talk to people in their homes and whatnot. And so, with the city directory you filled out these little cards—that's all you did—and you just went from home to home. Well, my sister didn't want me to do it. She said, "Oh, they just pay the minimum wage." I said, "Well, the money's not the important thing, it's what I'm wanting to do." And I said, "At least I'll have enough to buy my lunch." And she said, "Well, what about all that walking?" She says, "That's a lot of walking on that job." And I says, "Well, can I borrow your vehicle?" And so she said, "Yes." So I borrowed her station wagon. I'd take her to work in the morning and then I'd go after her at night, and that city directory thing really got me interested in Alaska and Fairbanks. Some of the things I ran into were out of this world. Sometimes I'd go into a house where they'd be having a party and they were so intoxicated they couldn't even give me their name and address, you know for the little card. Sometimes I'd be looking for a number and the house would be missing and I'd say, "Well, where's this house number?" And they'd say, "Oh, that was moved over to so-and-so street." So pretty soon I found out these houses were moved around like checkers and I'd look for houses and there would be a basement, just like holes in the ground, because the people would've built a basement with the idea that later they would add the upper stories, but somehow they never got the money ahead, so they were living in basements. I found a lot of people living in basements. One house, one cabin, I chased almost all one afternoon trying to find it, and I finally found it, guess where. On top of the city dump. It was a little cabin and it had been moved from one owner to the other and finally been donated to the Girl Scouts and then to the dump.

Jim: Nobody lived there anymore.

Tom: Nobody lived there, and when they got through with it, they had discarded it and I'd been chasing that house all over town. Well, anyway, all these incidents, learning how to avoid being bitten by dogs—cause I got bitten about three or four times—I had to learn how to have a magazine rolled up and beat off the dogs and go next door and call and have the people tie up their dogs and whatnot. Well, anyway, all these incidents with this job was just getting me more and more interested.

Jim: Excuse me, how did you get more and more interested in this job with all those dogs biting you? I'm amazed that you would want to continue on with this line of work, with the number of attacks that you were having.

Tom: Well, not particularly the work. The work was just sort of an excuse to get in and talk to people. I was talking to numerous people that were very interesting—all different walks of life—and the fact that Fairbanks had a frontier flavor about it. You know, like when I first came into Fairbanks I was just amazed. The dust was flying—this city had been here since the gold rush and it still hadn't paved the streets. Noble Street, for instance, was real potholed, and I'd landed at Eielson, they'd brought me in to Traveler's Inn and the bus went around behind there on Clay Street, and the dust was just flying, you know. It was things like that. I had been reporting in Virginia, Florida, Missouri—those states, you know, they're developed and whatnot. They're all sort of about the same, and here this was just such an unusual, different community.

Jim: You saw a lot of things to report on in Fairbanks, Alaska, then, Tom.

Tom: Oh yes. And while I was going around on this job with the city directory, I ran into Mr. Cliff Cernic, who was the editor of the *Fairbanks Daily News-Miner*, and I went in, and when he found out that I was in journalism and I found out he was the editor of the *News-Miner*, well he invited me in for coffee and cookies and he showed me the new children's books he had written. Before you knew it, he was asking me if I was able to come to the *News-Miner* to fill in and that he was expecting that one of his reporters was going to be leaving soon to take a job with the *Honolulu Star Bulletin*.

Jim: Was that in 1960, Tom?

Tom: Yes. I'd just been doing that city directory two or three weeks. He thought that this Jim LeBeck was going to be leaving in about a month or so, but then amazingly, the next week he called and LeBeck was leaving earlier than expected and he asked if I would come and fill in, and I said yes.

Jim: We have a call, Tom. Welcome to Alaska Gold Trails. Do you have a question for Tom?

Caller: I sure do. I would like Tom to explain, if he could, what seems to be the prevailing attitude in the state, and I've heard it expressed here in the borough too, big mining. Big mining companies are OK but I don't see much support for the family operations. I wonder if he could comment on that.

Tom: Well, for a number of years, the way I see it is that a number of the federal agencies and state agencies too would like to get rid of mining. In fact I had some Fish and Game people tell me that they'd like all the small miners wiped off the countryside. They said that they were polluters, that they attracted bears—that their garbage and stuff attracted bears—and that they thought it would be much more environmentally pleasing and so forth. For some reason it's hard to put over to them the economic benefits of having the small miner, and the things that they've accomplished. Of course a lot of the people that work for the government have their secure salaries. Does that answer your question?

Caller: Well, you've come along quite a ways on it. But the question was, why does there seem to be support for the large mining ventures and, like you say, they kind of want to eliminate the small one?

Tom: Well, the government people, you see, want to have revenue coming into their coffers. The state is taking money in from the oil leases on the slope and what they're trying to do is police the minerals and then the state or federal coffers will get the funds from both the lease fees and from royalties. So they are trying to make the same kind of thing that they've got going with oil, applicable to other minerals.

Caller: OK, a follow-up question is, for those Fish and Game people that want to wipe out the small miners, what do they propose that those people do to earn their living? What do they think those people are going to do? Are we all supposed to get government positions?

Tom: Well, it doesn't make sense, you see what I'm saying? They have their jobs secured so they can't empathize with someone out there trying to make a living in other endeavors.

Caller: It seems so strange and so odd that the bureaucrats would desire to wipe out this frontier spirit that you're talking about—the independent people that are trying to make it on their own.

Tom: Well, ever since I've been here it's been going in that direction. So I can only presume that it will continue. Just look at the environmental restraints that have been put on it. The placer mining is practically having to close down because of not being able to meet the environmental regulations that have been put forward. And you have things like some of the larger mines making the water clean enough to drink and then having to dump it back into the muddy river. It doesn't make sense.

Jim: You have really brought up some great points here, and I want to thank you for talking to us here on Alaska Gold Trails Thank you very much for the call. Tom, tell us about your introduction to the *News-Miner* staff.

Tom: Well, I began work there during that summer, and I was planning to go back to school that fall, but I became so inclined in stories that by that fall they were asking me if I would postpone and go back to school at the second semester, and what decided the question was Mr. Cernic was leaving the *News-Miner* and he had been the *Time and Sports Illustrated* correspondent, and the bureau chief came up from San Francisco and Mr. Cernic had recommended that the correspondency be given to me. Of course, it wouldn't work for me to take it and then stop in a month or two, so I reluctantly agreed to go back to school the second semester, and in the second semester I was more inclined than I was the first semester, so I stayed at the *News-Miner* for about two years, and then I helped start the *Tundra Times*.

Jim: The *Tundra Times*, was that with Howard Rock?

Tom: *Yes.* And I put in for the grant for the *Tundra Times* and we got the grant. We started that paper—an Indian, Eskimo, Aleut paper—and it's been going ever since.

Jim: How long did you work for the *News-Miner*?

Tom: About two years.

Jim: And then how long did it take you to start and develop the *Tundra Times*?

Tom: Well, we started the *Tundra Times* on Oct. 1, 1962, and the lead story, which I wrote, was the Secretary of the Interior, Stuart Udall, came to Fairbanks, speaking to the Chamber of Commerce, and he promised that the historic native land claims was the number one problem to be settled. Here's a copy of that first *Tundra Times* paper, and you'll see it's got Mr. Seeliger, who I think was president of the Chamber then, introducing the secretary, Mr. Udall. Well, I worked with Howard for one year, and I trained him in all phases of journalism, and then I went back to school for nine months, and then I came back and became editor of *Jessen's Weekly*.

Jim: Where did you go to school, Tom?

Tom: University of Missouri, School of Journalism.

Jim: Then you came back and joined Mr. Jessen at *Jessen's Weekly*.

Tom: Yes, and I was editor of *Jessen's Weekly* then, and I was editor during the flood—I mean from that time, from 1964 to 1967 and in 1967 we had the flood. The plant over there was under about six or seven feet of water, and those linotype machines were just sort of rusted in place and the whole plant had to be redone over. And we got an FDA (Food and Drug Administration) loan and then they figured that the loan was so large we had to go daily to bring in the revenues to pay the loan, and so we went daily then. And then in a month or so we went Sunday, and I was editor of the first Sunday paper. One time I was editor of a weekly, daily and Sunday. I was meeting myself coming back.

Jim: Tom, tell us about some of your adventures with *Jessen's Weekly*, after the flood.

Tom: Oh, after the flood? Well, it was quite an ordeal to recover from the flood, I remember that. I spent six weeks trying to save photographs—washing them, and drying them, painting them with chemicals and well, starting a daily paper, there was quite a lot to that. Also the fact that the flood had done so much damage to our files and oftentimes we'd try to come up with file pictures or information, you know, and it wouldn't be there because we had to throw it out. We had to sort of shovel out our files to the dump, after the flood. Let's see, you're saying interesting stories that I covered?

Jim: Let's have one. How about your most interesting story.

Tom: Well, I think the most interesting story is the one that's been put out that I covered, that was while I was with the *News-Miner*. It was a Kentucky tourist, William Waters, who was lost in the wilderness up in Charlie River country. He was a retired railroad worker and he had come to Alaska and he liked to fish very much. He'd fished a lot in Canada, and he went up to Circle City and he parked his car there at Circle, and he started fishing and he disappeared. And he was turned in; no one had seen him, his car was sitting there such a long time, and the police made an investigation. They got bloodhounds. They thought he had gone out in the water and drowned. I was covering the police beat then, and I had talked to some *News-Miner* pressmen who had been up there at the very time that he had disappeared, and they believed that he had wandered off further and hadn't drowned at this place where they had been searching, because they had found a lean-to where it had a Lucky Strike cigarette package, and it was the kind of brand that he smoked. Anyway, this man was lost. He started out for the foothills and it took him three days to get there, and in the meantime he ran out of water and he started drinking out of chuckholes, and then he reached Birch Creek and he started going down—he'd read in a book that if you got lost you should go south, so he was following Birch Creek south, which went for several hundred miles with hardly anything on it, real twisty, and as the summer wore off, as it became fall, the temperature became colder, and the only thing he was eating was rosehips and berries, and they began to disappear and it began to get cold, and finally he gave up. I think he had something like 17 matches, and he would build a fire and then he would try to take pieces of the fire and build a fire a little further down. Finally he ran out of matches, it began to get cold, and he picked out a sort of a decayed log, and decided that his time had come. Luckily some moose hunters from Fairbanks—Ray Casola, who had won the Yukon 800, and Millie Webb— were up there moose hunting. And Ray and Millie went by in a motorboat and that gave him a lot of hope. He got down to the riverbank, through a lot of tall vegetation, and when they came back down the river, why he tried to wave and attract their attention, but it was right at dusk and they didn't see him and went by. So then he went back disgusted, thinking he had missed his only chance of being rescued. And the next day they came by again, and that time, even though he was weak and had trenchmouth and whatnot, he was able to wave them down and they came by and got him and they brought him into the hot springs resort. They gave him beer and some things to eat, which they probably shouldn't, him having trenchmouth. Then they gave him a hot bath, in water so hot he could hardly stand it. Then they put him to bed and put nine yarn blankets on him. The next day they brought him into St. Joseph's Hospital in Fairbanks, and they couldn't find a thermometer that would measure his temperature—I mean his body was below 92. He made medical history, because he had adapted to the cold, and he lost over half his weight—he looked like someone who had come out of a concentration camp. Well now the reason that that's the most amazing story that I covered is that I talked to him when he first came in, in the morning, and I asked him, "These sisters won't let me come back unless you tell them that I'm to come back every night." So he did, he told them that I was to come back every night. So then, of course, other reporters tried to get in and they had no permission, but I did. So from there on for oh four or five weeks I came every night. The most amazing thing to me about this story was, you know you can go out when you have a garden and you think you can see vegetables and things growing, but in this case, this man's appearance changed from day to day for about 10 days, and I took pictures of him, and his recovery was the most amazing thing I think I'd ever seen and reported on.

Jim: How I wish we were not out of time. Tom, thank you very much for that story, and I also want to thank you for sharing your time with us on Alaska Gold Trails. Thank you for coming.

Tom: You're very welcome, Jim.

Sandra Stillion
with
Jim Madonna
March 9, 1989

Jim: I want to introduce our guest today, Sandra Stillion. Sandy, welcome to Alaska Gold Trails.

Sandy: Thank you, Jim, it's a pleasure to be here.

Jim: I've been looking forward to this for a long time. You've had quite a history coming into the country and watching Fairbanks grow, since the early 1950s, all the way up to the present time. Give us a little background, where were you born, Sandy?

Sandy: I was born in San Francisco.

Jim: Oh, a city girl. What in the world ever drug you up to Alaska from the city?

Sandy: Well, that's sort of what my mother wondered too, when Dad decided he wanted to come to Alaska. Dad had been up here working for two summers, prior to 1954, and at that time, I had an aunt and uncle who had been up here those prior two summers homesteading. And so, for that third year they suggested to Dad that it might be a good thing for him to bring us along. So he convinced Mom, and we set out, sort of caravan style. We had an old bus. I think it was an old 40-foot, pre-1940 school bus that had been converted for sleeping arrangements, cooking arrangements, and the back end of it was sectioned off for a horse and some goats.

Jim: I see. Was this the precursor of the recreational vehicle?

Sandy: Yeah, I believe it was.

Jim: Sandy, what did you have in mind, as you moved northward? What did you expect Alaska to be like?

Sandy: Well, I was only 11 at the time, and to me it was a grand adventure. I didn't really know where Alaska was, I just knew it was full of mysterious sounding things. Dad is a carpenter, and the military was experiencing a lot of construction on the bases, and so there was a lot of work for carpenters.

Jim: And how far did you make it? Did you make it all the way to Fairbanks?

Sandy: No, as a matter of fact, we didn't. Mom put out the skids at North Pole, I think, and said, "We're not going any further." So we settled in North Pole.

Jim: Before you ever got to Fairbanks? You didn't even come the final 10 miles into Fairbanks?

Sandy: No, I don't even remember when I made my first trip into Fairbanks.

Jim: Is that a fact? She said, "That's it."

Sandy: That's it.

Jim: Ten miles from Fairbanks. I can't believe it. The big city not far away. Could you see the lights?

Sandy: No. No lights. In fact, the lights of North Pole, which was barely a blink in the road, was the biggest lights we'd seen for some time.

Jim: How many people were in North Pole, at that time?

Sandy: I don't recall. Maybe 150, a couple hundred. I don't know for sure. I know school was just a handful of kids. We had multiple grades in each room.

Jim: Oh, that's interesting. Tell us about it.

Sandy: We had an old oil-burning space heater. You know the tales of the classrooms where you had to rotate seats so you could take your turn at getting warm? We did that a little bit.

Jim: I get the picture. What grade were you in when you arrived?

Sandy: I was in the fifth grade, when we arrived.

Jim: Did you graduate from grammar school there?

Sandy: Yes. Right at North Pole.

Jim: Did they have a high school?

Sandy: By the time I was out of the eighth grade, they had just built Lathrop (in Fairbanks). So, Lathrop was a brand new school when I started high school.

Jim: You mean to say that you didn't have the joy of attending Main School?

Sandy: No, I didn't, I'm sorry to say.

Jim: Oh, that's too bad. One of the historical sites. A memory that I have when I first came up here was attending Main School. Well, it must have been interesting to walk into the newly constructed high school here in Fairbanks, with all the new rooms. And you didn't have to rotate around a big heater to keep each student thawed out.

Sandy: It was a big change.

Jim: When you got to Alaska, what did you think about North Pole and Fairbanks after you'd had a chance to roam around a little bit?

Sandy: I was pretty much thrilled with the remoteness of it all. We had to use an old pitcher pump to pump water into the house. One of my oldest memories of living out there was trying to get that doggone powdered milk to mix up, to get the lumps out of it. We sort of grew up with powdered milk and canned milk. To this day I can't get enough fruit, because in those days fruit was a seasonal thing. It came in just certain times of year and you only got so much of it, and that was it.

Jim: That's right. I remember that.

Sandy: So, those are some of the things I first remember when I think of the early '50s in North Pole. No television, no telephones.

Jim: Oh, what a hardship.

Sandy: Right. Remote.

Jim: And how close was your nearest neighbor?

Sandy: Oh, really just across the street. We were right there in a little settlement of North Pole. They had a few streets and I don't remember just how many dwellings were there.

Jim: But in general they did have a few streets but the houses were single separate dwellings, not duplexes.

Sandy: Yes and a couple houses per block, something like that. High-density living.

Jim: Once you went to high school at Lathrop you continued on at high school there?

Sandy: I also spent a little bit of time going to high school out at Eielson—Ben Eielson High. At that time, we had the option to attend whichever high school we wanted to, but we had to provide our own transportation, and so one of the girls' fathers, that worked out at Eielson, used to take us out there. And everybody in town knows Chuck Rees, and that's where I first met him, out there. He was just a young man. He was driving shuttle bus at Eielson.

Jim: I'll be darned. Tell us a little bit about that time of your life. When you came into North Pole and Fairbanks and attended school at the various locations, perhaps grammar school in the fifth grade, tell us a little about what other kinds of activities you did in North Pole as children.

Sandy: Well, my aunt had horses, and so I spent a great deal of time horseback riding, summer and winter. We could horseback ride bareback, up to about 30 below. Anything colder than that, it just wasn't fun anymore. Wintertimes we used to be pulled behind cars on old car hoods, and those were our sleds. We spent a lot of time sledding up and down Badger Road, when it was still a gravel road, and there was little or no traffic out there. We read a lot in the wintertime. Summertimes were of course a great joy for any kid back then when we were cooped up so much of the winter. We spent a lot of time rafting up and down the slough that now runs right through the center of all the activity out there.

Jim: What do you mean you rafted up and down the slough? What was going on there?

Sandy: I don't know where the raft came from, but we had found an old raft there on the slough, and we got some big long poles, and we used to pole up and down the slough and thought we were really exploring. We might have went as far as where the new SuperValue is now, but to us that was a long distance back there in the slough.

Jim: Well, that was frontiersy, back there in those days, wasn't it?

Sandy: We thought it was. I was intrigued with the whole idea of it. I remember, that summer was my first experience with mosquitoes too.

Jim: What kind of protection did you have?

Sandy: We didn't have any, that I remember. Actually, it was kind of a frightening experience. I was out in the spring and all of a sudden I had a swarm of mosquitoes around, and I ran to the house for protection.

Jim: Tell us more about this raft. You know, I've got it in my mind that this is a Huckleberry Finn type affair, in which the kids were on a log raft floating down a small stream.

Sandy: Yes, it is. I don't remember it specifically being all logs, might have had some lumber nailed to it. But that's what it is.

Jim: Did you ever get in trouble when you were a kid, doing small pranky-type things?

Sandy: No, there really wasn't anything out there to do that was prankish. We did have outhouses and they were too big and heavy to turn over.

Jim: That's right. I remember moving the outhouses. That used to be a corker. Yeah.

Sandy: Well, maybe the boys did that, but the girls didn't.

Jim: I see. And tell us a little bit about life as you saw it in Fairbanks. What was the atmosphere like in Fairbanks and North Pole, in terms of frontierism. I know that some people have said that there were a lot of log houses around and cabins, as well as frame houses, but we didn't have the modern stucco-type houses that we have today. Did you witness Fairbanks with its little log cabins for the most part, or had the frame houses and more modern-style houses come in?

Sandy: Well, even the nicer frame homes, some of those were built in the early '20s, over there on Cowles and Third, Fourth and Fifth. Some of those homes have been there that long, but yes, there were. There were a lot of the log homes, maybe a few boardwalks on the outer edges of town. I think one of the things I remember most distinctly was the old steel-girder bridge that crossed the river. You know, now we have a nice cement bridge, but at that time, it was the old military-style steel bridge that crossed the river.

Jim: And that steel bridge was where Cushman ended in Fairbanks, right where the new cement bridge is now.

Sandy: That's right.

Jim: Sandy, tell us, did you ever have any scary things happen to you? Did you ever have anything that was peculiar and perhaps dangerous because it was in Alaska, rather than some place like San Francisco—something that wouldn't necessarily happen in the conterminous United States?

Sandy: Yes we did. Probably what is indicative of the harsh sub-arctic temperatures that we have here and the lack of modern conveniences that we had at that time. Our family had a near fatal incident out there at North Pole. It was in January 1955, and the temperature was 40 or 50 below, as everyone seems to remember. And we didn't know it at the time, but the super-cold air had kept the coal gases from going up the chimney. We had a coal stove in the basement, as most people did out there at that time, and somewhere during the middle of the night the gases had built up in the house and had started to fill us with carbon monoxide. My little sister was the one to wake up, in the early morning hours, and she was nauseated and sick and had woke me up, and I realized that something was wrong. I couldn't seem to get out of bed. I tried several times, and every time I'd try to get up I'd fall back down. My little sister managed to get down the stairs and into the bedroom where Mom and Dad were. Dad got up and instantly realized something was wrong, and even today he doesn't really understand exactly why he knew so quickly what was happening. But we weren't able to breathe very well at that time, and couldn't stand up well. So Dad had told us to get down on the floor, and he opened all the doors so we could get some fresh air in there. I had two brothers and a younger sister at that time—just four of us. Dad sent Mom, who wasn't feeling well herself but wasn't quite as affected as the rest of us because they slept in the bedroom with the door closed and the window slightly cracked. Mom made it over to the neighbor's house—Ruth Cunningham (many people know Ruth from out there) was the one she contacted, and Ruth, in her earlier days, was a registered nurse. She came over to the house with another neighbor and realized that we were in pretty bad shape. They got us up and took us out into that cold air and we spent the remainder of the night being held up, literally, on each arm of Ruth, and walking up and down the streets. We'd walk until we were so cold we had to come in and warm up, and then Ruth would warm up and take a couple of us kids and head back out, walking up and down the streets with us. We managed to all survive, but it was quite the topic of conversation for awhile.

Jim: I can imagine it was. Were there any side effects or recognizable headaches or anything of that nature that went along with that?

Sandy: Well I've had people wonder if we didn't all suffer brain damage.

Jim: Lets change gears here for a minute. There were a lot of colorful people around Fairbanks probably at the time that you came here, in the early '50s, people like Hulga Ford and Eva McGown, and they were, I think Eva was considered the hostess of Fairbanks.

Sandy: Yes, she was. She was a very prominent figure at that time, and I didn't have the pleasure of knowing her personally, but she was the official hostess for the city and quite a grand lady to listen to. She was on TV every now and then. She did not escape the Nordale fire that occurred a number of years ago; it burned down the old Nordale Hotel. We didn't know Mrs. Ford either, but she was a mysterious fascinating lady who wandered the streets of Fairbanks and always looked like she was in need. And of course, come to find out she was quite a wealthy lady. She carried a lot of mystique for us, though. We used to like to talk about her.

Jim: Was there anything that might have occurred, I don't know what might bring a story to mind for you, but I know you came to Alaska and you spent the rest of your life here. Is that right, or did you go out for a period of time, or have you stayed right here?

Sandy: No, we've been right here. As a child, anyway. As an adult I have been pretty much all over the United States for short periods of time, and of course always choose to come back. I have a tour company and I do tours in the summertime, and I like to tell people that we've just been here so long now we don't know any better.

Jim: It grows on you, does it?

Sandy: Yeah, it does.

Jim: Give us a little bit of information on your tour company. First, what's the name of the tour company?

Sandy: Gold Rush Tours.

Jim: Gold Rush Tours. And how does that work?

Sandy: We have sightseeing tours around town. It's about a 40-mile local sightseeing trip that takes in all the downtown area—of course it goes out and covers the pipeline, out there by the gold dredge, comes back in over the hill and takes in the Dog Mushers Museum, which was a big hit for visitors last year. We go around and show them the permafrost house there on Farmers Loop, which is always an ooh-and-ahh stop.

Jim: Kind of hard to believe a house is breaking in half, isn't it.

Sandy: They are very much interested in that kind of thing.

Jim: And how long have you been operating the tours?

Sandy: Gold Rush Tours? Three years.

Jim: Did you originate the tours, or was it already established?

Sandy: No, we bought an existing company.

Jim: I see. And who's your target? Who are the people that you're trying to attract to the tour?

Sandy: Most of our reservations that come in are the RV caravaners that come into town. There's a host of those companies now, across the United States, and coming to Fairbanks has become very popular. The minute they get into town they like to take a sightseeing tour, a city tour, to learn what we have to offer and a little bit of history. So, they usually contact a tour company and we're one of the largest small companies in town. I have a little more flexibility than the larger companies do, and so we're pretty popular with those groups.

Jim: You're strictly local.

Sandy: Yes.

Jim: How about local people, can they take your tour?

Sandy: Most certainly.

Jim: Do you think they would benefit from it?

Sandy: I've had a lot of local people take my tour. I encourage my friends to come along whenever they want to, and have actually pulled a few on board, and they're always amazed at how much they did not know.

Jim: Sandy, I was thinking that people from around Alaska who moved into the Interior of Alaska, might benefit, if they just arrived, by taking a tour to see what was available in Fairbanks, and they might very quickly become educated on the characteristics that we have here that are of a pleasant nature. And so, you say that you have had a number of the locals go on your tour.

Sandy: Oh yes, we have. And I'm always proud to take anyone who has lived around here on the tour, and see if we can teach them anything—and we do. We not only give them some of the history of Fairbanks and the area, and some of the more colorful history too, but we give them the economical information that they might not realize is useful.

Jim: How long is the tour?

Sandy: We have a tour every morning that runs five hours. Covers all of those areas and more, that I mentioned, and ends up at the beautiful Pump House restaurant for lunch. Then we have the same tour in the afternoon that covers the same route, but does not involve the luncheon, so it just takes three hours.

Jim: I see. A 40-mile tour. When you go over to the skyline what is the view like? Do you get a pretty good panorama?

Sandy: It's a beautiful view of the Fox area out there. We like to point out those areas that have been mined in the past and overgrown and now are residences. We also like to point out the fact that Blue Babe, one of the main attractions at the University, was discovered out there by one of our old time miners, Walt Roman.

Jim: Sandy, you're currently involved with Alaska Women in Mining, as the president, is that correct?

Sandy: Yes, it is.

Jim: And is that a fun job?

Sandy: Yes, it is. It's an interesting job. It's a job that I'm proud to have. We've had I think just four presidents so far, since we've been incorporated, and it's a position that I'm pleased to be able to fill.

Jim: Tell us a little bit about Alaska Women in Mining and what they do and what kind of position they hold regarding mining, the community and the public in general.

Sandy: We became an official group in 1985, for the purpose of promoting educational, social, and scientific opportunities for people who are interested in our mining industry. Mainly gold mining, but we have a lot of coal mining that goes on, and it all falls under pretty much the same category. Small miners are a target area that need to be helped and maybe even protected. We have a few fund-raisers each year, and the proceeds from that go towards promoting mining education. We have a scholarship that we sponsor. We have also sponsored some of the studies that have been done on mining and the effect on the streams in the area.

Jim: Didn't you come out with a book, a cookbook on mosquitoes or how to prepare a mosquito?

Sandy: Yes we did. It was a tongue-in-cheek, fun-type little book that we, or actually they did before, I really became involved with it. Every once in a while you'll see it on a stand somewhere, for sale yet.

Jim: Well, I've just recently seen it on a stand at Alaskan Prospectors, and if you've ever wanted to know how to prepare mosquito, especially for the tourist trade, I suggest you pick up one of those books. It tells you in step by step fashion on how to prepare a mosquito. I'm sure that you'll enjoy it, much much better than previous ways that you've prepared them. But I've got some wild stories about mosquitoes, but I won't tell them today, Sandy. What other kind of revenue-generating activities have you done? Do you have a quilt or something that you're doing?

Sandy: No, we've talked about doing one. Quilting, across the United States, is becoming very very popular, and we're looking into putting together one as a fund-raiser that might be indicative of our heritage in mining. About this time every year we put on the Gold Diggers Ball, that we get pretty excited about. It is the final event of the Placer Mining Conference that goes on every spring at this time. This is the 11th Annual Placer Mining Conference, that'll be held over at Alaskaland the last few days of the month, and ends up Saturday night, April 1, 1989 with our Fourth Annual Gold Diggers Ball.

Jim: I see. You know, it's interesting. I want to get back to the Gold Diggers Ball in just a minute, but next week's guest will be Tom Bundtzen, who is the chairman of the Placer Mining Conference, and he'll be here to give us a full description of the many papers that will be delivered, and of course these papers span the entire spectrum, all the way from recreational to professional papers, and it's an opportunity for those people out there in the north country here and anywhere else to come and find out what placer mining is all about and get a little bit broader understanding on how to become rich and famous through the mining industry, here in Alaska. So, with that, you say that the Gold Diggers Monte Carlo Ball is the final event, is that correct?

Sandy: Yes, it is.

Jim: And that's the fun part of it. Tell me, are you going to have some music?

Sandy: We're going to dance to the music of Sand Castle. They're a well-known band around town. We've used them in the past, and chose to use them again this year.

Jim: What other kind of events are you going to have? You know, I've seen brochures on the Gold Diggers Monte Carlo Ball, and the girls are kind of scantily dressed and the men are in various costumes with vests and armbands, and they reflect probably a late 1800s 1920s type atmosphere. Is that the theme?

Sandy: That is the theme of our Gold Diggers Ball, is that era, and we encourage everyone to come in some kind of costume. The ladies like it because there are a variety of costumes for that period of time. Some of them like the can-can dresses. It's kind of neat to watch, when you climb into a costume like that, how you just sort of take on that role, and so some of our can-can-dressed ladies become floozies at the ball.

Jim: Explain this to us. Some of the upstanding ladies of this community take on the role of a floozy and they sell what?

Sandy: Yes. They sell dances for a dollar, like they used to have in the old days.

Jim: And what do they have on, again?

Sandy: They wear shorter can-can dresses. Then we have the ladies there standing guard, who maybe might be at a Sunday tea, with the outfits they have on.

Jim: Oh, the prudish kind.

Sandy: Right. They're taking notes, and watching over everything. We have ladies who love to come in the long ball gowns. We have a variety of costumes there, and we have ladies who choose not to come in costume at all. So I want to encourage everyone to show up, and the more in costume, the more fun. We very often have, and plan to have this year, a costume contest.

Jim: You know, last year, or was it the year before, you had a costume contest, and that was so fun. I lost. Tell me, there's some lady there that plays the madam of the whole affair. Who is that? I mean, not necessary that you tell me who it is, but what does she do, go around and make certain that everybody's collecting for the dances? Is that the deal, or what's going on there?

Sandy: Yes. As a matter of fact, that's a role that I like to play. I'm not the only one there. We have the Golden Days Dancers who will show up and do some entertaining for us, and a lot of people out there are real familiar with Ricky Chagnin, who is also sort of a madam of the Golden Days Dancers. I like to play that part too. I sort of wander around and, being overall coordinator, I answer a lot of questions, make sure things are going OK, and just in general make sure that our ladies are showing all of our people a good time.

Jim: I noticed that this is on a Saturday, and it's on, of all days, April first.

Sandy: Yes. This year it falls on April first.

Jim: And what time does it start?

Sandy: Eight o'clock. Eight o'clock the music starts. We shut down the casinos about one o'clock, a little before, and we start with the prize auction or drawings, and we're usually finished by about two. It's a full evening of fun. And I didn't get to mention the fact that the fellows like this real well, because of the costumes involved too. They can come in their flannel T-shirts and grubby blue jeans and suspenders and look just like an old miner of the time. They can come maybe looking like the dandies in the casinos of the day, with the vest and the little hats. Or they can show up in their polyesters. We don't care.

Jim: You don't care how they come. Just come and enjoy.

Sandy: Just come and have a good time.

Jim: We're going to be running out of time here in just a minute, Sandy, but is there anything else that you'd like to say regarding where people can buy tickets, or something of that nature?

Sandy: You can purchase tickets through the Alaska Miners Association office. You can purchase them through any Alaska Women in Mining member, or that night at the ball.

Jim: Where's the Alaska Miners Association office?

Sandy: Upstairs at the NC Machinery Company.

Jim: OK, is there a phone number they can call if they want to get a ticket?

Sandy: 456-6650, I believe is the Alaska Miners Association number.

Jim: Sad to say, we have run out of time, Sandy. I want to thank you for joining us on Alaska Gold Trails.

Sandy: It's been a pleasure, Jim. Thank you.

Oden Stranberg
with
Jim Madonna
June 1, 1989

Jim: Good afternoon ladies and gentlemen, today our guest is Oden Stranberg. Oden, welcome to Alaska Gold Trails.

Oden: I appreciate being here, Jim.

Jim: Well, Oden, we've talked quite a bit on the phone and had a nice conversations before coming up to the studio. I understand you're a mining engineer, is that correct?

Oden: That's correct. A consulting mining engineer.

Jim: Were you born in Alaska, Oden?

Oden: Yes. Born in Anchorage in 1941.

Jim: Did you live most of your early years in Anchorage?

Oden: Lived through the middle of high school years in Anchorage, and then moved on up to Fairbanks and finished high school in the class of '59, Lathrop High School.

Jim: What was Anchorage like? Have there been quite a lot of changes since the time you lived there during the period of your grammar school years, or not?

Oden: Oh, to say the least. Anchorage is a teeming metropolis. I can recall when G Street going through town was a gravel road and it was really a lot of fun in the old days. But it's a nice town now, too.

Jim: There were some creeks running around there that the kids used to always go fishing in, if I recall correctly, and now alongside those creeks there's big towering buildings and not much room for fishing any longer. Do you see that change in the atmosphere down there, a little bit? Changing from more the town atmosphere into the city atmosphere?

Oden: Oh definitely so, but I think that in Anchorage, the town's tried to preserve some of the areas—like the old golf course has been preserved and still is the golf course to me. And Chester Creek has become a green belt area, and Ship Creek still remains about the same. So there's still a few things that are unchanged there.

Jim: You say you came up during your high school years to Fairbanks after leaving Anchorage. Do you have any idea, Oden, about how many people were in Anchorage when you left.

Oden: It's been a long time, but 25 to 30 thousand is what I recall.

Jim: What, we're talking about is a factor of ten here, aren't we?

Oden: Yes. A tenfold increase at least.

Jim: When you came to Fairbanks, you left a town of 25 or 30 thousand, you came to Fairbanks. Was that kind of a shock to you, to come to such a small town? Or was it the same size as Anchorage at that time?

Oden: Fairbanks, as I remember, was in the neighborhood of 15 to 20 thousand at that time. There wasn't a big change. It was a little cooler in Fairbanks. We went from 15 degree weather in Anchorage to 50-60 below in Big Delta, when we moved up, It was quite cold in Fairbanks also, when we got into town, but it warmed up the following day, on New Year's Day, and the water started to drip off the melting snow on the eves. So Fairbanks welcomed us.

Jim: That's quite a remarkable variation in temperature within a 24-hour period. Do you remember it as an exceptionally warm year, or was it just an irregular day?

Oden: It was an irregular day, as I remember, because the next day or so the temperature went right back down again.

Jim: Now during that period of time Lathrop High School must've been just about a new school.

Oden: It certainly didn't show many signs of wear, although they've maintained it very well. When I go back there to high school functions once in a while, it sure looks good now.

Jim: What were the facilities there? Did you have a swimming pool connected to it at that time? Was the Mary Siah Pool there?

Oden: No, neither the school pool nor the Mary Siah Pool were in. Our major recreation there was the gymnasium.

Jim: Mostly basketball, was it?

Oden: Basketball, volleyball, all the indoor sports.

Jim: And what were the major outdoor activities in the Fairbanks area that attracted you? Were you into skiing or dog racing or any of the other kinds of wintertime activities?

Oden: Well, not a great deal. There was certainly some ice skating along the way, and maybe a little bit of skiing, and the dog races, of course, during the season.

Jim: At that time did they hold the dog races on the Chena River or had they moved them out to Stoddard?

Oden: They were right on the Chena River at that time.

Jim: Let's see, what year was that, can you remember?

Oden: This was when I came into Fairbanks, in1957.

Jim: In '57. When I was here, just a few years earlier, they ran the dogs in a 20-mile race on the Chena River. Fact is, I think all the races were held on the river, and earlier, I believe about 1951, they used to have car races on the ice as well. And then, as soon as the car racing became very popular they moved it out to two different circular tracks that they built—one was located next to the Rendezvous Club, if I recall correctly, and that became a big summertime sport at the tracks. I don't know if they continued it on the river or not. But I remember that the ice carnivals were running on the river. Were the ice carnivals running in 1957, when you came?

Oden: Yes, they were. We didn't get to a lot of the activities, but I know they were going on.

Jim: What brought you up to Fairbanks from Anchorage?

Oden: My father was wrapping up his mining engineering degree at the University of Alaska, and he moved our family up in mid-year, 1957. He finished his degree work up. In the summer periods we spent the time out in a Kuskokwim mining camp, and then as he finished up and moved back to the Anchorage area, I continued, and started school in the mining engineering curriculum at the University of Alaska, in 1959.

Jim: Just during statehood time.

Oden: Yes.

Jim: And you also got your bachelor of science degree in mining engineering at the University of Alaska?

Oden: Yes. Finished up there in 1963, with a bachelor of science degree.

Jim: Are there any names that are still floating around that you might have gone to school with? Are some of the teachers still associated with the University or still around Fairbanks?

Oden: There's quite a few people. Some of the prominent ones, I know that Earl Beistline was dean of the College of Earth Sciences and Mineral Industries then, and Donald Cook, who is presently head of the College of Earth Science at the University now, was my department head at that time.

Jim: I remember, Don was the department head when I first came, back in the early 1970s. Now he's Dean of the School of Mineral Engineering.

Oden: Yes. They're great men. I see them every once in a while and they continue to have many words of wisdom any time I see them.

Jim: Earl retired, I guess about six years ago. He's been pretty active in the mining community ever since. I see him at a lot of the meetings. I've read in the paper he's been pretty active throughout his life here in Alaska. Oden, tell us a little bit about your father and what he's done in Alaska.

Oden: Well, Dad was born in Flat, in 1915, which was a town of over 1,000 people at that time, and he mined in Flat as he grew up, and then the family interests spread out and he and his brothers and sister became involved in a company called Stranberg Mines Inc. and operated a number of placer properties in the Kuskokwim district and one up near Utopia Creek. And they continued that activity until the early '60s when the $35 gold price pretty well brought an end to that work.

Jim: Well, your dad, then, must've been well-acquainted with the Miscovich family.

Oden: Yes. They all, as I understand it, practically grew up together out in that part of the country.

Jim: Are you familiar with any of the activity that went on during the Iditarod gold rush?

Oden: Oh, a limited amount of knowledge there, Jim. I think my father is really the one that can tell the stories about that at some time with you. I know that it was a real gold camp and there's apparently quite a bit of activity out there now, so there's some companies that are starting to take a look at the source of the placer gold, which was the original production target out in the Iditarod.

Jim: I was talking to Johnny Miscovich here, over the past year. During a couple of conversations we had he said he was uncovering the disseminated ore minerals in a lode deposit that they suggest might be the source of some of the gold in the area. It is a decomposed bedrock that he is washing straight through the sluice and collecting the valuables from. It was interesting to see just how he mined that particular type of lode deposit. I don't know, perhaps you heard him give a paper surrounding the Golden Horn Mine out there at Flat. I think he gave it at the recent placer mining conference here.

Oden: No, I didn't hear the paper, but I have stood on the ground at the Golden Horn with John and recognize it as being a portion of a probable major hard-rock gold deposit, which Alaska's going to be hearing a lot about in the next few years.

Jim: Over the years, Oden, have you visited a lot of the hard-rock gold properties. I know there's been a couple come on line. I was wondering if you have seen others that have high potential and might be going into production here in the near future.

Oden: Oh here in our own backyard there is a tremendous potential on Ester Dome and at Cleary Summit. The surface has just been scratched by the Silverado group on Ester Dome. We're going to be hearing a lot more about that operation, I'm sure. I've seen that from surface and underground and as the vein systems get developed there is going to be a good production unit brought on-stream there. I should say continue on-stream, as there's already a 250-ton-per-day mill. Just out of town near Cleary, the word seems to be that there's some real significant gold finds being made in several lode deposits.

Jim: The Vetter property was one of the most interesting. It peaked the interest of a lot of people when Rudy Vetter, the owner, who has been on the program, showed some of the vein gold that he had extracted. And of course the gold is just peppered through the quartz, and some of the samples ran up to around $6,000 a ton. Of course, the amount of that material that was available was pretty limited, but it was impressive to look down at a stone that was roughly the size of a softball and see it just peppered through with gold particles. He had some impressive ore that he had sliced up and made available, especially to my students at the University. That property is on Cleary Summit.

Oden: Yes. And that's one of the significant properties at Cleary that I was referring to. It could well be part of a production effort in the near future, from what I can tell.

Jim: Getting back to your father—he was born in Flat and he got his degree here at the University of Alaska. Has he worked strictly in Alaska with his mining background?

Oden: Generally, yes. I know that he's currently active in the mining field and is doing consulting jobs as they come along. The last major one that he did was to drill out a major reserve in the Kuskokwim district for a Lower-48 client. And it appears that that project after a mis-start, is going to get underway again this summer.

Jim: Explain to us, when you say you "drilled out a property" for a client in the Lower-48, what does "drill out" mean?

Oden: In this case it was a placer target on a stream called Bear Creek and a churn drill was flown out to the project—which by the way, we were talking about Earl Beistline a minute ago, it was his churn drill that was rented for the job—and 50 or 60 drill holes were poked into the ground on lines, and then a reserve estimate was prepared, and the amount of gold discovered in the drilling was sufficient to warrant a medium-sized mining operation to go ahead—a placer mining operation.

Jim: We don't want to get into the details too much, but when you say medium size, are we talking 100-yard-an-hour plant or something of that nature?

Oden: In the neighborhood of 100 to 200 yards an hour.

Jim: I see. And would under 100 yards be considered a small placer mining operation?

Oden: In the classification I use, yes.

Jim: And over 200 probably a large operation?

Oden: Yes.

Jim: That's standard just about across the board, isn't it, Oden?

Oden: That's what I would say. People use different classifications.

Jim: This property that your dad worked on, when somebody says a medium-size operation, there were suitable reserves for a medium-size operation to commence there. Would that mean that they had five years of reserves blocked out?

Oden: Well this particular property has in the neighborhood of 7 to 10 years of blocked out reserves, and then beyond that if further drilling goes the way we think it will, it's probably a 20-year project.

Jim: I see. And based on 100 yards an hour then, this will make a good living for how many people?

Oden: The operation would probably be peaking at about 12 people total on the project—Year in and Year out.

Jim: And out in that area, what would you call the length of the season?

Oden: 120 to 130 days. You can generally run between about the middle of May and the middle of October in that area. And when I say 120-day season, that would be the actual sluicing season. There's a number of weeks of prep work at the front end to get going.

Jim: Most of the operations that we're talking about are operations that use earthmoving equipment like Cats and loaders and draglines and backhoes to load into a processing plant. Using the model of Bear Creek, or any model you might choose, could you run down how the style of an operation might begin during the initial stages when somebody suspects a stream valley has a valuable gold deposit in it, right through the development stage and into the mining of the property? How a person might set up the mining equipment based on results of an evaluation? I realize that's a large chunk.

Oden: I might digress just a moment. There's another type of placer—a buried placer or an underground placer—that has quite a bit of potential in the Fairbanks area. And that type of operation you'd use smaller machinery and might entail shaft-sinking and drift work, and drilling and blasting the frozen placer material. But that's a digression, and then on to what you were talking about, Jim. One of the first things to undertake when looking at a drainage and suspecting values is to look at the USGS and Bureau of Mines or other records. There might be public records covering what people have done on the drainage before. And then, after going through that material and somewhat substantiating what you suspect, it may be that some field reconnaissance and some pan sampling and so on could be in order.

Jim: Once it's established, from pan sampling and surface examination, that there is enough values, the prudent man rule says that the person doing the investigation or interested in the property will put up time and money to open up a mine. I think that's the criteria for staking a claim, is that correct?

Oden: Yes.

Jim: And once he's established that there is significant amount of gold there to entice him or her to put additional energy into the project, what would the next step be?

Oden: That'd be some type of rational prospecting of the ground that would block out gold reserves or metal reserves, and that could take the form of test pitting, hand or by machine, drilling, or actual bulk mining on a somewhat small scale. And those are only a few ways of checking the ground.

Jim: Bulk mining of the material is perhaps just as accurate a way as any to evaluate a piece of property, but most times in the past we've been using churn drills. You spoke of churn drills. To describe them briefly, a churn drill is the same kind of drill that many people have seen drilling water wells, that seem to pound their way down through the gravels or through the soil. And then following the bit pounding its way down a few feet they will use a bailer to bail the broken rock out of the hole and then through repeating that method they would drill down to bedrock. Do you find that most people in Alaska today are using this churn drilling method of evaluating the ground as opposed to bulk sampling? Or is it the other way around?

Oden: Well churn drilling, as a lot of people will tell you, is an old-time method of evaluating ground that's still very valid now. Churn drilling itself is a rather slow but accurate process. And there's several projects going on in Alaska this summer that are using the churn drilling technique. Bulk testing is sometimes necessary where the churn drill hole itself will not give an adequate sample to give an accurate evaluation of the ground, and it might be dug out in a bulk test at a rate of say 5 to 10 yards an hour to get a recovery of metals and evaluate the ground. Because churn drilling is slow, and labor factors being as they are, a number of operators have gone over to a reverse-circulation rotary-type drilling that's been used quite a bit at the major gold deposit at Valdez Creek in deep rocky ground. The evaluation of ground has a lot to do with the ground itself, as to the type of equipment that's selected to drill it or to test it. Some ground in the placer district up around Wiseman and east over into the Chandalar District has gold that's coarse enough that normal drilling techniques will give indications of value, but actual shaft sinking is really needed to get the bulk material out to test it. Or in lieu of shaft sinking, some type of large-diameter rotary drilling, in the 18-inch and up diameter range.

Jim: Once the property is evaluated or drilled and we find that there's suitable gold there for mining, you're going to have to make a decision, based on the characteristics of the ground, I assume. Probably the depth of ground will play a role in the kind of machinery you select. The type of gravel, whether it's flat or round, and the size of the boulders would probably also play a role, wouldn't it, Oden?

Oden: Yes, it certainly does. The digging section, be it stripping material or the material to be mined, will govern the machinery selection, as will the overall size of the deposit. And there's any spectrum of sizes of machinery and type of machinery that would be selected. It's difficult to make an overall generalization, but a lot of times you can say generally that one thing or the other becomes critical in bringing a deposit into production. In one of the Kuskokwim deposits that I'm familiar with, for example, the removal of 25 to 30 feet of frozen muck is the large expense item, whereas the actual processing of the five to eight feet of pay section is the easy part of the job.

Jim: You know, in the Fairbanks area, I read a couple of articles and I've heard some people who've mined in this area say that the major gold was within the last 5 or 10 feet above bedrock, and also trapped within the first foot or so of the fractures within bedrock, and we're talking now about maybe 50 to 100 feet of muck overlying 50 to 100 feet of gravels. And all the gold, the real gold values, are down there within the last five feet. So a person has to select the equipment that can deal with that depth. Chances are when you gave us that introduction about drift mining, that perhaps the drift-mining method in many cases, in this area, was the best approach.

Oden: Any way you cut it, when you get in this business, you're forced to become a materials-handling expert.

Jim: That's true. I just heard about this recently—in Canada they're starting to drift mine using some sophisticated equipment and some sophisticated techniques. Spiral drifts that spiral around and using rubber-tired equipment to go down to the bedrock-gravel interface and bring the gravel up again. I have recently worked with a fellow out near Tenderfoot who put in a drift mine, and he used all the old-fashioned methods, with the exception of on the surface he has some of the more modern machinery. But underground it was all steam-thawing and I remember when I went down the shaft, as soon as I got down to the floor of the drift and looked back in there, there was this little light, probably 50 feet away, and there were these two guys mucking the face out. And it looked like I had just walked back in history by about 80 years. It was just as I had visualized it when the '98ers were working in the Klondike. It was a remarkable sight, kind of a thrilling experience for me. At any rate, those are the kind of things one imagines when these old-timers dropped these shafts to bedrock, perhaps 30-40 feet, and in the Fairbanks area up to 200 feet. And then they would drift out laterally looking for that paystreak. Well, the objective then, during this drilling and this bulk-sampling operation, of course, is to define what we call the paystreak.

Oden: That's right.

Jim: I was talking to Ernie Wolff the other day. He was probably one of your teachers too, wasn't he.

Oden: No. I don't think I had him for a teacher, but he is a friend.

Jim: He made one comment, he just lit up like a lightbulb when he said, "Jim, when you're on the pay, you really know it. When you're on the pay— you're drilling across the channel and when the gold is coming out of the hole, boy you're really happy."

Oden: You're even happier when you're digging it and running it through your processing plant.

Jim: Are you ever. We've brought our gold-mining activity up to evaluating the property, and of course once the property's evaluated, you have to select the proper type of equipment, is that correct?

Oden: Yes.

Jim: Just quickly here, Oden, when we're talking about equipment for these mining operations, in a small operation, if someone is going to go out and buy good used equipment, what kind of money could they expect to spend on a small operation to initiate his plant?

Oden: A good Cat for $35,000 and a sluicing arrangement, $50,000— $100,000. And if you put everything together—the tractor and the sluice plant and pump and so on—for a small operation you could probably get into business for in the neighborhood of $250,000.

Jim: I wish we had more time but the trail has come to an end. This has been fun. Oden, thank you for joining us here on Alaska Gold Trails today.

Oden: It was a pleasure being here, Jim. Thank you.

Mary Lou Teel
with
Jim Madonna
October 27, 1988

Jim: Welcome to Alaska Gold Trails, ladies and gentlemen. Our guest today is Mary Lou Teel. Hi, Mary Lou, how are you today?

Mary Lou: Hi there. I'm just fine, thank you,

Jim: One thing that I've learned about you is that you're active in the mining community in Alaska, and have been for a number of years. However, you had your beginning in Michigan, is that correct?

Mary Lou: Yes. I was born in a little town called Millersburg, back in 1932. It's a small farming community.

Jim: And you were raised on the farm?

Mary Lou: I was raised on the farm, with everything that comes along with a farmer's daughter. That's what I am.

Jim: That's kind of a broad view. Tell us everything that comes along with being a farmer's daughter. Could you perhaps clarify some of the steps that are involved?

Mary Lou: Yes, I think I should. We had like what was called Old Macdonald's Farm, where we had cows, horses, chickens, pigs, sheep, the whole kit and kaboodle, so therefore I learned to milk cows at an early age, to feed the chickens and pasture the horses and cows.

Jim: You fed the cows.

Mary Lou: Yes.

Jim: Did you do the other part of the work that is required to clean up after the cows?

Mary Lou: If you mean the shoveling, yes.

Jim: Along with that, was there plowing and other things?

Mary Lou: Yes. Plowing and cultivating, planting big gardens, and we raised practically all of our own food, and then some for sale also. That was the way my folks earned their living.

Jim: You know, when I was a young lad, I went to a one-room schoolhouse. It was a farm community, and we had all eight grades in one room, and it was interesting to note that in that school there was a bell tower, and the kids got to ring the bell to start school in the morning. Did you have anything like that?

Mary Lou: Yes. Only the school that I went to was in our small town, and it had four rooms in it, and we had the school bell there. And lots of times the teacher, as a reward for the kids that were good, would allow them to ring the school bell.

Jim: You would ring the bell at what time? To just start school?

Mary Lou: Time to come to school, recess, noon, and that was it.

Jim: I see. And how big was Millersburg?

Mary Lou: Millersburg was a very small community located over on the Lake Huron side of Michigan.

Jim: So all those people who know about Michigan would recognize it.

Mary Lou: Yes, they certainly would, and especially if you say that it was up close to the Straits of Mackinac, just about 50 miles from there.

Jim: And how big was it, in terms of population?

Mary Lou: Oh, I think when I was growing up there we might've had 600, not many more than that.

Jim: 600 people in the town. That meant there was probably what, 40 in the school?

Mary Lou: That's probably a good estimate, counting town and some country kids. The country section outside of that had their own little schools, and most of those were one-room schools. And our particular school went to grade 10, and then we had to be transported for our last two years of high school into what we called the city school, which was actually just a little bit bigger town about 10 miles from where I lived.

Jim: Was that kind of a social shock to you, or were you prepared for that?

Mary Lou: Well, I was kind of prepared for that, because being a little bit more outgoing than my sister was, why I was into a lot of the plays at school and a lot of the activities, especially if they had anything to do with sports. So, with playing basketball and a few of the sports, why, I did get to go to some of the other towns for some of the activities.

Jim: Mary Lou, let's change gears here and ask you the big question. And the big question, of course, is, what was it that attracted you to Alaska? Was there some magnetism, or a job, or what?

Mary Lou: You know, actually, in the fall of 1951, I was married to an Air Force man, and he was transferred here to what was called at that time Ladd Air Force Base. And so that's how I came to be up here.

Jim: I see. And what was Fairbanks like when you first arrived, in those years?

Mary Lou: It was a neat place to come to. I'd always thought that Alaska would be a great place to come to, and when my husband was transferred here, I thought, "Ah, gee, I'm going to get my chance to go to the frozen north." And so, arriving here, on September the 28th, 1952, I got off this plane in Weeks Field at that time, and it was just wonderful, even though it was night and there was a little bit of fog around, I just had to see everything there was to see. So the next day we did a little touring, and it was a wonderful place. We still had the dirt streets, the board sidewalks, and the little pigeons running around, and I loved it.

Jim: So you have seen it, through the years, as it grew, changed and modernized a bit, but you still see the old structures sitting around, and remnants of what it was like in the earlier days. You know, when I first came in, the military used to set up installations on the street around town and play army games. Were they still doing that in '52?

Mary Lou: Yes. It was just kind of phasing out.

Jim: Tell us, how long did you live here, while your husband was in the military? Was that for a long period of time?

Mary Lou: Well, we were up her 'til 1955—56, and then he was transferred outside for a few years, but it wasn't our choice. We extended up here just as long as we possibly could, until they said, "Nope. This is it." So we went outside for a few years, and then, this being our first love, we returned back here. And I've remained ever since.

Jim: And what year did you come back?

Mary Lou: We got here right after statehood.

Jim: That means, in ongoing time, you're a pioneer.

Mary Lou: Yes, and I had returned off and on for visits, but not 'til then to stay.

Jim: Well, when you first came up here, what kind of activities were you involved in? Were you involved in outdoor activities—fishing, hunting?

Mary Lou: Yes. Being raised on the farm with my dad, who's an avid fisherman and outdoorsman, why, I continued my hunting, my fishing, and one of my favorite spots to go was down to Tangle Lakes. One could only drive partway and then had to backpack the rest of the way into Tangle Lakes. We did a lot of fishing and a lot of hunting.

Jim: That's down by where Paxson is?

Mary Lou: Yes. Down off the Denali.

Jim: That's a beautiful spot and a lot of people continue to go down there and enjoy that part of the country. Tell us, when you came back to Alaska, in 1959, was your husband still in the military?

Mary Lou: No. My husband came back to go to work in civil service. By that time the name of the base had been changed to Wainwright.

Jim: Well, what got you involved and interested in mining? I understand that you own a number of claims around the state, and you've been actively involved in the mining community. What was it that drew you to that particular field of interest?

Mary Lou: Well, I guess, being a person of the earth, why I've always wanted to do this. It's one of the things I thought would be so neat to have a piece of Alaska of my own—something where I could go, enjoy, dig, and yet get a little bit of gold and maybe make a living. I was up at Circle Hot Springs, in 1969, and was real interested in it. There were just a few people that were getting back into mining at that time. I'd taken a drive down the Deadwood Road, 'cause someone had told me they were mining down there. Well, I got there and there was this washout, so I turned around and came back. That night why, I saw a pickup with a Michigan license plate, so I went up and asked the gentleman, when he came out, where he was from, and it happened to be a friend of my uncle's, from back home, whom I had known. And he said he was mining down off Deadwood. I asked him, could I just please go down and watch and see what they were doing. So he offered to help me stake my first claim, and that's how I got started.

Jim: So you staked your first claim on Deadwood Creek, is that right?.

Mary Lou: Yes.

Jim: Tell us, Mary Lou, what did you do? How did you start mining your claim? And why did you want the claim? Did you just have to taste the adventure of mining in Alaska, was that it?

Mary: That was partly it. And another one was having a job working in town in an office. I worked for the department of highways. I wanted a place to get out of town, where it wasn't too far, yet I could drive and there would be some recreational facilities there. So, I just decided that this was it. I got some information, not knowing much about it. Everyone up there was just real helpful. At that time there was only myself, Bob Rockburn, and I believe Hap Stringfellow, on the creek, the whole length of it. And so I started out with a small rocker, which was given to me by one of the old-timers up there, Simon Silbiloff, and then he helped me build a little sluice, and so I had a bucket and my pick and my shovel. And that's how I started out. I'd pick and shovel for a little while, then I'd run the rocker. And, then I'd put it down through the little sluice, but I had none of the modern conveniences that we have today.

Jim: Did you get any gold? Any big nuggets, or little nuggets, or what kind of gold did you get?

Mary Lou: I started out doing some fines, until Simon come down and told me, "Gee," 'cause he was also a geologist, and he came down and said, "I think maybe if you start digging over in this section here, you might do a little bit better." Well, his advice was great, because I got my first two real nice nuggets out of there the fall of '69, and then another real good one in 1970, and those three I still have, 'cause I had them made up into a ring. And I did quite well just with my little pick and shovel, because I had very little overhead, and I'd leave here Friday night, after work, take my 357, my German shepherd, and my tent, and that's how I lived up there for oh, I'd say, the first four or five summers, until I was able to get a small trailer— and when I say small, it was small.

Jim: Well, you know, that's the kind of thing a lot of the people in the Fairbanks area dream about doing, and I think we can still go out and do those kinds of things, if we have the adventurous nature, and people should understand that they can still go out and find a creek someplace and do a little panning and a little sluicing. Tell us more about that gold that you were getting out of that stream channel. We want to hear about the big nuggets and the fine gold and more.

Mary Lou: Well, we didn't progress a whole lot. Like I said, I still continued to do my picking and shoveling and eventually graduated to having a larger sluice box, which we set up directly in the stream, where I could just let the water run through—then I didn't have to carry water by the bucketsful. I operated this way for quite a few years, and I will have to say that I was real satisfied with the outcome of what little input I could get through it. Then I had several offers to lease the property, but I wasn't quite sure whether I wanted somebody else to mess up my little piece of Alaska there, so I put it off for quite a few years, and then finally I decided that well, OK, I couldn't get out of the ground any more than what I was doing with just my meager way of doing it, so I leased it out to some very good miners. They were new miners to the area, but they proved themselves to be not only good neighbors, but good honest people.

Jim: Look, Mary Lou, you say you leased it and you mined. Where do you sell your gold?

Mary Lou: Down at Oxford Assaying and Refining.

Jim: Mary Lou, as you pointed out, you did take a lot of gold to Oxford Assaying and Refining, and you've been up in the Circle Mining District for a number of years now, and you leased the property out. You had some success doing that. Can you give a little bit more information. How did these people mine that property?

Mary Lou: Well, they started out with a D-8, D-9, a loader, and one of the larger sluice boxes, which had been designed by one of the fellows here in town. And they started out with not a whole lot of knowledge, but a whole lot of desire and all, so therefore, with what little knowledge I had, I was able to help them a little bit. We had done a lot of remodeling on the original sluice box, and then they got into it and did very well. They had a lot of help from the miners up there on Deadwood, because by this time we had our little, I guess it was the mini-boom, up in that area. So our creek at that particular time ... I always used to refer to it as my creek, because I kind of felt that way, and at first I wasn't too pleased with all the intruders up there, but I knew that this was progress, and so it all turned out real well.

Jim: You must have had a lot of experiences with the different miners up there, and what they were doing, the kinds of equipment they used. When you first went up there, were they using big Cats, like the D-8s and D-9s that you see today, pushing gravel into a sluice box? Is that the kind of mining that we're talking about?

Mary Lou: Well, when I first went up there there were a lot of them starting out with a lot smaller Cats and things, because the value wasn't there as far as selling the gold. But as the price of gold increased they did start then with the D-8s. Then in the later years they started with the D-9s, and a lot of them got started with a few more loaders. Where before we used to have to have the loader push the dirt into the sluice and then run down around and take the tailings out, well, as gold went up in price and miners were I guess a little bit more fluent, or maybe a little bit more daring, why they had another loader and operator to move tailings, which saved a lot of time.

Jim: When you first went up there, were they mostly single-channel sluice boxes?

Mary Lou: Oh yes, yes. Just the small little ones, that you just kind of built yourself—put your plates in it and used rugs—or army blankets was one of the first things I used—to catch the fine gold. Where now they have all the fancy things, with the drilled plates and things like that.

Jim: It's interesting to note that in the 1970s that we began coming out with the more advanced multiple-channel sluice boxes. Have you seen any of those sluices? The Hector sluice box is one of those.

Mary Lou: Yes. And fact is, Hector built one for the leaser that I had up there on Deadwood, and it worked very well. They seemed to be real satisfied with it. They recommended it to several of the other miners there, not just on Deadwood but in the Circle Mining District.

Jim: It's interesting to note that Hector's started manufacturing those multiple-channel sluice boxes, in Alaska, in the late 1970s, and they did find a lot of popularity in the mining industry, and probably the reason for that is because these multiple-channel sluice boxes reduce the particle size down, so that the high-specific-gravity materials were more efficiently extracted from the aggregate, and as a result, the miners recovered more fine gold and became more successful, so Hector's really made a contribution to the mining industry in the state of Alaska, through the development of his multiple-channel sluice boxes. And I'd like to add that just recently he built a large plant for Polar Mining Company, which has been particularly efficient. So with that, you say they did start the multiple-channel sluice boxes up there in the Circle Mining District. And you probably saw the mini gold rush take off. I think it started back in 1975 really, when President Ford signed the bill that would allow gold to be traded on the open market without any problems. You saw that blossom and bloom and at first you were a little hesitant about all those coming into the country.

Mary Lou: Yes, I sure was. I guess I thought that I'd found a little corner up there where it's peaceful and quiet and you could take your friends and relatives up and they could sluice or they could pan a little bit, and it was just really kind of neat to me to be able to show the next person that came along how to pan and get the most out of it. So I guess I will have to be very truthful and say that I was real reluctant to see all these people invading the creeks up there.

Jim: A little bit possessive, were you?

Mary Lou: Yes, as a matter of fact.

Jim: But it's turning out good, isn't it.

Mary Lou: Yes, it has, and it has sure brought in a lot of money to our communities, and of course I can't say enough for the mining industry. Not only because of what it brings back into the country, but because of the type of people that you meet in the different areas, in gold mining.

Jim: In a couple of conference presentations I broadcast the point that Alaska has the most well-developed placer mining industry in the world, and we're looked upon as the model by the rest of the world. Some people raise their eyebrow at that, but you have had to have gone around to the different placer mining industries in the various countries, to recognize how high-level our placer mining industry is. We have advanced in terms of environmental improvement to the point where no other country can match us, and we're continuing to move towards better environmental controls. The miners are becoming more and more sensitive to those kinds of things, and I think they're doing a fine job. They're working in harmony now, and I think that we have probably the model that will stand for a long time. And I have to point out that, we have the placer mining conference here in Fairbanks, and people from around the world want the *Proceedings,* because those *Proceedings* have everything from fine gold recovery to environmental papers included in them, and of course this kind of information is important to have for the mining industry worldwide. So I think we've done a really good job in that respect. And by the way, Mary Lou, I think you have a phone call here. Let's see what we've got. Hi, welcome to Alaska Gold Trails. You're on the air with Mary Lou Teel.

Caller: Yeah, I just heard you say something about the efficiency and the fact that Alaska's modeling the gold mining industry, and I just wondered if you'd comment about how that relates to other countries. Like, Russia evidently has such a massive gold reserve, and I guess other countries do as well. How do they obtain that gold and do they have a placer mining industry?

Jim: Well, you know, we're fortunate to have had speakers from Russia over here at the placer mining conference on a couple of occasions, and of course they were here on a fact-gathering mission as well as delivering certain types of information, and yes, indeed, they do have a large placer mining industry. However, the information that has been provided, to date, wasn't that extensive, so as yet we do not have a full understanding of what's going on there. One characteristic which seems to exist throughout their placer mining industry is that it is labor-intensive compared to technologically advanced methods. That's about as good as I can answer that question, pertaining to Russia. If you want me to talk about other countries, like Canada, Australia and the conterminous United States, reference those areas specifically.

Caller: Well, I was just wondering if the placer mining industry was returning the greatest percentage of their reserves, or if it came from hard-rock or other types of mining. I'll hang up and you can talk about that if you wish.

Jim: OK, well thanks for the call, sir.

Caller: You bet.

Jim: Sorry to say, folks, we've run out of time. I want to thank you, Mary Lou, for joining us this afternoon, on Alaska Gold Trails. We had a lot left to talk about. Sorry we ran out of time.

Mary Lou: Thank you, Jim. I've enjoyed it.

Helen (Beaver) Warner
with
Jim Madonna
December 1, 1988

Jim: Hello ladies and gentlemen. This is Alaska Gold Trails and I am your host, Jim Madonna. Our guest today is Helen (Beaver) Warner. I've been looking forward to this interview for a long time, Helen. Welcome to Alaska Gold Trails.

Helen: I think I've been trottin' along those trails for quite awhile, Jim.

Jim: I think you have too. You've been a long-time Alaskan and have participated in the placer mining industry for many years. Helen, you have a rich background, let's start with where you were born and what kind of area you came from.

Helen: Well, I was born in San Francisco, California, and I was raised in a more rural setting, more north bay setting, back in the days when that was country—chicken capital of the world.

Jim: Chicken capital? How does an area get a name like that? What makes it a chicken capital?

Helen: Well, I think it was because they produced the most eggs of any little given area. So it was known as the egg basket, and called the chicken capital.

Jim: Why wasn't it called the egg capital?

Helen: I think the farmers thought the chickens came first.

Jim: I see. We have a phone call. Let's see what's going on here. Hi, you're on the air.

Caller: Yes. Jim Madonna. This is Gene Foley.

Jim: Hi, Gene Foley, how are you today?

Caller: Oh, just fine. I wanted to call you up and publicly thank you for your class this last week.

Jim: The placer evaluation workshop held by the University of Alaska Mining Extension?

Caller: Yes.

Jim: Where did you hear about the course?

Caller: I heard about it on Alaska Gold Trails on KFAR radio when I was driving downtown here two weeks ago.

Jim: It pays to listen. Look, thank you very much for the call. How did you like the course?

Caller: Oh, I liked the class very much. I was especially impressed because of, not only the technological aspects, but the fact that your instructors were also successful mining people. They brought a lot of expertise into the picture beyond the technical.

Jim: Well, these people have been around a long time, they've had a long history in the Alaskan mining community and I think that we all prospered in having exposure to them and their experience. We just can't thank them enough for their contribution.

Caller: Well, I'd like to thank them; it was a great course.

Jim: Let me mention their names—Milt Wiltse, from the Division of Geological and Geophysical Surveys; Del Ackels, who is a long time miner in the interior of Alaska; and Doug Colp was there, who has spent decades in the industry. And of course Ernie Wolff also helped me out on the program. So, you know, these are all knowledgeable people in the industry. It was a pleasure to be with them. Thanks again for your call, Gene, and I hope you come and take more classes at the University.

Caller: I plan on taking more, Jim. Thanks again.

Jim: Helen, we're back with you, and we were talking about eggs.

Helen: And chickens.

Jim: Well, tell the audience where you grew up in this chicken capital of the world—to what age?

Helen: Until I was about 15.

Jim: Where did you go then?

Helen: Klamath Falls, Oregon.

Jim: What in the world did you do in Oregon?

Helen: Finished growing up.

Jim: Did you go to college, following your high school years?

Helen: Yes. I left Klamath Falls, went one year to Stanford, then transferred to a small school outside of Portland, Pacific University, and that's where I got my bachelor's degree.

Jim: Following your bachelor's degree, did you go into industry, or what did you do?

Helen: I took off after graduating with a bachelor's degree and a whole hundred dollar bill I received for a graduation present and went to Los Angeles, where I went to work in the space industry. I had a degree in math, and computers were just coming into the common industrial sector. So I went to work for Northrup Space Laboratories and worked on the guidance system for Project Apollo and Project Ranger.

Jim: Oh, that sounds exciting. How long did you work at that?

Helen: I worked at that for three years, and then I went back to school and ultimately earned a master's degree.

Jim: And where did you go to school?

Helen: Oregon State.

Jim: And did you complete the master's degree there?

Helen: I completed most of the course work and went to Livermore and worked for the Atomic Energy Commission until I came up here to Alaska and finished my master's here at the University of Alaska Fairbanks.

Jim: Oh, you were working in Livermore. Just exactly what were you doing? What did your job center on?

Helen: I was working in a division called geochemistry division and I was a mathematician. I was maintaining two of their production computer programs on yield analysis and on accounting and decay curve analysis.

Jim: When you say decay curve, are you talking about the disintegration of atoms like uranium to its daughter isotopes? How does this apply to industry?

Helen: It depended entirely on the program and what had generated the decay that was being analyzed. A lot of the work down there at the time was done under a project called Ploughshare, which was peaceful applications of nuclear energy.

Jim: Tell us about the people who worked there.

Helen: They were tremendously wonderful people.

Jim: Well there was one person that you met down there that was particularly wonderful. What was his name?

Helen: You mean when I was taking a graduate class in radio chemistry and nuclear physics?

Jim: Is that what you were doing?

Helen: Yes. That's where I met my husband.

Jim: Oh. What was his name?

Helen: Henry Warner.

Jim: Henry Warner. And tell us, what did Henry do there? Was he working in the same place that you were working, or did you meet him at school?

Helen: Actually, they would teach classes from the University of California at

Davis or University of California at Berkeley, right on the lab premises. And both Henry and I happened to have registered for a course in radio chemistry and nuclear physics. Henry was the principle research technician for chemistry, so he worked over in Building 312, I believe, or some wonderful designation, and I was over in Headquarters for Radio Chemistry. We sat next to each other in the class.

Jim: Oh, sounds like it had potential.

Helen: It was wonderful.

Jim: Beaver, tell us a little bit more about your introduction to Henry.

Helen: It was really rather calm. We were arguing about valence.

Jim: Valence. Now that sounds like a term that's a mystery to a lot of people. Valence. Does that have anything to do with positive and negative charges?

Helen: Yes, it does.

Jim: Sounds romantic. Tell us about that.

Helen: We were discussing—now this is indeed how we happened to get started—whether chlorine had only one valence, or whether perhaps it could behave with two different valences. And how you would establish whether there was one or two different ones. That led to a longer discussion, which ultimately led to a gold mine in Alaska.

Jim: Well, how did it happen that you decided to come to Alaska and look at gold mines? What kind of conversation could continue on the path from valence to gold mines?

Helen: Well, we did discuss the fact that gold was one of the more noble metals. Henry was involved in mining down in Nevada. They were doing a lot of the testing underground in those days, and he did a lot of mine sampling for them. And my mother had been up here and had been looking at some mining property, and conversationally I mentioned Mother and ultimately got around to the fact that Mother knew a man who had two gold mines. In essence he had a spare.

Jim: I see. And so you and Henry must have made some plans to come up and work on the spare. What year was that?

Helen: That would be fall of 1963, and we came up in the spring of 1964. We have been here ever since.

Jim: Sad to say Helen, we have once again run out of time. I guess it is true that "All good things have to come to an end." Helen (Beaver) Warner, thank you so much for joining us here on Alaska Gold Trails, today.

Helen: Thank you, Jim. Its been a pleasure.

Arnold "Swede" Wasvick
with
Jim Madonna
Petersburg, Alaska
December 19, 1988

Jim: Today our traveling microphone has followed the trail to the town of Petersburg in Southeastern Alaska where our guest is Arnold "Swede" Wasvick. Welcome to Alaska Gold Trails, Swede. Just for the record tell us how you got your nickname.

Swede: My name is Arnold Wasvick, but everybody calls me Swede. I got it during my high school days at a basketball tournament in Juneau in 1927. It's been a moniker that's really stuck.

Jim: Were you born in Alaska or did you come from Outside?

Swede: I was born in Ballard, which is a suburb of Seattle. In fact at the time I was born, in 1910, there were more Norwegians in Ballard than there were in Norway.

Jim: How long did you stay in Ballard?

Swede: We stayed in Ballard for probably eight or nine years. Then my dad moved the whole family up here in the early '20s so I've been here going on 65 years now. However, my dad came directly from Norway to Alaska. He was a fisherman from the old country. He came up here in an old halibut steamer in 1905.

Jim: Did you come directly to Petersburg?

Swede: Yeah, we came directly to Petersburg. My mother had a sister living here. So that's how we happened to come to Petersburg. My dad came up in the spring and later sent for the family. My mother, three sisters and I came up on a steamer, the old *Admiral Rogers,* and we've been here ever since.

Jim: What was Petersburg like in those days? Can you tell us a little about its development?

Swede: Well, I sure can. Petersburg was a town of about 900 people. We had plank streets. Main Street was planks. All of the streets going up the hills and out into the residential areas were all on planks. It was a clean little town. We didn't have such a thing as dust, gravel, mud and stuff like that, in those days; lots of muskeg. We just kind of hoped that it would stay that way, but the fishing industry, of course, developed quite a bit more. It was primarily a fishing town. We didn't have any timber industry here. We had a little bit of logging, but nothing that would really bolster the economy. It was fishing. We had halibut fishing, salmon fishing, shrimp fishing, crab. All of the seafoods that were produced at that time were here and that was the main industry.

Jim: Was there any prospecting and mining going on during that time?

Swede: Yes, there was some prospecting. In fact, I worked at the old Maid of Mexico Mine, which is down in Woewodski Island, one year. They were trying to develop a mine, but the shortage of money and because of various other conditions, they didn't seem to be able to get the thing going.

Jim: Do you know the history of the Maid of Mexico Mine? What kind of mine was it?

Swede: It was a hard-rock gold mine, primarily gold, but they also had some silver. We worked up the hill, and our big problem was that we couldn't get water to the stamp mill. They didn't have the money to run a pump from the lake, which was a quarter mile away. When they tried to develop the mine, they had an engineer come up from a big mining corporation in Vancouver to evaluate it. I think the results were pretty good, but for some reason they didn't follow through on the development

Jim: Do you think the ore reserves were there, but the technology required to extract the gold wasn't quite developed?

Swede: When I was out there, this was in the early '30s, they had a vein that was very very rich, but the darned thing pinched off and they lost it, and they didn't have the money then to go looking for it. That was the story that I got. I didn't know anything about the mining end of it, but there's been an interest in that mine ever since. Right now, there is some development going on down there on the island. Whether it's ever going to amount to anything, why we don't know, but Doug Colp told me, a couple of years ago, that somebody is going to find a big deposit down there some day if they just keep exploring. It's in a mineral belt, I think like Chichagof out on the west coast. It kind of comes down through Duncan and this way. They've staked everything in the whole Duncan Canal including Woewodski Island and I think even over on the mainland. It all seems to run in one geological strata.

Jim: Let's return to when you were a little younger, following your arrival here in Petersburg, and of course, you said the streets were all made of wood, and it was quite a clean little town. What year did you come here?

Swede: We arrived here on the 15th day of March 1924. I was almost 14.

Jim: Did you go to school with Doug Colp?

Swede: Oh yeah. He was behind me by quite a ways. In fact he was in grammar school yet, I think, when I graduated. He was in the same class as one of my sisters. I graduated in '29. I think he graduated in '34 or something like that. I'm not sure. Oh, I knew Doug. I fished shrimp with his dad.

Jim: Harry?

Swede: Harry, yeah. Several winters I was out with him.

Jim: Well, you and Fred Magill must have also been schoolmates, or very close? I guess Fred was about the same age as Doug wasn't he?

Swede: I think so. Of course, I've known Fred ever since he was a little kid too. I was a little bit older. I don't think they were quite in high school yet when I graduated from high school.

Jim: There were a series of fox farms around about that time if I'm not mistaken?

Swede: Oh my, every island, every island in the area, all the way from here to Juneau and out of Juneau...every island had a fox rancher on them. That was a big thing for a while, but that petered out. The price of fur went down and they couldn't even afford to feed foxes. They just turned them loose. Early on, they were selling breeding stock for probably $1,500—$2,000 a pair. Then the skins got down to the point to where they were only worth about two dollars. It just cost much more than that to feed them. So, that just went by the wayside, but it was a booming thing for, I think, probably about eight or ten years. Every single island or rock had a fox rancher on it. That contributed quite a bit to the economy here, of course; all of those outlying fox farmers all came to town here to shop, you know.

Jim: One thought just passed my mind about Petersburg. The locals have a name—what do they call Petersburg?

Swede: Little Norway.

Jim: Little Norway. How did Petersburg get the name Little Norway.

Swede: Well, it was started by a Scandinavian in the first place. Peter Buschmann was a Norwegian. The fishermen who were in this town, well all of the civilian stock that was here were Norwegians. At one time, we had one Jewish fellow in town, but he didn't stay very long, and we had one colored fellow that was here for a few years, but he finally died. That was all we had. The rest were all Norwegians. We didn't have an influx of all the other nationalities until the timber industry took over. Then we got everything in here. Like the Lutheran Church, that was the main church. We had the Catholic Church, the Presbyterian Church, and now my goodness, there must be 12 or 14 denominations here now. So it just shows the mixture of people. In fact, I went to a meeting today for the 17th of May committee that puts on this Norwegian Independence Day Festival on the 17th. There was about two of them that I knew. The rest were strangers on it; they all know me it seems like, but I don't know them. I don't have a personal contact with a lot of those people. It's really been interesting.

Jim: When you graduated from high school, Swede, what did you do?

Swede: Well, I went fishing. That was the natural thing to do was to go fishing. Oh I worked around town. I got different jobs. I worked in a couple of stores. I wanted to go into business for myself. So I gave that a try after awhile. I got married when I was about 21 or so, and we started raising a family. We have five daughters here. I just got a new great-great-grandson here the other day. The family is getting bigger. We must have 17 or 18 greats (grandchildren) now and then great-greats coming up, so it's been a pretty prolific family as far as the reproduction is concerned.

Jim: Doing your part to keep little Norway going?

Swede: Yeah, we had to keep Little Norway going. We have a lot of people here who aren't Scandinavians, so it's beginning to be kind of a melting pot now. Seems like all good people here, all contribute to the community and are proud of the community. I'm really proud of this town, the way we've got it laid out after we went through some growing pains, reconstruction and new construction. I'm just like everybody else—you bitch and gripe, but after it's all over why, it's really nice. You can see that yourself. You walk down the main street now and it's really a nice little town.

Jim: It's always been a pleasant little town. I've enjoyed it every time I've come to visit. I remember the first time I came to teach, which was probably 12—13 years ago. I entered my first class, and there must have been 35 or 40 people attending.

Swede: Oh, did you have a class here?

Jim: Oh yes, I've taught four classes in mining and prospecting here. I teach the University of Alaska Mining Extension Program.

Swede: Oh you do?

Jim: This is the fourth course that I'm putting on now, as a matter of fact, but in that longer first class—a four-week prospecting and mining course, the Petersburg students turned out and just welcomed me with open arms. It was such a good feeling to be welcomed like that. The fact of the matter is, Swede, it's kind of interesting that Petersburg had the reputation of being a little bit standoffish early on. I was expecting all kinds of things. I walked in, I found it just the opposite of its reputation. They opened the doors, they open their arms, and right away they accepted me and it was very friendly.

Swede: That's pretty much the characteristics of this town. It's always been that way. We've always been grateful to have people come in and visit with us, teach us and show us. There was a time that I was kind of interested in this mining business, but you know, I got broke into fishing pretty early. I'd rather stand up to my elbows in fish slime and gore than go out here and dig around in a bunch of hard rock. I'm just a seaman at heart. We put in some tough days out there in the old gulf. Anyway, after you've been on the beach for a couple of weeks, why you feel like you're ready to go again.

Jim: You have been fishing then most of your life here in Petersburg, is that correct?

Swede: Oh yeah, well the last 20 years I have cooked out in a logging camp. My wife and I ran the cookhouse for Muir's Logging Company. We started in Thomas Bay and wound up out at Point Alice out on the west coast. So I've been more or less in the food business pretty much my whole adult life. I started the Pastime down here where the restaurant is now. The Homestead, I built that place and I had that for about 10 years. I was in the mercantile business for awhile. I finally sold that, and then I went fishing again. I fished for quite awhile until it started to get to me; charley horses and rheumatism and one thing and another. So I quit and I went to work in the woods, and I stayed there for about 20 years.

Jim: Cooking?

Swede: Cooking, and then I retired.

Jim: Tell us more about what you have done in your life and perhaps some people in Alaska that you might know that would be interesting to interview?

Swede: The only one that I know of in town here that has ever been interested in mining is Fred Magill.

Jim: It is interesting you brought up his name; I just had a lengthy interview with Fred and it was quite interesting. He's had a lot of experiences.

Swede: Yeah, he has. Then there was Dave Omer now who passed away. There used to be a group of us that grubstaked some of these old guys that were prospectors. You know we'd buy them beans and bacon.

Jim: Omer, I've heard of him; Fred referred to him. What did he do? Can you give us any information?

Swede: Dave Omer, he did a lot of prospecting. They have the shrimp cannery here. He was out prospecting. Well he'd go by himself and be gone for several days, and he was always kicking around looking for something out in the rocks. His dad, Earl, was the one that financed the old Maid of Mexico Mine.

Jim: Oh, that's right. Omer was the one.

Swede: He was the banker for the Maid of Mexico at the time when I was out there for several years until they just couldn't do it anymore. It just didn't develop for them, but there was some potential there. Hard-rock mining in those days was really an expensive way to go. Every time you fired a round of dynamite out there, you know, it cost them quite a bit of money for powder and time. Then, if they missed it, like they did...they had this vein, and I was told that they hit a stringer there, that they sent some samples down south and it ran $20,000 a ton. That was at $20 an ounce too. The gold looked like it was painted on the rocks, and that's what they were looking for, but they lost it, and they never had enough money to go hunting for it again. Maybe that's all there was, I don't know.

Jim: Let's change gears here for a minute, Swede. A lot of the Pioneers have related stories to me regarding close scrapes they've had in life, or they had a very scary extraordinary experience or a more memorable experience. I was wondering if perhaps you might have had a very close call or an experience that was memorable that you would be willing to share with us.

Swede: Well, I sure have had a couple of close shaves. I've been shipwrecked, and had to swim ashore.

Jim: In the frigid waters of Southeast Alaska?

Swede: You betcha it was.

Jim: Tell us that story, Swede.

Swede: It was in the summertime and we were fishing down towards Portland Canal. We had just delivered some fish, and we were on our way home when we ran into some engine trouble coming up along the coast. We couldn't get it going and we drifted onto a breaker. Of course, it smashed the boat up to where she sunk. So we all had to take to a skiff. We had life jackets on, jumped into a skiff and was going ashore. The sea was running pretty heavy, and it swamped our skiff. There were three of us on the rig and we were all in the water, and we swam ashore while the water batted us about. So that was one of the hairy experiences that I had. We got up on the beach, no shoes on, walking along on the barnacles and one thing and another. Finally, a cannery tender came from down towards Tree Point. As luck would have it, they were in close enough where they saw us on the beach. We were standing there waving our shirts and one thing and another, and they picked us up and took us to Ketchikan. So, that was one of the close calls that we had in the summertime.

Jim: What recommendation would you have for anybody in a boat after that experience, Swede—safety jackets?

Swede: Oh, heavens yes. If you have to abandon the boat, you got to put on the safety jacket, no matter how good a swimmer you are, because you can run into all kinds of things. You can run into a kelp pack. I did. You can run into undertows, currents and different things you know. If it's cold enough, you can cramp up and not make it.

Jim: I imagine it was plenty cold in that water.

Swede: It was. It was, but it wasn't so cold, and we didn't have to go that far. We probably had a couple of hundred yards to go. Our big problem getting ashore that time was going through the kelp that lies along the edges, but after we got through that why we got up on the beach. Like I said, we walked along, we were heading for Tree Point. We were going to walk down toward the light, which was about oh, I don't know seven-eight miles down the beach. As luck would have it, we were picked up before that. I can't remember the name of the boat now. It was a cannery tender.

Jim: You said you have another experience that might be of interest, Swede. What would that be?

Swede: Well, I've had some hunting experiences alright, but none of them have been dangerous.

Jim: Do you have any exciting bear stories that might be thrilling?

Swede: No, but I've got a wolf story. I was duck hunting one time up in the head of Duncan Canal years ago. I saw what I thought was three or four deer out on a sandbar, oh gee, a mile or a mile and a half away. I had a telescope on my rifle that I had with me. We usually carried it because there were a lot of deer in the country in those days. So when we were duck hunting, we usually had a rifle handy in case one showed up some place. Through this telescope, I picked up these animals. I thought they were deer. So I got my Buddy (cocker spaniel) and I thought, "Well, let's walk up there. Maybe we can get one of those guys." So we got down into a slough—it was MacDonald's Slough—it's a little river that comes down through the middle of the mud flats. In order to keep under cover, we stayed down in this creek bottom, and walked up as far as we could until we got where we wanted to cross over the mud flats to where these animals were. I had a little black cocker spaniel with me, who was my hunting partner. When we got ready to cross the flats, we got up on the bank and here's a pack of seven wolves right out in front of us. They were coming across the flats toward us. So I got up on the bank and I started shooting, and I got one the first crack. They were within 150 yards of us, you know. Then they start milling around, and I missed a couple of times. Finally, I got another one, and shot some more, and then another one. Then my dog was going to go over there and get smart. This little black cocker spaniel ran over there like he was really going to show off. Because of the way they were snapping and growling, why, I was afraid they'd get him. So I worked on this other wolf and got my dog back. Well, in the meantime we discovered that it was a mother with six half-grown pups. She started moving toward the timber, trying to get the pups to follow her. As it turned out, I got four of them, and the other two and the mother got away.

Jim: There was a time here in Alaska when there was a bounty on wolves, is that correct?

Swede: That's right. There was a bounty on them at that time. I just had a brand new telescope on my rifle and I paid for it with the bounty off those wolves.

Jim: Let's see, there was a bounty on wolves, seal and eagles. Three animals for which the rules have changed. The seals and the eagles are protected, more or less. The wolf isn't, but there is no longer a bounty on wolves.

Swede: No, not anymore. I think you can trap them now or hunt them for their pelts.

Jim: Times change, don't they.

Swede: Oh, I should say. One of our supplemental incomes was hunting seal and eagle. We used to go out bounty-shooting on weekends. In fact, shooting bounty was where I paid for all of my ammunition. Towards the last, gosh, we were getting six dollars for a seal scalp and two dollars for a set of eagle claws, and four bits (50 cents) for the tail feathers. It was a pretty profitable situation. If you could go out and get 10 or 12 eagles in a day and a half a dozen seals, you could do pretty well. But now that's all protected. And, I have no desire to kill anything anymore.

Jim: Let's change directions here for a minute, Swede. Is there a Christmas that, perhaps something happened where some adventure took place that might set one apart from all the rest of the traditional Christmases you ever had?

Swede: Well, we've always had pretty nice Christmases, but I missed a Christmas one time. I was out trapping, and I was down in Rocky Pass. They were supposed to pick me up on the day before Christmas, and by golly, the weather set in. It started snowing and we were having such snow squalls, they couldn't get out there with the plane. That was the one Christmas I wasn't at home. That was the only Christmas I ever missed.

Jim: What thoughts went through your mind when they couldn't get out to you the day before Christmas?

Swede: Well, I was concerned about my wife and the kids not having their daddy home. From what I understand, they really missed me too, because I was kind of the Santa Claus around there at that time.

Jim: Well, tell us Swede, did you have any concern about your own welfare? Were you out in a squall or were you pretty well set?

Swede: We were pretty well set up. There were three of us out there and we worked every day and were just watching the weather. I was finally picked up, because the plane made it around the big snow storm and swung on in. It was Quinton DeBor. I don't know if you ever heard of him. He was flying here at that time. He tried every day for four or five days to get me.

He had to get Swede to town—that was his idea, you know. He finally came sailing in, and we were out in the middle of the sound in a skiff moving from one trapline to another. I just jumped in the plane. The plane left the other fellow in the skiff. I went into town in my old trapping clothes. I hadn't shaved in three weeks. I was kind of a sight when I came into town. The family had never seen me like that. It was quite an event, but we had a good Christmas afterwards. They saved part of the festivities for me.

Jim: Even if you were late I bet it felt good to be home with your family?

Swede: Yeah.

Jim: One other question: We are having this interview on the 19th of January 1988 and you just finished your service as grand president of the Pioneers, is that right?

Swede: September. It goes from September to September.

Jim: I see. I just wanted people to know that you had served in that capacity and now you are, more or less, a consultant for future presidents.

Swede: That's right. We discuss subjects or topics that come up for the good of the Grand Igloo. We are a committee, a kind of standing committee, to be referred to. If there's something that comes up, the past grands will study things and make recommendations.

Jim: Elaborate a little bit about the Pioneers of Alaska. What is required to become involved with the organization? How many years do you have to live in Alaska?

Swede: Well, you have to be in Alaska for 30 years. You have to be a good citizen. You're investigated if you apply for membership. It's very seldom that anybody is ever turned down. In fact to my knowledge, I don't know of anybody. Anyway, it requires 30 years of residency to join the Pioneers. It's a social thing. We do have committees like in the legislature. Now, we kind of look out for the senior citizens and the pioneers, and keep up on current events and things that involve the Pioneers. Gosh, it's a big organization; it has pretty near 8,000 members now so it's a pretty big outfit, and it's really a big voting block for one thing, you know, politically. Then, here a few years ago, they nominated me as a grand officer.

Jim: What is a grand officer?

Swede: Well this is of the Grand Igloo. This is when we have our conventions and all of the Igloos in the state come together, once a year, and we have this election, where we select new officers, and then we discuss all the business of the different Igloos and Auxiliaries, and see what we can do, as far as the legislature is concerned, for the betterment of the Pioneers. That's primarily our function—to take care of the old pioneers. Some, of course, have it a little bit better than others, and we try to fix it up so that everybody can have an honorable and a decent lifestyle after they get older and non-productive. That was one of the main things as far as the Pioneers Homes were concerned. I was instrumental in getting the senior citizen building up here on the hill.

Jim: In Petersburg?

Swede: Yes, in Petersburg. We can bring a lot of pressure to bear on the legislature when there's things that we want to have done.

Jim: I could imagine—an 8,000 voting block, and growing everyday, is a significant group of voters.

Swede: Right. Yeah, I think we're growing everyday, not very much. We lose a few every year, but then I think on the whole we're gaining.

Jim: Regarding the Pioneers, there are Pioneers Homes around the state of Alaska, do you have a handle on where these homes exist. Where's the number one Pioneer Home?

Swede: Number one is in Sitka. That's the first one. Then we have one in Anchorage...well, let's see, maybe we have two in Anchorage. We have one in Palmer, and we have one in Fairbanks. We have one in Ketchikan, and now we're getting one that should be available for occupancy this year in Juneau.

Jim: So we have several Pioneers Homes strategically located around the state that are taking care of the people. What are these grand officers? Are these people the governing body?

Swede: That's right. The grand officers are the governing body. If there's any pertinent things that come up, usually it will be the past grands, the grand president can call together for any advice that they want. They don't conduct any business, but they recommend things to the Grand Igloo. That's at the convention. Last year, we had the convention in Palmer. We have it in different places. Next year, it's going to be in Sitka. Two years ago, it was in Valdez. So we try to hit all the communities that can handle a convention. It's quite a chore, you know, there are about 600—700 people come to these conventions, and trying to house them, feed them and keep them busy for three or four days is a major project.

Jim: Tell us about the steps in the grand order of things.

Swede: Well, I can tell you the way I went through it. I started out as a trustee. I was a trustee for two years, I think.

Jim: Do you have to be recommended for this position?

Swede: Yes.

Jim: So, how did you become nominated for the position?

Swede: Well, I really don't know. I can't think of his name now. Poor guy, he passed away recently. Anyway, at one of the conventions, I was approached and asked if I would be interested maybe in being an officer of the Grand Igloo. I thought, well, why not? I was elected as a trustee, and I think I was a trustee for two years. Then again, Danny Plotnick; do you happen to know Danny Plotnick?

Jim: No I don't.

Swede: He was from Juneau. He was in this Farmer's Home Administration deal when I was working on this building up here, so we had a lot in common. Anyway, just before we went to the convention, Danny Plotnick called me from Juneau—He was on this nominating committee—and asked me if I would be interested in going through the chairs of the Grand Igloo. Well, I hadn't given it any thought. I figured well maybe I'm too old for that, I was past 70, and I thought, gee whiz I don't know whether I can hack that. Anyway, they finally talked me into it. Then they asked for the recommendation from our delegation to the convention from the Petersburg Igloo and the Auxiliary, and of course, they recommended me. So then I was on the slate. Then they had the election. The nominating committee brings in a slate of candidates. Usually, the candidates that they present at the convention are the ones that are elected. After all, they all have been studied to find out what their qualifications are. There's really no campaigning or anything like that. So that's how you get on the Grand Igloo officer slate. Then, you usually start...like Doug (Colp), I think he's sergeant-of-arms, which is out by the door. Then you go from sergeant-of-arms, you're moved up to chaplain. Then you go from chaplain to historian. Those are all steps in the chain. Then you go from historian to second vice-president, and then first vice-president. You have to serve in all those capacities for one year, and then you go from first vice-president to grand president. The grand president's duties is the installation of officers of all the Igloos and Auxiliaries. So a year ago today, I was in Valdez in 15 feet of snow on my tour. Evelyn and I spent nearly, well we did, we spent five and a half weeks on our tour.

Jim: And Evelyn's your wife?

Swede: Yes, she's my wife.

Jim: You were installing officers.

Swede: We installed all the officers in all the Igloos. In July, I instituted a new Igloo in Big Delta, so I made a trip up there. Then I was in Fairbanks for the tail end of Golden Days, so that was part of my official visitations and duties. I was to do all of that, that I could and I had a good time and enjoyed it. Then in September, at the Grand Igloo Convention, I presided. That lasted for four days. So we finished all our business and everything that was required and had a big blowout at the end of the session.

Jim: What a fine contribution. You seem to have really enjoyed your time in office.

Swede: Yeah, this was a wonderful experience both for Evelyn and I.

Jim: Once you finish this tour through the steps of becoming the grand president, what happens after that.

Swede: I'm a past grand president, and I am on the executive committee now, all of the past grands are on the executive committee. That is an advisory board.

Jim: So you need a lot of exposure at the legislature?

Swede: Well we do. I was up there twice last year. I testified once, and I was up there for a couple of things just to see how things are going on. Your presence, by golly, influences some of those guys that you really want to work for you. We have good representation; we've been doing great up there.

Jim: Do the Pioneers support any other outside activities?

Swede: No, we don't get into anything political or anything like that. We have a lot of members that are interested in that, and they can maybe do those things on their own.

Jim: That's a personal thing though?

Swede: Yeah, about the only thing that we have taken up in the Grand Igloo that has been more or less a political football has been the longevity bonus. At the last convention, we voted for this annuity situation to finance the longevity bonus. We all went along on that. We don't finance anything, any politicians or anything like that. We do have a lobbyist in Juneau to keep us posted on everything that's going on during the legislature. His notes and reports are sent to the grand president now and sometime all of the past grands will get a little information on it or we do it by telephone. I was really busy during the legislature. It keeps you up all of the time. I wouldn't believe it, but when I turned over the gavel as grand president to the incoming president, my blood pressure went down 31 points. I couldn't believe that. I never thought for a minute that this job pressured me, because I didn't feel like it, but my blood pressure was always up there. I just couldn't believe it. My daughter's a nurse. I live right down here next to her, and she came up and said, "My gosh, Dad, you're sure in good health now, compared to what you were here awhile ago.

Jim: Who is the new grand president? We better check his blood pressure.

Swede: A fellow by the name of Ed Kopp. He'll be here next week.

Jim: I see, and where does he call home?

Swede: He's from Homer. He's a retired FAA man I think or CAA or whatever it is. He's on his tour now and he'll be here in Southeast this next week.

Jim: Do you have any other experiences you would like to share with us.

Swede: I don't know if you want to hear about my most recent trip to Fairbanks or not.

Jim: Sure, we do. Tell us.

Swede: Returning to Fairbanks, to me, was a special treat. It was the first convention I went to in Fairbanks. I hadn't been there in 49 years—from the time we were up there and played basketball. When I came back, I gave a report from the Petersburg Igloo to the Grand Igloo and then I mentioned the fact that I had been there in 1929 and maybe some of the old-timers would remember when we were there because we won the All-Alaska Basketball Championship in Fairbanks.

Jim: In 1929?

Swede: In 1929, our high school won the state championship. I was wondering whether there was anyone in the audience that remembered that or had been there at that time. We had called a recess, and I walked out into the foyer, and there was a fellow by the name of Miller, and Johnny O'Shea, and one more. John Butrovich was on the team but he wasn't there at that time. There was three of them there. I can't think of the other one's name. Anyway, did we ever have a reunion.

Jim: Reminiscing over that game.

Swede: It was really something, that series. We played three games. The scores were 56 to 55 and we had the 56. We won two out of three. When we were in Fairbanks, Leonhard Seppala was there, who was the great dog musher. Do you remember, that took the serum to Nome.

Jim: Oh, right.

Swede: He took us for a dogsled ride out to the college (University of Alaska). So I'd been out there in 1929.

Jim: And to go with Seppala too, that was an extra treat.

Swede: That's right, with Leonhard Seppala, and at that time it was called the Alaska Agricultural College and School of Mines.

Jim: I think it was called that up until 1935. Then it became the University of Alaska.

Swede: Yeah, and I think Bunnell was the president. A fellow by the name of Ryan—I don't remember if he taught in the college or whether he taught at the high school, but he was our referee at the ball game. Later he became the commissioner of education. So that was a particular good treat to visit with those people, and a lot of them remembered. More recently when I was up there for the installation of officers, I mentioned it again...it was in my resume, something about playing basketball up there. I wanted to know if there was any of the people at this banquet who remembered the games, and lo-and-behold, there was five women that came up to talk to me about it. They had been the song queens and yell leaders at those basketball games. After the games there was a mystery: We were there during St. Patrick's Day Ball, and we went to this ball and the girls wouldn't dance with us boys from Petersburg. We were kind of ignored after winning this championship, so we left, and I asked one of the girls about that. I said, "What was the deal? How come?" What had happened was the boys had put us off limits to their girls. If they danced with any of us boys, they'd had it as far as the local boys were concerned. I asked them if that was the truth. This one gal, she hung her head, kind of in shame, and she said, "Yep, by golly it was." She said, "I went home and another girl and I cried for days after that series was over." That was one of the highlights of my trip, unraveling that mystery, and of course returning to Fairbanks three times during my tenure as grand president. Then, I met people in every single town I was in that I had known from years back that remembered me through different things, fishing and other activities.

Jim: That was a good one. Are there any other stories you would like to share with us, Swede?

Swede: Well, I don't know, it's all fishing and hunting as far as I'm concerned.

Jim: You still like going out sportfishing?

Swede: Oh yeah, I have my little boat here. I got a little 19-foot glass-bottom, and I go out during the summer. I have it at home now. I don't hunt anymore, but the one activity I can do is fish. If conditions are right, I go out and shoot birds, but I'm not as active that way. This will be two years in May, I just had a knee transplant. Well that kind of slowed me up, but I'm getting along fine now. I don't get around quite as much as I used to, but I am 78 years old, and there are still plenty of things to do.

Jim: Well Swede, something just happened here recently that is a blessing for me. Mrs. Magill made the comment, "There are plenty of opportunities left in Alaska for people who want to reach out for them." I feel that here just recently, there was an opportunity that made itself available to me, and that was, of course, to interview pioneers and people like you. During the interviews I take a personal approach, and when I leave I feel that the person I have just interviewed has become my personal friend.

Swede: Well, that's the way I feel. I don't think I have an enemy. I've always been able to make friends, and I've always enjoyed people. I've gotten teed off a time or two at different ones, but I cannot carry a grudge. I've been that way all my life. Sometimes it has been good for me and sometimes it hasn't, but in the long run, I got everything I want—a wonderful wife and a good family. What more can you ask for?

Jim: That is the most important, isn't it?

Swede: That's right. I've been pretty healthy. I've had a few minor things, but gosh, after 75 or 80 years…I don't think the old carcass was made to last as long as we can make them last now. I think that's why we break down. Gosh, we live to be 80, 85, 90, even up to 100. Why, the old carcass wasn't made for all that stuff, I don't think. If we didn't have all of this modern technology why we'd be six feet under a long time ago. When I went down to have this knee transplant, it was just like walking into a spare-parts room at a garage. Everything you wanted was right there. The doc says, "Whatever you need, I'll put it in."

Jim: Just pick it out and we will rebuild you.

Swede: He said, "I'll take it out, and I'll put it in." And that's what he did. He took an x-ray, and he said, "We can fix that." I wasn't too excited about it. I thought, "Gee whiz. I don't know if I want to go through this or not." But there was a friend of mine who had just had orthoscopic surgery on his knee. It just took care of him. So he says, "Let's go see this doctor of mine, see what he says. You don't have to do anything, just see what he says." So the doc took an X ray or two and said, "Oh yeah, we can take care of that." He talked me into it. The next morning, I was on the table, and that's all she wrote.

Jim: Now, how long has it taken you to recuperate from this? Are you ready to go now?

Swede: My knee is just as good as it ever was. I was in constant pain for about four years. What happened to my knee was the cartilage in the joint just wore out and the bones were just rubbing together and aching all of the time. I got rid of that, and now my good knee gives me more trouble than anything. I favored it so long I think I have to rehabilitate that a little bit. I had him X ray that, but he said that it wasn't worth him going in for an operation to do that. He said, "You'll get over that eventually."

Jim: How long was the recovery, Swede?

Swede: Oh, I was hurting for maybe six weeks, but after the pain and sore-
ness from the operation left it was fine. I had to be careful. I walked
with a walker for about two months. Now it's fine.

Jim: Well, Swede, all these good interviews have a habit of coming to an
end. I want to thank you very much for permitting me to come into your
home and share some time with you and learn about what you've done
in your life. I'm sure that many of your friends around the state are
going to enjoy this interview when it gets written up. Thank you so
much for your time.

Swede: Well good! You are so welcome. It's a pleasure to tell you the
stories about the old times.

Nedra Waterman
with
Jim Madonna
Haines, Alaska
January 17, 1988

Jim: Again our trail has led us to Haines, Alaska. where we are with Nedra Waterman. Two things, Nedra: First, I want to welcome you to Alaska Gold Trails on your 41st wedding anniversary, and second, it is time to tell your side of the story about life with Wes Waterman.

Nedra: Thank you, Jim. I heard your interview with Wes, and I am ready to tell you the true story.

Jim: Nedra, tell us, where were you born, and if I can be so inquisitive, just what year was it?

Nedra: Well, I was born in Vancouver, Washington, in 1918. I'm not ashamed of my age. I came to Alaska in 1944, landed in Anchorage, no job, 50 dollars in my pocket. That was on a Monday, and on Thursday, I went to work for dear ol' CAA. I worked for them for, oh, a little over two years, met Wesley Willard (Waterman), and that was the end of that.

Jim: Tell us what CAA. stands for.

Nedra: It means Civil Aeronautic Administration.

Jim: What did you do for them, Nedra?

Nedra: I worked in the bookkeeping department.

Jim: Then, you met this chap, this good-looking chap. Tell us how'd you happen to meet him? What sequence of events led up to meeting Wesley Willard? Who's this Wesley Willard guy?

Nedra: Well, I was between jobs. So I went to Talkeetna to visit people I had met and knew. He came in from the mines, pretty inebriated, one night. About midnight he came into the store that the people I was visiting owned. That's when I met him. A few days later, I saw him in Anchorage and he didn't remember me, of course. Then we saw each other occasionally, and finally, at Christmastime we went out, and January 17, 1947 we were married. We met in September—September 26.

Jim: Where were you married?

Nedra: In Anchorage. At the Episcopal Church on Fifth Avenue, Father Finn married us.

Jim: You were working for CAA at that time.

Nedra: No, no, no, I had left CAA, and was running a little sandwich shop in front of a bar, can't even remember the name of it.

Jim: Now Wesley wasn't frequenting that bar and happened to see you at that sandwich shop, did he?

Nedra: Oh no, I met him in another bar. Then he used to come into the sandwich shop. He would rarely eat—he just came in to see me.

Jim: Tell me, what was Anchorage like in those days? What kind of town was it? Did it have dirt streets and a frontier-type environment? How many people were there?

Nedra: My but you ask a lot of questions at once. I don't have any idea how many people. Fourth Avenue was the only street paved, and it was paved from C Street to L Street...pretty rowdy, more bars than businesses on Fourth Avenue. There were all kinds of elements there. A lot of the old time Alaskans were still around in those days. It wasn't as citified as it is now.

Jim: Did they have annual events? Did they have the Fur Rendezvous then?

Nedra: They had that then.

Jim: What was that like? What kind of action took place there during Fur Rendezvous?

Nedra: Well, I don't know too much about the Fur Rendezvous. I know there was a lot of drinking. Of course, there always was, no matter whether it was summer or winter, Fur Rendezvous or what. They used to have a parade on the Fourth of July...and I remember one year, the mechanics down in the railroad yard entered a name for the Fur Rendezvous Queen—May O'Connor. Little did anyone know that it was Malamute May. She had been a dance-hall girl in Dawson, she and her sister. She was quite a character. She didn't win, but she did make a pretty good showing because no one knew who she was. I don't remember many other things going on. When we left there in '61, Fifth Avenue wasn't paved yet.

Jim: So it was still a frontier town in '61 then?

Nedra: In lots of ways, yes.

Jim: Tell us something, what was it like marrying Wesley then spending your honeymoon by going up to the mining camp? How did you like that? What was life like for a woman in the mining camp, especially for a young Cheechako woman, fresh into the country?

Nedra: Well, I sure didn't know what I was getting into.

Jim: If you knew then what you know now, would you still have married him?

Nedra: I don't know. Oh boy! That was a loaded question, Jim! I could go into a lot of stories about that but I won't. I might have. I really didn't know him and he didn't know me.

Jim: You just kind of got married, that's it?

Nedra: We just kind of got married and took it from there. I always said he married me for money because I had a little bit more than he did. By the time we went mining, we didn't have a dime. Like he said, I ruined Cache Creek. I said if I was going to live out there six months, I was going to live like a human being, and I did.

Jim: Did you like it? Did you meet a lot of nice folks out there?

Nedra: Yes, yes a lot of good folks. It was a different way of life for me. Vancouver, Washington, where I was born, was a very small town, but I had not lived with an outdoor privy and no running water and lights, and such. We got out to Fall's Creek where we landed, after we were married. He had built a wannigan, but he hadn't brought enough lumber for an outhouse. So he had a board and he measured it between two trees. Well, he measured it for his legs, not mine and I was pregnant, and I had quite a summer with the outhouse. Pretty near fell in a couple of times.

Jim: Tell us, when you came back out of the mining camps, what did you do following that period of time?

Nedra: Well I was pregnant. Of course, I didn't know his folks and he didn't know my mother and we promised to go home for Christmas. So, I went home in October and he was going to work until Christmas and come out. Well, he came out at Thanksgiving and he called me up and I didn't think it was him on the phone except he said a couple of things that made me believe it was him. Then we stayed in Portland and Vancouver until he came back to Alaska in April, and I came up in July with our oldest daughter.

Jim: You played stay-at-home mom with the family, then?

Nedra: Yeah, I stayed just family, and two years later, we had another daughter. So I was raising children, and of course, we lived in villages where there wasn't a great deal of work.

Jim: Where did you move to then.

Nedra: Well, let's see. We lived in Talkeetna when Kathy was born.

Jim: What took you to Talkeetna?

Nedra: Well, I married him.

Jim: Oh, I see, I understand that. That is when you were mining out of Talkeetna?

Nedra: Yeah, he mined the first year we were married. We were married in January. We were stuck in Anchorage for two weeks. There wasn't a train, it was so cold. When we finally got a train to Talkeetna, it was eight hours to go 120 miles and nearly froze. We lived in Talkeetna then until March of '49. Then he went to work for CAA, and they shipped him off to Bethel, and they said there was no housing for the baby. We were stuck in Anchorage and I got pretty mad, so I went up to the regional office where I had worked, and I was bitterly complaining, and the next day they called, and he was relocated to Tanana where we could all be together. So, Julie was born when we lived in Tanana.

Jim: How did you like Tanana?

Nedra: Oh I did. On the Yukon River, there was about 40 white people and the rest natives. They had the tuberculosis hospital there. It was a lot of fun. We had a lot of good times there. You made your own good times. It was like Talkeetna. You made your own good times in Talkeetna. In those days there was no road into Talkeetna. You went by railroad. I can tell you some off-color stories about Talkeetna if you want.

Jim: You bet I want. Tell them, please.

Nedra: We would take Sunday walks. We had our oldest daughter and her baby carriage. It was a nice perambulator baby carriage we pushed down the street and this Annie D. came up to us. She was one of these native girls that was picked up from the Eklutna School, these old-timers when they would want a cook and a woman to live with, they'd go down there and they would marry one of these girls out of the Eklutna School. Well, there was two of them I guess, they were the two Annie's in town, Annie D and Annie R. Oh, they used to fight, but this Annie D came up to us while we were walking and she looked at the baby, oh, how cute, and she looks around at me and says, "You know Missus. I don't know what the matter with Wes, but he never ever go to bed with me." Everybody else in town was always going to bed with her.

Jim: That's all there was to it?

Nedra: That's all there was to it.

Jim: How did you respond to that? Did you beat the hell out of Wes?

Nedra: No, I just laughed. What could you say. Just because everybody else slept with her.

Jim: Just everybody except Wes.

Nedra: I know another story about Annie D too, but I don't think you want it on there.

Jim: Well go ahead. Whatever you say I will put in the story.

Wes: Hell, why not!

Jim: You stay out of this, Wes!

Nedra: Well, when I went to Talkeetna to visit before I met Wes, the store-keeper where I was visiting, his wife and I were walking down the street. There were two "Annies" in town: Annie D and Annie R. They had a fight. Annie D had Annie R down on the ground and was peeing in her face.

Jim: What was that all about?

Nedra: Well, she peed in her face and got up and walked off and left her laying there. I don't know what the fight was about.

Jim: Any more stories from Talkeetna, Nedra, or anyplace else for that matter?

Nedra: Well this was long before my day—I think it was '42. Freida DuVault had a roadhouse.

Jim: And this was Talkeetna?

Nedra: Talkeetna, yeah. There was a big flood. So from the lower end of town, by the river, they were takin' everybody to higher ground by a boat, and Freida was so drunk she wouldn't get in. "I'm not gittin' in any goddamn boat," she says, "I'll swim." She swam up to where the water was shallow, but then she hit dry land and she was polluted enough that she kept swimming. I guess it was quite hilarious, everybody got quite a kick out of it.

Jim: Any more, Nedra?

Nedra: Well, there was Belle McDonald. Gramma Belle came to Alaska before World War I and she homesteaded in the Matanuska Valley in '18. She lived there in Talkeetna, and she was quite a character. One year she got chickens in—about 300 chickens—and she knew every one by its name. Mack, her husband, would steal eggs from her. He'd get out there and steal the eggs and trade them for a drink. She wanted to sell some of them for roasting chickens, but she could never decide which ones she wanted to sell. Before I ever met Gramma Belle, when I worked for CAA, in Anchorage, one of the engineers came in, and he'd been up to Talkeetna. One of the ladies I worked with said, "How's Gramma Belle?" He says, "Oh she's doing pretty good, but the river got high, but she said it was only up to her ass this year. Last year it was up to her tits." In her store, the floor was quite wavy and she put up a plank to walk across. Bless her heart, she was a dear soul, and we thought a lot of her. She lived with Wes and me. She'd been quite ill in the hospital in Anchorage, and we lived in Anchorage at the time. Of course, everybody said, "If there's anything we can do, Belle, you just let us know." But when it came time that she could leave the hospital, but not well enough to go back to Talkeetna, they all disappeared. So we said, "Well, she can come and stay with us for a time." Well, she liked the

TV real well, and everybody that came to the house enjoyed her stories. After a while she got well enough, she could go home. One time, I said to Wes, "All my washcloths disappeared". I couldn't find a one of them. He said, "Go look in Gramma Belle's suitcase." Sure enough, there they were, neatly folded. She thought they were nice little cloths to have. She went back to Talkeetna, and she was finally in the Pioneer's Home in Sitka and that's where she passed away a number of years ago.

Jim: She was a real true pioneer of Alaska.

Nedra: She was an Alaska pioneer, yes.

Jim: What was her name again?

Nedra: Belle McDonald, sometimes Wes called her "Railroad Belle." I never heard her called that. Up the line they called her Goat Mary. She raised goats, and she lived on this property that belonged to Lusack and Cap Lathrop. Anyway, she wouldn't get off because she had squatter's rights. They called her, Goat Mary, and if she was ever on the train and you were on, you heard everything. She talked to everybody. Sometimes she was so loud everybody in the car could hear her.

Jim: Those stories were fun diversions, but now back to Tanana. When you left Tanana, where did you go?

Nedra: Kenai.

Jim: How long did you live there?

Nedra: Five years. I didn't like it as well as other places. You're on the highway. It wasn't as friendly, I didn't think. One lady told me, "Well you'll like Kenai because nobody pays any attention to what you do or where you go." Well, we were there awhile before we had a car. One Sunday, my two daughters and I took off after Wes left for work, and we came home when he came home. That night, before I retired, three people came and asked me where I had been that afternoon. That's minding their own business isn't it?

Jim: You didn't have experiences like that in the villages?

Nedra: No, no.

Jim: Well that's because the villages are so small, everybody knew what you did.

Nedra: Yes, everybody knew where I went.

Jim: From Kenai, where did you go?

Nedra: Anchorage.

Jim: Oh, back home? To the big city and little sandwich shop out in front of the bar!

Nedra: Yeah. No...well, I guess it was still there when we went back. We were there about four or five years and then Wes had to take his retirement. We went to California, which I don't recommend.

Jim: Not for an Alaskan?

Nedra: No, or anybody!

Jim: When you finally came back, about 14 or 15 years ago, you returned to Alaska, this time to Haines, where you've made your home. In fact, it was about that time that I met you.

Nedra: Yeah, we were running the Townhouse Motel.

Jim: Right, I stayed there when I came down and taught here at Haines, and Wes took the prospecting course.

Nedra: Yeah, and you stayed several times after that.

Jim: It was never the same as when you ran it, Nedra. Thank you for the interview. Knowing you both all these years has been a pleasure. I'll never forget you.

Wes Waterman
with
Jim Madonna
Haines, Alaska
January 16, 1988

Jim: We have followed the trail to Haines, Alaska, where we are meeting with Wes Waterman, a colorful character in Alaskan history. Wes, welcome to Alaska Gold Trails. How are you today?

Wes: Well, I'm pretty good today, but I have been better.

Jim: Tell us about where you came from. Were you born in Alaska.

Wes: I was born in Portland, Oregon. I lived there mainly in around Portland. I lived there until I came to Alaska in February, 1940.

Jim: What year were you born, Wes?

Wes: 1915.

Jim: That suggests that you came to Alaska when you were 25 years old.

Wes: Well, almost, almost. You're right close.

Jim: You went to school there, around Portland. Did you work after school, or maybe the question is, did you finish school, Wes?

Wes: No, I didn't.

Jim: Well, tell us a story about that.

Wes: Well, I'll tell you, it's a good story. It's kind of a long one I guess. Some people think I was crazy. Well, maybe I was. I even thought I was for awhile. My dad had taken a homestead up by Mount Hood. It was a timber claim. I was a young buck at the time. I was in high school and I was up there and we were getting ready to set up a little railroad-tie mill. So they were going to log and cut the timber on it. I was blowing stumps and splitting big logs, wind poles and whatnot to make the road up to this little tie mill. Well, I'd had a dynamite cap that I'd been using. I was going to throw it away. Like some stupid kids, like they are, I'd never thrown it away. I always put it back in the can with the other dynamite caps. Well, I had one final shot to make one afternoon. It turned up that was the only cap there. Well, it had corroded over the end of it. I broke that corrosion putting the fuse in and that damn thing went off in my hand. So that kind of left me a mess. At the time, I think I was a junior in high school. One of the doctors said, "Well don't make him go back to school for a while, let him get over the trauma of this accident." So I didn't go back to school at all. Hell, I just progressed from bad to worse, I guess.

Jim: What kind of damage did it do to you, Wes?

Wes: Well, I lost part of my left hand and I lost my right eye. So, that was about all though. Like I said, I was pretty well torn up and scarred up for awhile. Hell, I feel I did alright, even with the girls.

Jim You never went back to school then? Wes, tell us, before this incident occurred, did you pass through your grades in school or did you have some difficulties getting though kindergarten on through that junior year in high school.

Wes: Well, what is kindergarten? We never heard of kindergarten in those days.

Jim: I've dated myself. You're obviously a lot older than I am, Wes.

Wes: Well I might be older, but I don't know. Sometimes they say older is better, but just like my dad said, "Kid, we didn't have any dummies in our family, and you may not have much of an education, but you still have some smarts." I still got a few. My 73rd birthday is coming up awful darn close here now. My wife and I are going to celebrate our 41st anniversary here the day after...oh hell, tomorrow!. Don't knock it. Boy if she's listening now, I'm apt to catch hell just over this. Jim, now don't make me laugh.

Jim: Wes, tell us what you did after you recovered from the dynamite-cap explosion. Did you go to work someplace or did you just continue to chase girls?

Wes: Well, I finally went up and saw the guy who had the little tie mill going. He put me to work out there in a cut-off saw. It was hard work. Between the cut-off saw and the slab pile, it tried to make a man out of me I guess, I don't know. I can remember several times getting in from a party the night before just in time to change clothes and go to work, but that was normal for kids in those days. We didn't have any dope in those days. I never heard of any dope in our part of the country. We did have a fellow who made home brew. We knew a bootlegger where you might get a pint of moon (moonshine). These things come natural to kids.

Jim: What was the magnetism that drew you to Alaska, Wes? What started you thinking about the north country?

Wes: Like a young buck will, a girl got a hold of me, and we ended up getting married. I think that I wasn't quite 21. I think we were married about four years, and I don't know, she thought the pasture was greener on the other side of the fence or some darn thing. I guess you might call it that. Anyway, we split up. So, I had a friend—we used to bum around together all the time even though we went to different schools—his name was Hans Greiger, and he had come to Alaska the year or so before and he was working on a survey crew outside of Anchorage there at Elmendorf. It was

Elmendorf then. They hadn't even started Fort 'Rich' (Richardson). So I got a letter from Hans. He says to get my butt up there and we can get plenty of work with good pay in the spring. I said, "It's still wintertime." He said, "Well then, you'll be early." So anyway, I said I would scrounge up enough money to buy a steerage ticket. I got on one of the Alaska Steamship Company's boats and made my way up to dear ol' Seward. Well, I got off the boat and onto the train, and I ended up in Anchorage,

Jim: Wes, tell us, what was the ship you came up on, and tell us about steerage. What is steerage?

Wes: Steerage. Well that's a cheap way to travel. You wasn't traveling first class. See, you had a bunk down in the lower end and you ate mess down there with the crew, I guess as you want to call it. Now the steamship company, what was there in those days? Only Alaska Steam. I have ridden three of the old Alaskan Steam ships. It was hurting my feelings deeply when they were taking them off of the line and all you could do was fly. Then here in the later years, they put in a ferry system. Well, that leaves a lot to be desired, I'd say.

Jim: What kind of food did they serve you down there in steerage, Wes?

Wes: Well, I don't know. I've had a lot worse and I've had better. Down in steerage, you eat with the crew and most of those crews eat pretty good.

Jim: How was the accommodations in terms of bunks? Did you have good bunks? By the way, some of my friends who have come up steerage often said they sometimes got a little bit seasick down there in the lower part of the ship. Was that true?

Wes: Well, I guess it's true. I never did, but a lot of people got seasick in the top decks too. I don't think that seasickness was just for the lower decks or the people who didn't have enough bread to pay for a cabin up topside. But anyway, those were good ol' days. Hell, I don't begrudge those who say how tough things are now up there on the North Slope. If they had come up to Alaska in 1940 and had to live the way we did at times, they'd think that they are (now) living in the Waldorf Astoria on the top floor.

Jim: Wes, give us some information regarding the trip from Seward to Anchorage on the railroad. What kind of trip was that? Is the railroad the same today as it was then?

Wes: Well, I don't know whether it's the same today or not. I haven't traveled it for so many years that it isn't even funny, but I hear that they still run. I don't think they run passenger lines. Well, they do run passengers to Whittier, because they have a ferry connection there and they do take vehicles to Whittier. I used to make a trip to Whittier quite frequently because I worked for the FAA, the Federal Aviation Administration, and we had an outer marker down there at Whittier and I had to service it once a week. So I say, Whittier was no stranger to me in those days. Of course, this wasn't in the early time, this was along in years after I came. It seems like it was from '57 to '61, in those years.

Jim: How long did it take you to get to Anchorage after you left the ship?

Wes: Oh, I mean it was just a day, by the time you loaded up and boarded the train. In those days it was a two-day trip from Anchorage to Fairbanks. They always had a stop at Curry; that was the midway point, as they said. They had a railroad hotel there you stopped at. They used to have some good parties there.

Jim: Did you travel to Fairbanks or did you stop off at Anchorage?

Wes: Oh I stayed in Anchorage for awhile. Then I left Anchorage and went to Fairbanks, because the military informed us that they were disregarding Elmendorf or Fort Rich as a military base. Everything was going to go into Ladd Air Field (Fort Wainright) in Fairbanks. So everybody was getting ready and so I and another fellow I had met on the steamship coming up, went to Fairbanks. We got there around the first of April.

Jim: What was Fairbanks like at that time? Was it a pioneer town? What kind of activity was going on when you arrived?

Wes: Well, there was not much activity. It was a day I remember especially, because we got there and the next day, the first part of April, the sun came out and it got warm. You'd see everybody in town was gathered around the buildings soaking up the sun. It was real balmy. That was the earliest the ice ever went out at Nenana. It went out the 20th of April I think, that year, and that's been the earliest that it's ever left the river.

Jim: About how many people were in Fairbanks at that time? Can you remember?

Wes: Well, I didn't count them, but there wasn't too many. It might have been right close to 2000.

Jim: Where did you get employment?

Wes: Well, I arrived in Fairbanks and it was three or four days before I got work. There again, I was almost broke, didn't know what I was going to do. So I was going around, looking for work and ran into Sig Wold. He had the trucking outfit. I don't know whether Sig is alive or not. Well, we got to talking and he said he was going over there in Garden Island. He asked me if I wanted to walk along. We walked out to the old Miner's Lumber Company sawmill. He said, "Do you know anything about these?" I said, "Well, a little. I've worked around them for several years." He said, "You're just the kid I'm looking for." So I went to work for Sig. Well, I got acquainted with a girl in one of the employment offices, and I told her if a job came up out in the dredge or out in the mining camps or something for a guy to get out in the hills, let me know. Well, I had worked out there for two or three weeks.

Jim: That was for Sig Wold at the sawmill, right?

Wes: That's right. Well, I finally got a call from this gal and she said, " If you want to go to work out in the mines come down here tomorrow morning." So I showed up. Of course I stopped and told Sig what I was thinking about, and he cussed me up one side and down the other, which I guess he deserved the right to.

Jim: Yeah, he was losing a good hand. He knew it.

Wes: I don't know. It worked out. I went down on American Creek down out of Tofty, and I worked there all summer.

Jim: Doing what?

Wes: Well, we was driving thaw points mainly, for a dredge operation. I was on the thawing crew. We just did everything that had to be done. When they needed the hard labor and the heavy work done, they put me out, and I would cut sods for a new dam and load it on a Go-Devil (sled) for the Cat to come out and pick up, and that was quite a job. I forget, Jim Matthews I think or maybe Ted Matthews—Jim or Ted anyway. Ted was the real boss and Jim was our foreman. He said, " Go out and put all you can on this Go-Devil." So I did. I went out and I cut moss all day long, and sod, and stacked it up. He sent a Cat out to get it and the Cat hooked onto it. He didn't know if he was going to pull it or not. Of course, I was down driving points by this time and he stuck that Cat so deep in the mud and the muskeg out there that I guess they had to get a couple more Cats to go pull him out. So then I caught hell for putting too much on the damn Go-Devil.

Jim: Tell us about this cutting sod. How big a piece did you cut, and how did you stack it and so forth?

Wes: Now you're working my brain again, see? Well, the sod is what they would build dams with out in the creek. They would back up the water. The thawing crew and the dredge had to have quite a bit of water, but they reused it. They would take the sod down where we were driving points, and they would stack it and make a dam that was maybe 10 feet wide at the base. The sod chunks were, I imagine, oh, a foot and a half wide, maybe two feet long, like square blocks. They were cut maybe eight inches deep, depending on how thick the sod was. Then, you pick those up and stack them on the Go-Devil. Well those things were heavy to begin with. Jim had kind of been riding my butt every now and then, so I thought, "Why, I'll fix him." I put a load on that Go-Devil no Cat would ever pull. So then I caught hell again. But anyway, that's what they used the sod for, was to build those dams. Then they had pumps to pump the water from these dams and back up to the thaw points, where it was used to thaw the ground. We had to keep working ahead of the dredge.

Jim: When you talk about points, these are a series of pipes you drove down into the ground? Do you recall how far apart they were? Were they in a grid system?

Wes: They covered an area from two to three hundred feet wide and two to three hundred feet long. There was a field on each side of the main water line. They pumped water through a 30-inch main pipeline. It was a big one, easy to walk and carry everything on. Then they had the smaller off-shoot lines that went out to the thaw points on each side of the main line. Like I said, you were looking at a field of 300 by 300 feet, maybe even bigger. This was the area. The thaw points, which were connected to these offshoot lines by a flex hose were about 15 feet apart. These were driven down to bedrock. You would be driving the point—if you hit a rock, or something, you had a head on the top of that point; you could beat on it with a hammer or you took a pipe wrench and twisted it until you went by the rock that was holding it up, and you would continue driving it down until you were sure you were in bedrock. They would pass water through them to thaw the ground, for a couple of days anyway, maybe longer.

Jim: So they would let this surface water run through the pipe to thaw the gravel?

Wes: That's right.

Jim: Did you drive the pipe all the way to bedrock at one time, or did you have a series to go around to? Tell us how you did that.

Wes: Oh no, you traveled from one point to another. You could only drive down as far as you had thawed. If you'd keep working these points, maybe you hit the same point every 20 minutes or so. As they dropped down, then there were areas in between them that it took quite awhile for water to thaw. That dredge didn't like to hit frozen ground when it was working.

Jim: It would damage the dredge then, if it ran into some frozen ground?

Wes: Well, it would make it jump around a bit.

Jim: As you drove the thaw points down, water was continuously running through the point, is that right?

Wes: That's right.

Jim: Every 20 minutes then you might make your cycle from point to point. Maybe what, 10 or 20 points? How many?

Wes: I forget now how many.

Jim: How deep was it to bedrock?

Wes: Oh I'd say around 15 feet, something like that. Of course, they'd stripped the top moss and everything off. We were through the muck and at the top of the gravel.

Jim: You had to thaw that 15 feet of frozen gravel or all the way to bedrock. Once it was thawed, was the ground ready to dredge?

Wes: That's right.

Jim: That was about 1940, wasn't it?

Wes: Yeah, that was 1940.

Jim: Who owned that dredge? Do you recall?

Wes: Hmm...I think it was American Creek Operating Company as far as I can remember. I don't remember just exactly who it was. It wasn't the big corporation. I think all of the bosses were from the School of Mines there at the University.

Jim: How long did you work with that dredging company?

Wes: Just the one summer.

Jim: What did you do after that? Where did you go to work?

Wes: The next spring I went to work near Old Talkeetna. I had gone out to visit the folks a little bit during the winter and told them what I thought of Alaska. Coming up on the Alaska Steam, I met this fellow, oh...his name will come to me in a minute...So anyway, he talked me into going with him. He said he needed somebody that had driven a tractor, a Cat. He had a little Caterpillar 22 with no blade, no nothing, but we used it for freighting. This was quite a trip from Talkeetna out to Bird Creek with that. We went up and over Black Creek Summit there out of Petersville at the roadhouse then down into Cache Creek, then up Cache Creek , then from the top of Cache Creek over into Bird Creek. Made quite a trip.

Jim: Was he running a placer operation out there?

Wes: That's right.

Jim: What kind of equipment was he using in his placer operation?

Wes: Just all hydraulic monitors. We would run three monitors, but lots of water. We were running three four-inch monitors with lots of water.

Jim: Explain the source of water and how the water got to the nozzle and exactly what happened there.

Wes: Oh! I just remembered the guys name that ran the Bird Creek operation, it was John Johansen.

Jim: Did John Johansen own the placer mine out there?

Wes: Well he was one of the men in the Alaska Exploration and Mining Company.

They had this property there on Bird Creek. They worked it every summer.

Jim: Now explain how they worked that, Wes?

Wes: As I said, they used three monitors with four-inch nozzles—they used a lot of water. I think they had 300 and some foot of head.

Jim: When you say 300 and some feet of head, what do you mean, Wes?

Wes: That means the ditch that fed the water came into the pinstock, and the pipeline that came down to the mine was 300 feet above us. That gave us quite a bit of pressure.

Jim: From the tip of the nozzle, now if you have 300 foot of head on the nozzle, how high could you squirt that water out of the tip of that nozzle?

Wes: I wouldn't try to jump that high. That head of water coming out the end of that four-inch nozzle would push most anything. I mean anything that is moveable. Any building or framework, it would just tear it up.

Jim: You would spray this high-pressure water out of that nozzle against the exposed face of the cut. Is that right?

Wes: Well, the cut where we worked was almost, I'd say 90 to 100 feet thick. I always maintained it was a glacial dump—clay boulders, everything—the glacier or glaciers dropped all their residue when they thawed at this given point and it filled up this canyon. The glaciers had been cutting away at old gold deposits that had been creeks or placer ground in earlier times and it was all mineable. We were mining in a blue clay. The placer gold just came out of this clay. You could tell that it was placer gold. We didn't get many big nuggets, but then again, there was a lot of coarse gold. Norman Steins was there in the early fall of '41, and they did some prospecting. He was quite excited about it because they found gold so high in this clay deposit. Consequently, this would slough—in the wintertime as the ground would freeze the frost would penetrate into this clay, when it thawed in the spring, it ran just like soup. It would slough down into the pile at the bottom of the face, then we would just wash it away. The big boulders and the big clay deposits would drop off. We would have to blast them to break them up so that we could get rid of them. Big rocks we would have to either bust up with a hammer or we had a stone boat. When we got enough of a crew together, we would roll it on that stone boat and move them with our little 22 Cat. We usually hydraulicked and washed the gravel into the sluice boxes.

Jim: So right from the face, you washed the material with the hydraulic monitor. That's an art, isn't it, directing that material right into the sluicebox with high pressure water?

Wes: An art? Yes I guess it is kind of an art. Either you become good at it or you better get out of the business.

Jim: Wes, tell us, from the sluice box what happened to the tailings.

Wes: Well, we were in kind of a unique position there. The sluice box went down and through where they had cut a little V through the edge of this bedrock down into a canyon. Bird Creek had cut its own canyon separate, and so we had a natural drainage. I mean, the sluice box dropped the tailings off the end maybe 20 or 30 feet to the bottom of this canyon. Even at that, during summertime, there was an awful lot of gravel and mud gather in this canyon from the sluicing. Sometimes, during the course of a year, we would have to set up another big monitor (six-inch) down there on the bank to blow those tailings further down the canyon. We had to divert all of the water through it. As I said, it had a six-inch nozzle on it. It takes quite a stream of water to run a six-inch nozzle with 300 foot of head, I'll clue you in.

Jim: How long did you work out there with Johansen in the Petersville area?

Wes: Well, let's see, I went out there in '41. We worked there '42. It seems like Uncle Sam needed me January of '43. Took a poor ol' one-eyed man into the Army and sent him out to the end of the Aleutians. Then in '46, when I was discharged from the Army, we went back into Bird Creek. None of the Johansens were back in there at that time; we were just trying to do the assessment work. After the war, mining was zilch. It was not a very good proposition. The price of gold was down and everything else was climbing sky high, but I came into town with a bunch of gold and that's where my wife met me.

Jim: What town was this that you came into?

Wes: Dear ol' Talkeetna.

Jim: Well, you came into the city of Talkeetna, and your wife-to-be was waiting there for you.

Wes: Practically. She's shaking her head. I'm going to let her tell her own story on this and then I won't catch so much hell over what I say.

Jim: Well, go ahead. This is your story, Wes. We will get her version later. Tell us how you met your wife.

Wes: Well, me and my buddy who had come up to go mining with me had come in from the creek. We were out at the old CAA (Civil Aeronautics Administration) building. Of course, after a couple of bottles of booze and a couple of hours went by, it seems like things were winding down. We decided that the party was wearing off and we went into town to get some more booze. Of course this CAA, was a little bit out of town, out at the airfield. I went into the Barrette and Kennedy. It was a store at the old place. We got us a bottle of booze. Somebody said, "We've got to have something to mix it." So they brought out a big bottle of Coke. They said,

"Hell, we don't got any glass to mix it in." I said, "You guys aren't much at all. I'll show you how to mix booze." I pulled the cork out of the bottle of whiskey and I pulled the cap off the bottle of Coke. I put them both in my mouth, tipped them up and let them run. I said, "They'll mix goin' down just as well as anything." I look over, and this blonde gal is standing there. She's just kind of looking at me like, "Boy, this guy's a weirdo from way up in the creek." Anyway, so that's where I met my wife. After I mixed my drink, and it had gone down, I looked at this gal, and she looked at me like she thinks I'm crazy. I don't know, maybe she's crazy too. It wasn't no time after that we got married. I must've been crazy, but not bad.

Jim: You think you made a good choice, Wes?

Wes: Well I don't know. That was 41 years ago.

Jim: How long after that did you get married—a day, a week, a month, a year?

Wes: Oh let's see. This was in almost the first of October wasn't it? We got married…well my oldest daughter was born on the 13th. We got married on the 17th. Of course, there was a year's difference.

Jim: That's one way to remember it, Wes. Did you continue to work out there in the mine after you got married?

Wes: In a way, yeah, but I didn't go back to Bird Creek. Maybe this was my big mistake. Of course, my wife didn't know what she was getting into. I have to give the gal credit. She's willing to try. We went out in March sometime. We went across the river, loaded up the Go-Devil. I had built a Go-Devil as we call it. In fact, I had two of them—that had barrels of fuel and gasoline on one, and then we had lumber and everything else on the other one. I would take one out far enough, then I would drop her and the things off by the roadhouse, then I would run back and get the second load. So we made it on over into Cache Creek. At times, my wife didn't think that we were going to make it, but then we did. Using that lumber, I built a regular little wannigan on the Go-Devil. That's what we lived in all summer. My wife claims she spoiled Cache Creek, well everybody thought she did. She had a cookstove. She had a double bed with an innerspring mattress on it. Oh she was right up top drawer. She had linoleum on the floor. We had curtains at the windows. Cache Creek had never seen this type of thing before. Everybody else slept on old Army cots or a folding cot. That's all you got by with all summer. Here we were in a nice summer bed, living high on the land. Well, that didn't last too long. We mined out there that one summer. The next year we worked in Talkeetna. Things were kind of rough mining, so I went to work for the railroad. Did you ever hear of a gandy dancer?

Jim: Tell us what you did as a gandy dancer, Wes.

Wes: Oh we replaced ties in the railroad bed, and anything that the section required, we would do it. I have a story—it's a bear story. I don't know whether you'd want a bear story. I thought we were mining.

Jim: I'd love to hear a bear story. Let's hear a bear story.

Wes: The railroad brought in a crew. They were Mexican and colored from the South and they were redoing the roadbed. In fact, this was when they changed a little bit of it. They had this one tall colored boy. He made a pet out of a bear. Their camp was above Talkeetna and he made a pet out of this bear that was coming into the garbage cans. I don't know how. They must have been there at that camp for two months. They left sometime in September and this guy had made a pet out of this black bear, a full-grown black bear. He would take a bottle of pop or a mickey of wine. That bear would open it, hold it in its paws and hold it up and drink it. It seemed like everyone else in those work cars were scared of that bear; when the bear would come inside, well out the other side they'd go. It was sometime in October before it started to snow. Well, our section crew was up and we were taking the switch out of the main line that was on this spur where the camp car was parked. We had been taking this switch out 'cause they didn't want any switches or anything for any of the snowplows to hang up on when it was wintertime. We were eating our lunch and I was sitting alone when I looked up and over at the edge of the woods. Here come this black bear poking its nose out. Just walked out there in the open. I said, "I betcha that's that bear that colored boy made a pet out of." Well, they didn't think that they were going to find out. "I said, "Well I'll find out." I stood up and I tore one of my sandwiches in half and I walked about a third of the way to that bear. I held this sandwich out and that bear came over to me and took that sandwich out of my hand and looked up and I scratched its ear. Everybody was standing back, "You crazy son-of-a-bi..." I won't say the words they did, but it wasn't too nice. Well I said, "Lordy, if he's not afraid of me and I'm not afraid of him, we get along fine." I turned around and walked back over and finished my lunch. Pretty soon the bear walked back over to the woods, disappeared, and there wasn't anything else to it. Well, we went home that night, somebody got talking about this bear, and some guy who thought he was going to be a big bear hunter shot that poor thing. Why, I'd walked right up to him. So, I was kind of put off about that. Somebody had a nice pet; it wouldn't hurt anybody, if you didn't hurt him. That's my bear story. Everybody said I was crazier than a loon for walking up to it.

Jim: Well that in one way is the nicest bear story I ever heard, and in another the saddest. Now back to your employment; how long did you work as a gandy dancer, Wes.

Wes: It was just the one year, then I went to work for the good ol' CAA, Civil

Aeronautics. The first assignment was out at Bethel, so we went out there. We were overhauling some of the big generators out there, D-8s and 8800s or whatever you want to call them. Finally the wife—she had worked for CAA, before we met, and she knew some people in CAA—she got us assigned to a station in Tanana. We went there real quick. So we were at Tanana for four years.

Jim: What year was it that you left Tanana?

Wes: We left Tanana in the early part of 1953.

Jim: Where did you go then, Wes.

Wes: To Kenai. We were stationed at Kenai for four or five years, somewhere along that line.

Jim: With the FAA?

Wes: That's right. Well it was the CAA then. We hadn't switched over yet. I was there for a number of years and then I transferred to Anchorage, where I stayed until I had to take my retirement.

Jim: What year did you retire?

Wes: It was '61.

Jim: 1961. Did you stay living there in Anchorage in 1961 or did you move?

Wes: The doctors told me I should move to a warmer climate, and a lot of swimming would help me as much as anything. We sold our place there in Anchorage and moved to the Lower 48, mainly California. I think that was the biggest mistake in my life. That was almost bigger than voting for statehood.

Jim: When did you come back to Alaska?

Wes: Oh, it was about 13 years ago.

Jim: It must've been almost 15 years ago, Wes, because 14 years ago you took a course in basic prospecting when I was teaching the Mining Extension short courses for the University of Alaska.

Wes: You're right, but I had just arrived when I took that course.

Jim: We have just run out of tape. We can finish this interview tomorrow. It will be your 41st anniversary, and I can interview Nedra too. That will be a lot of fun to see how she tells her side of some of these stories.

Wes: I'm looking forward to it. This is a lot of fun.

Jim: Good morning, Wes. It is January 17, 1988. This is your anniversary.

Wes: This is it. This is the ol' 41.

Jim: We were talking a little while ago about life on the lower Yukon and a fellow we both know by the name of Tuffy. I first met Tuffy when he was maintaining the gas line out at Barrow. What was Tuffy's last name?

Wes: Edgington. Tuffy Edgington. Everybody called him Tuffy. He was strictly a good egg.

Jim: Where did you meet Tuffy?

Wes: I met Tuffy in Tanana.

Jim: And how did you meet him?

Wes: Well, he was a comin' and a goin' all of the time. He had a little mine down the creek, Yukon River, just off of Kokrines. He had an old L-5 military observation plane he had fixed so he could haul Cat parts, and he could haul just about any darned thing. He used to come to Tanana because that was the closest place for him to do any extracurricular activity as you might say. We got acquainted. I worked for the ol' CAA there at the time. He would come in and he would spend the weekend.

Jim: Was Tuffy a big man or a little man? Describe his features to us, Wes.

Wes: Tuffy wasn't quite as tall as I was. I was six foot three. I'd imagine that Tuffy was close to six foot. He might have weighed more than I did, and his arms were long. In fact, he was the only man that I ever knew who would pick up a 50-gallon drum of oil with his fingertips and put in the back of a truck. And that was right close to 500 pounds. I didn't ever want to meet him in the dark and have him mad at me.

Jim: So he was a stout fellow, this Tuffy?

Wes: Well he was just plain strong. Don't say stout. He was heavy build, he was still a good egg.

Jim: I heard a lot of people say that Tuffy Edgington had a heart of gold. Is that right?

Wes: Well I never took it out and examined it, but there's nothing the man wouldn't do for you. I guess that's the main requisite of everything. If what you have and if someone needs some of it, and he'll share it with you, he had a heart of gold.

Jim: So Tuffy came into Tanana quite often from his mine up in the Kokrines. How was he mining up in the Kokrines? Was he hydraulicking or open-cut with Cats, or how was he mining?

Wes: He was mining with a D-8 Cat. It was just open dozing, you might say, onto a plate and sluice box. I guess there was enough creek water there; water wasn't any problem. I don't think Tuffy had a pump, didn't need one. I don't know what else he was using.

Jim: How long was Tuffy mining there?

Wes: I'd imagine five or six years anyway, maybe longer. I can't recall. I don't know whether he mined after he had his airplane accident or not. He was pretty well broke up in that. That was one of these odd accidents. He was flying from upriver somewhere into Kokrines and he had a native woman from over in the Indian village and he was taking her home. Rose, his wife, was pregnant and they were in the back. They had no seat facilities or safety belts in the back end of that old L-5. People would just crawl in, sit and hang on. Of course, don't tell the FAA this. So, he was flying down to the Kokrines. He was just about to land. His plane was icing up and he said, "I hope I can get it down." Well, he didn't quite make it. He was maybe 200 or 300 hundred yards off of the runway and he said it just wasn't flying anymore. So it went right into the ground. He said, "Oh my God, what have I done to the women in the back end?" Tuffy, he wore belts, he had shoulder harness, he had everything fastened up in there because he was always hauling mining equipment. He didn't worry much about himself. In this accident, the girls walked out of it, hardly a scratch on them and Tuffy was just broke to pieces. They took him by dog team to Tanana. He was in rough shape, and they flew him from there into Fairbanks. I don't know how many months he was in the hospital.

Jim: Do you know any adventures Tuffy had aside from that airplane crash? I think I heard a story about him transporting your wife's mother from one point to another. Relate some of those stories that you heard about Tuffy to us Wes, would you?

Wes: I just think a fella ought to use his imagination. There's nothing unusual about any of the things that Tuffy did. It was done by every one of the old-timers up there that was flying around. Anyway, my wife's mother was up visiting us from Vancouver, Washington. It came time for her to go home, and Byers was the plane that flew from Tanana to Fairbanks, and Tuffy wouldn't hear of us sending my mother-in-law into Fairbanks with Byers. He would take and fix up seat belts and put her in the back end of his plane and he would fly her to Fairbanks. So this was being done. They was all loaded up. Of course, he had to make...oh, what do we call it...a potty stop at Manley Hot Spring. We had friends there too. I didn't go along on this trip. I had to work. They stopped at Manley. After a few drinks and a potty stop, I guess they got back in the plane again and headed on upriver to Fairbanks. After awhile, the one wing of the airplane was dipping a little bit. So the mother-in-law reached up and shook Tuffy's shoulder and said, "Tuffy, what are you seeing?" "Oh, look at the geese and the moose down there," he said. My mother-in-law looked at her daughter, "You can't fool me, he fell asleep." Well, you know, sometimes a guy's tired and had a few warm drinks and this does happen, nothing bad. I'm sure Tuffy wouldn't have stayed asleep long enough to do any damage to the airplane, but that's the way it goes.

Jim: You have any other stories like that Wes, regarding Tuffy?

Wes: Yeah, but, no I don't think I better tell it. Tuffy was called Stud and he had the works to prove it, that's about as far as I can go with it.

Jim: You started it. Don't leave us in suspense; finish the story.

Wes: Well one time I had to get up and go potty when Tuffy and Roz were staying at our place there in Tanana. I went in and went to the bathroom and I happened to look over in the bed there where they were sleeping and he was laying out there stark raving nude...Lordy, you just wouldn't believe it. I didn't hardly believe it then, but I didn't have gumption enough to wake up my wife to get her out there to see that. It was something. He must have had a graft from a stud horse or something there at one time or another.

Jim: You think Roz was a happy woman, do you?

Wes: Well Roz made the statement there one time. She said that no woman was ever going to take that man away from her. If she even tried, she was in for one hell of a fight."

Jim: When we were talking earlier you said you were going to tell us about one of your most memorable festive occasions in the Bush of Alaska. Tell us about one of your Thanksgivings that was particularly memorable.

Wes: Well it was particularly memorable. I remember when we started out mining up off Falls Creek down near Cache Creek there. There was a bench that the dredge had left. It come Thanksgiving time, and the wife wanted to go to Jack Neubauer's. They were mining down at Spruce Creek, that came into Cache Creek there. They invited us down for Thanksgiving dinner. We had to walk down there, and the wife was pregnant at the time, and I had to carry her across Cache Creek a couple of times. She would hop up on my back and we'd go, and then we decided it would be best, instead of crossing the creek a dozen or more times going these four or five miles, to go up out of the creek and get up on top where there was a trail that was pretty easily traveled. We could drop right down into Spruce Creek and then walk right down to the camp. So that's what we did. We climbed up the bank...it must've been 100 or 200 feet up the rim of the canyon, in elevation anyway. We got up on top and hit a pretty good game trail. There were a few little gullies that we had to cross, but there was nothing big until we got down to Spruce Creek where we dropped down into their camp. It wasn't too bad going. I had a .38 Special revolver. A couple of spruce hens flew up in a tree, beside us. I thought why we might just as well have a spruce hen too, but that one spruce hen, he kept ducking his head. I'd draw down on it and let loose, but hell, all he would do is move his damn head. So I knew I wasn't going to waste too many shells and didn't have too many in my pocket besides that, so we didn't get a spruce hen that day. We finally went down there and had a good dinner, I think we stayed overnight and then made it back the following day. Everybody out in the creeks at that time, if you could get to another camp and they were better set up than what you were, you were always invited to stay. It seemed like several people always showed up.

Jim: So it was quite a festive occasion with all of the people congregating at the Neubauer's place for Thanksgiving dinner.

Wes: Well I don't remember how many people were there. I can't even remember how many people were in their camp. You know time flies and you get older. I never thought…well, you get old but it sure as hell beats dying young I guess.

Jim: Who are we going to talk about next?

Wes: I'd hate to mention any names. He was from the University.

Jim: Well Wes, just tell us the whole story. When did you first meet this guy?

Wes: Is the tape running? Oh hell, then I'd better be truthful now hadn't I? No more lies.

Jim: Tell it the way you see it, Wes.

Wes: Well, the wife was running the motel—the Townhouse here in Haines—at that time. There was a young fellow who came down from the University to teach a prospecting course. He asked me if I'd ever done any mining. I naturally said yes. Usually that's what a young fellow comes to Alaska for, to see if he can find him a little gold or something. Well, I found somethin' and I found a little gold but then I kept the somethin, which after the time passin' for 41 years we're still together. I don't know how much longer I can make it, but we're still at it. So I went to this course in prospecting, not that I was ever going to use it. Anyway, I still won't mention the guy's name. I think I forgot it. Anyway, we got to talking and he was interested in any mining adventures.

Jim: Did you tell him a story?

Wes: On a moose hunt, when I was stationed in Tanana with the CAA, I'd gone up the Yukon. I was up past Morelock Creek. I was coming down and I'd happened to see this old bull moose way down the river. I took a shot at it with an old .30-06 that I had. It was way too far. I more than likely overshot anyway by holding too far above him, and he went into the brush and up. We went on down the river in the boat. I pulled in and put the boat up on the bank. This other young fella and I went into the brush and started looking around. There was a little creek that came in there, so we walked up the creek. I got into some real pretty timber. That sure looked nice. The trees weren't too big; tall and straight. We went on through that and never saw the moose. I climbed up on a bank, it leveled off and here was a trail—a road. The trees were cut off. Some of the stumps were pulled out. It was just the start of a good road at one time or another. So we thought, "Hell, let's see where this goes." So we walked back up this canyon, and finally got to this brushed out place and ran into a real swampy area and here was a foot trail. So we just kept on up this foot trail. Pretty soon we come on an old mine shaft. Well, down across the creek a ways were two or three old cabins that were almost completely fallen in. We looked around the mine shaft for a little bit. There was an ore car and rails and everything coming out of the mine. I never did go in the hole to see what it was like. We went down to see what was in these cabins. Well, there was an old chest of drawers. It had all come apart and it was laying there, so I pulled out the drawers. In there was a bunch of papers. I just scooped up a bunch of them, tied them together, and I brought them home to examine them. There were a lot of good things in there. There were stories about this mine. It was silver, mainly galena, I guess, I don't remember. I never did look for any of the ore to see what it consisted of. Anyway, I told this story to this teacher in this prospecting course, and I gave him a copy of these papers that described this mine and said well maybe you'll get up there someday and look it over. Well, I've talked to him in later years and he says he never had a chance to get up in there. I've got the original papers. There's papers from old Judge Wickersham, and there is other ones from a fellow who was in charge of the road department in the territory at the time. Oh, there's just a lot of correspondence. A lot of it didn't amount to anything. In there was a bunch of stills (photographs), the type you used to see in front of a movie house when they had the silent pictures. You'd go to a movie house and there were these racks in front of it that had these pictures of different scenes in the movies—the actress and the actors and whatnot. There were a bunch of these photos and they were in extremely good condition. I don't know how everything else could have suffered the way it did, and then these things be good. They must've been good material. Anyway, they came home with me. There was a movie made by The Alaska Motion Picture Corporation or whatever they called it at the time. It was made filming a movie called The Cheechako, and this was filmed down in Girdwood. Now if you can imagine what Girdwood would've looked like. There was pictures of it there too, of Girdwood. They had unloaded the paraphernalia and were standing around in the front of a shed I'd call it. That must've been the accommodations in Girdwood at the time. Well evidently, they did make a movie. I have heard that a person can rent it from some of these old movie houses, but I have these old stills and we are going to try and get these into a museum or some place where they might be appreciated a little more than sitting on an old shelf where nobody would see them. Well anyhow, I guess to get back to the old cabins, I had these papers. There was this character. He is sittin' here beside me now, and it's my friend, Jim Madonna. I honestly don't know whether he's a character or not. He seems to think I'm one. Of course, there was a lot of people in Talkeetna back in the ol' days that thought that I was kind of a character. He took a copy of the report. Hell, it was from a geologist and the assay and whatnot of this ore out of this mine. Jim said if he got the opportunity he was going to look into it, and hell, we'd become rich, but hell, he said he was going to get up there, but he's so busy at the University, I don't know whether he chases the girls there or the other way around...I better hush up about that, his wife is sitting right here alongside of me.

Jim: I'll get us both out of trouble here, Wes. Do you have some other good stories?

Wes: Yeah, this is a story that comes to mind about when I lived in Talkeetna. It was about a devious and obnoxious fellow that no one liked or trusted. In fact they were a little bit scared of him. People said you better be careful here in Talkeetna because they had one fellow around here that was really obnoxious and maybe dangerous and paid no attention to anybody else's rights and privileges or even property. They didn't know what to do with him, so him and two other guys went to the edge of the river to check the ice. Well this guy must have got too close to it. I don't think they would actually push him into the river, but if you'd fall in the Talkeetna River at that place, there was no place to go but down and into the Susitna, and down under the ice for heaven knows how long. Anyway, there was three sets of track going to the river and only two coming back.

Jim: That is quite a story, Wes. Do you have any more?

Wes: Yeah. Now this happened when I lived back in Talkeetna. There was a young fellow that came up from Anchorage. He went to work there at the same section as the gandy dancer crew, and he was up working on the railroad. This one friend of ours, Fos, had a nice wife and this young guy got to playing around with her, and he got to braggin' about it. Oh, he could go to bed with her anytime, and he was going to take her away and marry her here in a little bit, and everything he was going to do. Well, ol' Fos, he didn't quite go for that so, he decided he was going to put a stop to it. They were working up on the railroad about a mile-and-a-half—two miles out of town, maybe a little further. Fos took his .30-30, walked up to where they were working, and he was talking to the guys. They wanted to know what he was doing, and he said, "nothin' much." He was just takin care of some business. He raised his .30-30 and put three bullets right through this guy's breadbasket. He said, "Well, that'll end that." He gave the crew his .30-30 and they loaded the guy up and of course, brought him back to town. Well, they sent poor Fos into town. They got to checking around and it seemed like the other guy was a deserter out of the Army and he was wanted here and there for crimes. Pretty soon they almost gave Fos a medal for getting rid of him. Where else but in Alaska, in the early days, can you put .30-30 slugs through a guy's belly and almost get a medal?

Jim: Thank you for the interview, Wes. Your stories deserve to be in print. I may never get to that mine on the Yukon, but I promise I'll see that your story gets into a book.

Jack Williams
with
Jim Madonna
October 12, 1989

Jim: Our guest this afternoon is Jack Williams. Jack is the director of the Fairbanks Historical Preservation Foundation here in Fairbanks. He's got a lot to talk about. And of course you know that there's been a lot of publicity about restoration of the riverboat *Nenana*, at Alaskaland, and Jack's going to give us some information about that. Jack, welcome to Alaska Gold Trails.

Jack: Thank you, Jim. It's a pleasure to be here.

Jim: Jack, give us a little background on where you were born, what year you were born, unless that's classified information, of course.

Jack: Not yet. I was born in Brewster, New York, in 1931.

Jim: Was it a city environment, town environment, country environment?

Jack: Very very small town, Jim. Actually, my folks left there when I was about four, so I don't remember much about it. And from there we moved to Mt. Kisco, New York, which I do remember a little bit about. It's again, a very very small town. After that, I went to school in Tarrytown, New York, called St. Vincent de Paul. I was about seven. And when I was about nine, I moved to Maine and stayed there until I graduated from high school.

Jim: When you graduated from high school, did you pull off...Let me put it this way, when I was in school, I remember, we used to pull a few shenanigans, once in a while. What kind of high school did you go to?

Jack: It was a boarding school, a prep school, called Freiberg Academy. It's a very old school. Daniel Webster was the first headmaster. The reading of some of his books on how he disciplined the students was very very interesting. I don't think a day went by when somebody didn't get birched.

Jim: Birched. I've been birched.

Jack: Yeah, so have I.

Jim: As I recall it was a memorable experience. Wasn't it fun?

Jack: No, it wasn't.

Jim: I used to get birched in front of the whole class. That's the part that hurt.

Jack: Well, Webster didn't elaborate in his journals whether or not he made a performance out of it or had an audience, but I suspect he did.

Jim: Tell us. Was there any good reason for you to be birched?

Jack: Not in my opinion.

Jim: Was this a local town high school, or did you have to come from around the area to go to it? A lot of times we think about rural areas and the young people come in and a few years back they would stay right in town in dormitories and go to high school.

Jack: That describes it exactly. It's a very rural community in western Maine, very close to the New Hampshire border, and there were many little towns around there that didn't have high schools. So those town kids, we call them, came to school from their home, and then there were a group of us that lived in the dormitories—boys and girls dorms.

Jim: That must have been interesting. Boys and girls dormitories. I can imagine all kinds of shenanigans going on.

Jack: Perhaps if they hadn't been separate dorms. But they were.

Jim: Even in separate dorms, I'm certain that the ingenuity of young people can overcome. Tell us, did you ever have any experiences where you defied the rules and regulations of dormitory living at the high school?

Jack: Well, in my senior year, we did have...well you might call it a regular escape pipeline, where we had a system set up to get girls out of one certain window on the second floor of the dormitory. Of course, in the wintertime it was too cold, but in the fall and in the spring we did that pretty successfully. Until we got caught.

Jim: Oh. You got birched?

Jack: No. We didn't get birched. Up there we got put on campus. We couldn't go downtown.

Jim: Aw, that's sad. How long did that last?

Jack: Well, that didn't bother me, because the fall of my senior year, the day after I'd arrived for the school year, Cliff Grey, our baseball coach and English teacher and dorm proctor, told me, "Williams, you're on campus 'til the ice comes out of the Saco." And I said, "Cliff, it hasn't even frozen yet." He said, "I know that." So I was already on campus.

Jim: Well Jack, tell us a little bit about your life after graduating from high school and before coming to Alaska.

Jack: Well, I graduated in '49 and went to California—San Mateo, San Francisco Bay Area. And stayed there for a couple of years and then came to Fairbanks in 1952 to work for the summer. I really didn't like it very much when I first got here. It was unlike anything I'd been used to. And when I left in the fall, it wasn't for very long, surprisingly, that I began missing it. I missed it so much I came back and enrolled in the University of Alaska.

Jim: Ah, good choice.

Jack: I think so. I've never regretted it. Although, on my way back, I did wonder what I was doing.

Jim: How long did you go to the University of Alaska? And what department or school did you attend?

Jack: The School of Civil Engineering. And I attended two and a half years there.

Jim: And you were preparing for what kind of degree?

Jack: A civil engineering degree.

Jim: What did you do following that period of time, in terms of work?

Jack: Well, through the civil engineering, which I found, by the way, I was not adaptive to—I'm much more comfortable with arts and letters and history and English—But, through the civil engineering I'd learned to survey, and in 1953 I began surveying and continued that until 1960, when there was about an eight-year break. After that break I went back to surveying and stayed with it until 1982, when I got hurt, and I couldn't survey any more.

Jim: What kinds of activities did you enter into when you were surveying, Jack? Where did you go? Did you just survey around town and plot out the city streets? Or did you go out in the bush? What did you do, here, in this surveying business?

Jack: Well, whatever was called for. I spent quite a bit of time construction surveying, in and around Fairbanks. And then various bush jobs, subcontracting for the Corps of Engineers, working on a lot of their Nike sites around town, and White Alice sites out in the bush. Spent a lot of time on the North Slope. I was up there in '55 on the DEW Line (Distant Early Warning Line) for a year, and that was very interesting. Down in Amchitka, working for Chris Berg. As a matter of fact, I was involved in the layout of the mile-deep hole that was drilled for the atomic blast, down at Amchitka.

Jim: Oh, is that right?

Jack: Yeah. That was very interesting.

Jim: I've got a little story about that. Can I?

Jack: Go to it.

Jim: I remember, when I was just a young lad, back there. What year was that?

Jack: Oh, golly when was that? '68, I think, something like that.

Jim: Yeah. I was just finishing at a community college in California—junior college. And I was emphasizing geology. And out in the paper, Dr. Bob Forbes, I'll never forget ...

Jack: Oh, I know Bob well, yeah.

Jim: Do you? He was working on that, and he was the head of the Geology Department at the University of Alaska at that time, and a big picture of Bob Forbes and a big article, regarding his statements and the explosion at Amchitka surfaced, and I'll never forget what I read, he says, "We don't have to worry about a tsunami." That's what I remember from that article. But what was more impressive to me, as a student, is that here I'd read about this Bob Forbes guy in Alaska, and at that time, even in junior college, I had made my plans to come back to Alaska and complete my education. That was, of course, '68, like you say. And who was my first instructor, in metamorphic petrology, but Bob Forbes. And there I was, sitting there. I'd finally become a student of this fellow who I'd thought was just a world class geologist—and he is.

Jack: And he is. And he was right. There was no tsunami.

Jim: I just wanted to comment on that and tell you a little bit about one of the people that I thought was pretty well known here and worldwide, and is well respected and as a matter of fact inspired me to apply for graduate school at the University of Alaska.

Jack: Oh, he is. He has international credentials, there's no question about that.

Jim: Thanks for letting me add that little bit of my history, Jack. Go ahead with the drilling story.

Jack: Well, I was only there for about three and a half months, and they drilled a pilot hole first, and then we laid out the blast hole. And they were very very specific, naturally, on the coordinates of the blast hole, and they hadn't really started drilling that when I left. After that, I came back to Fairbanks and went on the road from Livengood to the Yukon River, the TAPS (Trans-Alaska Pipeline Service) haul road.

Jim: You said you had an accident. Give us some background on that.

Jack: Oh, this was in '82. I was lifting when I shouldn't have been, and I injured my back—tore the ligaments away from the base of my spine, according to the doctor. And that ended the surveying career. But while I was surveying, it was very very interesting. And I have to say that I love the outdoors. I love being outdoors, and surveying is just the greatest job that you can get, because you're paid to be out in the woods. Sometimes you're going across country that has never been seen by anyone.

Jim: So, you were being paid to do what other people pay to do, is that it?

Jack: It was like a permanent or year-round vacation. Although, it has its drawbacks. Sometimes, it was just very very cold and the weather did interfere with us, but basically, all of my memories and all my feelings about it are extremely positive. I really liked it.

Jim: Jack, you were talking about your back problem. Has that healed up pretty well so that you function without problem now, or is that still painful to you?

Jack: Well, the subject is not painful, but the back is. It's just something you learn to accept.

Jim: What did you do, following your surveying experience, and, once again, how long were you surveying?

Jack: Well, from 1953, Bill Mendenhall, at the University of Alaska, was my very first party chief. We did the installation of utilities in Arctic Park, when they were first building Arctic Park, down here. And this is before he met and married Nancy. From '53 to '60, and there was a break there of about eight years, and then from '68 until '82.

Jim: Sorry to break the flow of conversation but you know, Jack sometimes all these buttons confuse me. They make me a little uncomfortable at times. As a guest do you feel comfortable on the show, Jack?

Jack: Oh, very comfortable. Absolutely. How long you been doing this now, Jim, three years? You'll get used to it.

Jim: Yeah. Another five or ten years, Jack, I think I might get it down. But the once-a-week routine is probably not enough to keep me going. It seems like the first five or ten minutes of every show, if it wasn't for my people who participated in the contest each week, I think that warms me up, and after that I'm set to go.

Jack: Reorientation time.

Jim: Reorientation. Yeah. And a lot of times they say, "I can't hear you. How come I can't hear you?" And I say, "Because I didn't push the button." At any rate, Jack, what did you do following your accident and after you'd recuperated from that?

Jack: Well, I started a small restaurant, called Souvlaki, and my wife and I were working that. I've been interested in Alaskaland ever since 1973. At that time the city owned Alaskaland had begun to rent out the small cabins for concessionaire space. I immediately took one and I've always thought Alaskaland would have a great deal of potential, more as a historic theme park than anything else, which I think is very important, to preserve our history.

Jim: What year was it that you rented the cabin in Alaskaland?

Jack: In '73 we started a small sandwich shop.

Jim: My wife had a cabin at Alaskaland. I think it was around '73.

Jack: That's when they first started renting them.

Jim: Yeah. She had a nice little shop there.

Jack: Which one was it?

Jim: I don't know. I forgot the name of it. Boy, she's going to murder me when I get home. Actually, well, maybe she'll phone us and let us know the name of it.

Jack: Well, did she enjoy it out there?

Jim: Oh, yes. She had a great time. She enjoyed dealing with the tourists. She is real capable in that area. Now, of course, she owns Alaskan Prospectors, which gives her the same atmosphere that she had out at Alaskaland. But I do recall a lot of people telling me at about that period of time. She was a student at the University, and they said, "She owns a beautiful shop at Alaskaland. It's well decorated and very impressive." At any rate, we went walking through there a couple of years ago, and went to all the shops. Visited every shop. And it's just beautiful out there. You can sit there and reminisce. And, why am I telling you this, Jack? Tell us your story.

Jack: What you're saying is interesting and I quite agree. Moving the old buildings to Alaskaland to preserve them was a stroke of genius. I don't know who's responsible for it, but the creation of a pioneer heritage park is very valuable, not only to ourselves but as a big tourist attraction. And through my experience at Alaskaland, Bill Walley appointed me to the Alaskaland Commission, and while on the commission, I learned that there was a possibility of some historic restoration on the Harding car—President Harding's car—Denali.

Jim: That's stored at Alaskaland right now, is that right?

Jack: That is at Alaskaland right now, yeah. And one thing led to another and we formed an organization called the Fairbanks Historical Preservation Foundation, dedicated to the restoration of artifacts, not only at Alaskaland, but all over the community. We did the restoration on the Harding car, with a $43,000 grant that the city allowed us to use. It was a grant given to the city by the state, for historic restoration of the Kitty Hensley house. However, the Pioneers of Alaska elected to lift the Kitty Hensley house and put a new foundation under it, at their own expense. And they did, thereby freeing the grant money for our foundation to use to restore the Harding car, which we did in 1987-88. It was rededicated to the public on Memorial Day of 1988.

Jim: The organization that you started here now is only a couple of years old then.

Jack: Yeah. All of the people on the board of directors were contacted in, I'd say, March of 1987. We were incorporated as a public non-profit organization in November of '87, and in January of 1988 we received our IRS classification of 501 C3—non-profit. So we are two and a half years old. We'll be two years old next month, legally. However, last March we were two years old organizationally.

Jim: Now, tell us, what is your title?

Jack: I'm the executive director.

Jim: The executive director. And you were the original executive director?

Jack: No. That's just recent. Originally I was the chairman.

Jim: Was there an executive director in the beginning?

Jack: No.

Jim: So, you were the head of it from the beginning?

Jack: From the beginning. I've been the executive director, I think, since last March.

Jim: Recently, in the newspaper, and this might be a real good contest question, we saw a picture of the *Nenana*.

Jack: Beautiful. Absolutely beautiful. A watercolor by Neville Jacobs.

Jim: Neville Jacobs. She's going to be on the show with me, here, in a week or two.

Jack: Great.

Jim: And I think we're going to have a nice chat. There is a lot of interest in the restoration of the *Nenana*. If I remember correctly, two months ago you had a big gathering out there at the *Nenana*.

Jack: That was very interesting, Jim. That was sponsored by the Pioneers of Alaska. And that was on August the 6th. The guests of honor were anyone that the Pioneers could contact who were original crew members. And we had 25 signed up in our guest book, who were original crew members, but there were more there. A couple I guess didn't see the book or didn't want to sign it, or whatever. But the gathering was a tremendous success. Mike Dalton is primarily responsible for putting that together.

Jim: Is that right? Mike's been on the show.

Jack: Well, Mike is very effective.

Jim: Give us a little background on the *Nenana*. Where did it travel?

Jack: Well, the *Nenana*, traveled down the Tanana, Nenana and Yukon Rivers. It was prefabricated in Seattle, in 1931, and brought to Nenana and constructed by Berg Construction Company. That company later became Chris Berg Inc. The construction was begun in June of 1932 and she was launched in May of 1933. And she's been on the river ever since. She was one of the largest riverboats in Alaska. She's 210 feet in length, with a 237-foot overall length. She carries a cargo of 300 tons, and she could push two barges, each carrying 300 tons. So she had a tremendous amount of power, with condensing steam engines that generated 600 horsepower, two of them. Her cargo—she carried everything, lumber, fresh vegetables from Nenana, mining equipment, grain, dried salmon, including the smell, and coal, gold, other precious ores, horses, dog teams, milk, passengers. She had a capacity for 58 passengers, but was authorized for only 16. She was just a vitally important link to the river communities. Her history, although brief, played a very important role in Alaska riverboating.

Jim: How long did she serve again?

Jack: She was retired in 1953.

Jim: When did they put the *Nenana* in Alaskaland.

Jack: Well, it was first retired in '53, leased for a year I think by Yutana Barge Lines—I'm not really positive about this, and I don't think they made a go of that with it, but it was leased by someone, and then in 1958 it was brought up the river, purchased by Greater Fairbanks Opportunities Companies. I believe Dutch Durr and a few of the old timers were involved in that and the Fairbanks Chamber of Commerce. And that didn't work out. She was then passed on to the City, and she stayed at the foot of Lathrop Street from 1958 until 1965, when she was moved into Alaskaland. A big trench was dug and she was floated in, and stayed there, in one place, until 1985, when she was moved to her present location, which is on a concrete grid, which is what she needs for the support underneath her hull.

Jim: By the way, the *Nenana's* had quite a history. Are you familiar with these following words? "*Nenana,* the last lady of the river."

Jack: Oh, yeah.

Jim: How 'bout a premier. Let me tell the people out there, our listening audience, what we're about to do.

Jack: Yes, do that.

Jim: Jim Bell wrote a song about the *Nenana,* "*Nenana,* the Last Lady of the River." It's premiering on Alaska Gold Trails today. I hope you have your tape recorders ready to go, because you're about to hear this new song by Jim Bell. And you've heard it for the first time on public radio, right here on KFAR and Alaska Gold Trails.

Song: "*Nenana*, the Last Lady of the River" by Jim Bell was played for the first time on public radio.

Jim: Well, there you have it. What do you think of that, Jack?

Jack: I think it's beautiful. I don't think Jim has written anything I don't like. He has over 200 songs. Extremely talented. This song says it. It has the emotion. It has the beat. It's wonderful.

Jim: To add a little to that, for those people who've seen Jim perform, and for those who haven't seen Jim Bell perform, we've had him participate in some of our conference gatherings, where he performed, and he always has standing-ovation type performances. Absolutely excellent. And, can you give us a little word on where he performs right now, Jack? Or in the summertime?

Jack: Well, at the Palace Saloon at Alaskaland.

Jim: You bet. So, if you want to take a look at what Jim has to offer, there's where you can visit him and catch one of his performances. And of course Jim Bell was one of the guests here on Alaska Gold Trails a few months back. We had a great time. Jack, you wanted to add a little bit about the historical business here in the Fairbanks area and Alaskaland, and what you might be doing. We have about two and a half minutes here if you would like to sum it up?

Jack: Well, I would like to mention that the Fairbanks Historical Preservation Foundation is committed to the concept of preserving our history and, through that, increasing not only our pride in ourselves but, for instance, the *Nenana*, when restored, could be a source of great community pride, and will provide an incentive for continuing historic restoration and revitalization at Alaskaland and throughout the community. By doing this we're going to add to our own well-being and independence, and we will be able to capitalize on our heritage and greatly stabilize our visitor tourist industry, which is a totally renewable resource that has not been taken advantage of. We believe that one of our greatest assets is our history, and it's lying all about us in ruins. It needs to be restored. It's going to be very very good for the community, philosophically and financially. I would like to name the board of directors, if I could, for Fairbanks Historical Preservation Foundation. The chairman of the board is Ken Murray, Kenneth H. Murray, young Ken. Joe Jackovich is a vice chairman. Jonathan Link is our treasurer, Janet Matheson, historic architect, is our secretary. Captain Jim Binkley was on the board until just very recently, and the press of other business forced him to resign, but his seat has been taken by Captain Skip Binkley, and he is a more-than-welcome addition to the board. He'll be at his first meeting tonight, at our board meeting. Jim Hayes, Tony Nigro, Ray Kohler and Steve Sanders are board members. And I might add that these people are all extremely and very very dedicated to what we're doing.

Jim: Perhaps you would like to comment on some of the concepts that you see in the future for Fairbanks in general. Maybe some preservations of other buildings in the Fairbanks area.

Jack: All of the old building in the Fairbanks area, if structurally sound or if structurally recoverable, savable, they should be preserved. A prime example of this is the Alaska Gold property on Illinois Street. It is a complex. I don't think there are many like it in the entire United States, if not the world. The administration building could be a wonderful mining museum, which we don't have. Mining is basically responsible for the growth of Fairbanks. The machine shop is operable—a belt-driven machine shop. The retort building, the gold room, could be restored. Tourists could see gold being poured into the original molds. That is one prime property, but basically, everything that we have, that is savable, should be saved, to our own benefit.

Jim: Our time has come to an end. Jack, Thank you for all the valuable information. I want to thank you for joining us here on Alaska Gold Trails today.

Jack: Its been fun, Jim. Thank you.

Part III

Where the Trail Winds

Part III

Where The Trail Winds

Following the Alaska Gold Trails radio interviews in 1989. the guests and I, where possible, have stayed in touch. The following summaries provide the reader with a brief history of these pioneers over the most recent years.

Ed Ashby—Ed still lives in Fairbanks where he is involved in selling surplus equipment. During Golden Days he enjoys participating in the "Mug-Up." He is also heavily involved as a volunteer with the Red Cross at Ft. Wainwright. When asked what was in his future he said, "I plan to travel in a small motor home, and I am currently looking for a traveling companion."

Jim Bell—Jim still lives in Fairbanks and although he quit performing in 1995 he continues to direct and write all the music, except the Can-Can, for the Golden Heart Review. In 1977 he was commissioned by Festival Fairbanks to write an original musical about Fairbanks for visitors, from a woman's point of view, *Fortunes: Tales of the Goldrush* was presented at the Alaskaland civic center theater, where it experienced terrific attendance and was well received. In 2000 he wrote another original score, this time sponsored by the Fairbanks Shakespear Theater. It included 20 songs for the show *Pinocchio* which ran successfully for three big weekends. Jim continues his work at the Palace Saloon at Pioneer Park during the summer and has joined with his wife to open a boutique. When asked what is in the future, Jim answered, "I plan to continue composing for the rest of my life."

Bob Cowgill—Bob passed away in Fairbanks, Alaska on December 18, 1994. He was creamated, and his ashes were scattered along the Chena River (Source: Janet Cowgill).

Janet Cowgill—Janet moved to the state of Washington where she bought a house in 2000. Two years later she moved to Virginia where she lives with her son. In July of each year she has been traveling to Alaska. In addition, she has been taking trips to Kentucky, Tennessee and Texas. When asked about her health she said, "I am healthy, although I do have some leg problems."

Bob Hamilton—Friends and family bid farewell to Bob Hamilton on October 12, 1993 in Fairbanks, Alaska (Personal communications Roblyn Dresser).

Jerry Hassel—Jerry still lives in Ester (near Fairbanks) where he runs a mining operation on Ready Bullion Creek. Each year he takes a couple of trips to Seattle to visit family. Several years ago he bought a duplex in Soldotna,

Alaska, where he stays several months each winter. When asked what his plans for the future were, Jerry responded, "I want to mine as long as possible, but when I retire I want to move to Soldotna."

Phil Holdsworth—Friends and family bid farewell to Phil Holdsworth on June 7, 2001 in Anchorage, Alaska (Source: Alaska Miner, July 2001).

Bob Jacobs—Bob and Neville continue to live in Fairbanks. He retired from Mark Air in 1985. Since that time he has traveled each winter to such places as New Zealand, Australia and Haiti. He is currently active in the Quiet Birdmen, which consists of retired pilots with 500 hours or more. When asked what was in his future, he responded, "I hope to begin traveling around Alaska with a trailer, stopping for extended periods to fully enjoy sites of interest."

Neville Jacobs—Neville continues her passion for painting Alaska landscapes, wildlife and Fairbanks history. Two of her paintings were selected for the telephone directory while others are exhibited in local art shows and carried by local art galleries. She has published articles in *Alaska Women Speak* and *Common Ground*. She is currently regional representative of the U. S. Tibet Committee and works for human rights in Chinese-occupied Tibet. Neville has traveled extensively visiting such countries as Manila and the Philippines, in addition to travel to the Florida Keys and other parts of the United States. When asked what the future holds, she replied, "I intend to continue to write, paint and do public service for the rest of my life in Alaska.

Ray Lester—Ray still lives in Fairbanks where he works for College Utilities for six months each year. He enjoys golf in the summer and bowling in two leagues during the winter. Ray continues to be interested in the gold and silver markets. When asked what was in store for his future he replied, "My family has placer claims with known reserves, and I look forward to returning to placer mining if gold prices continue rising toward a favorable level."

Leah Madonna—Leah still lives in Fairbanks where she continues to run her prospecting and mining equipment store (Alaskan Prospectors). In the summer she is also active in gardening, and during the winter she enjoys writing short stories. During the winter months she also enjoys traveling to the Tucson Gem and Mineral Show, and Quartzite, where she purchases minerals for the store and to fill customer requests. When asked what her plans are for the near future she replied, "I plan to continue running the store, on a limited basis, and will be traveling to the Brooks Range this summer where I will spend some time at Del and Gail Ackels' mining camp and do some metal detecting and prospecting."

John Miscovich—John still continues his work at Flat, Alaska, maintaining both his lode and placer properties and looking for someone who would like to turn them into working mines. Personally, he is writing a book on placer mining at Flat titled, *Curse Of Gold*. He chose that title to contrast gold's value and beauty as a precious metal and the brutal hardships one faces to extract it from the often unyielding clutches of the frozen earth. The book is due out by mid-summer 2005.

Maurice "Ozzie" Oswald—friends and family paid respects to Maurice on January 3, 1995 in Anchorage, Alaska (Source: Alaska People 3 March/ April 1995).

Tim Sander—Tim has retired and still lives in Fairbanks, Alaska, where he has a small practice in marriage-and-family counseling. In addition, he continues to offer support in Beginning Experiences, which is an international organization for English speaking countries that deals with grief arising from broken relationships. From time to time he fulfills his duties as a priest by filling in as needed at various Catholic parishes in Interior Alaska. He also continues his passion for flying by sharing his interest with interested students. His second greatest recreational passion, fishing, continues to fill all remaining extra time. Tim says, "I will continue my work and my recreational activities as long as I live in Alaska."

Mary Shields—Mary continues to enjoy her life as an Alaskan, living in a cabin/home at Goldstream. Each week during the winter months she mushes her dogs to her remote cabin 27 miles south of Murphy Dome (located approximately 15 miles west of Fairbanks). Since our interview on Alaska Gold Trails, Mary has begun a tour business called Alaskan Tails of the Trails, where people experience a true Alaskan lifestyle centered on dog mushing. When asked her feelings about Alaska, she replied, "I feel very fortunate to live in Alaska at this time in history, and I hope that future generations have the opportunity to enjoy these similar experiences."

Tom Snapp—Family and friends said goodby to Tom Snapp on September 8, 1995 in Fairbanks, Alaska (Source: Sister, Colleen Redman).

Sandra Stillion—Sandy has continued an active lifestyle. In 1990 she became commissioner for the Alaska Independence Party. New adventures and dreams came true in 1995 when she retired and joined her husband, Sam, in their dream of sailing. They sailed the Inside Passage and up and down the coast of British Columbia for the following seven years. In 2002 they decided to settle in Blaine, Washington, where they now live. Sandy stays active; she has served as a commissioner for the Fidalgo Pool and Fitness Center and has taken up gardening as a serious hobby. When asked what is in her future, Sandy replies, "I love gardening. The only thing I like better is spoiling my grandchildren."

Oden Stranberg—Oden 58, passed away on March 3, 2000 at Fairbanks Memorial Hospital (Fairbanks Daily News-Miner).

Mary Lou Teel—Mary Lou still lives in Fairbanks. In the wintertime she does a great deal of traveling in the lower states. She is active in the Pioneers of Alaska and continues to enjoy mining and staying up-to-date with the Alaska mining industry.

Helen Warner—Helen still lives in North Pole, Alaska. Her major interest is placer mining on Porcupine Creek, 125 miles North of Fairbanks near the Steese Highway. In the winter she teaches math at the University of Alaska. When asked what her plans were for the future, Helen said, "I have several research books which are currently in progress and hope to publish in the near future. I have been seizing the day for my entire life and will continue to capture the beauty of every moment for the rest of my years."

Arnold "Swede" Wasvick—Swede passed away on November 20, 1992 at Petersburg, Alaska and is buried in the Petersburg memorial Cemetary (Source: Daughter, Jeannie Norheim).

Nedra Waterman—Nedra passed away on May 17, 1997 in Haines, Alaska (Source: Eagle Eye).

Wes Waterman—Wes passed away on January 2, 1993 in Haines, Alaska (Source: Chilkat Valley News).

Jack Williams—Jack continued work with the Fairbanks Historical Preservation Foundation until 1997. In 1997 he began preparing Captain Charlie Adams' (the riverboat captain that brought E.T. Barnette from St. Michaels to the Chena River where Barnett started the town of Fairbanks) logs for publication into a book—*Cheechako Ghosts of the Klondike*. The book was published in 2002. He and his wife, Nancy, continue to operate Souvlaki, the restaurant business they opened in 1972 at Pioneer Park in Fairbanks. When asked what his future plans were, Jack responded, "I plan to continue selective historic preservation projects along with the business and some travel. Alaska is where my heart is."

Part IV

Appendices

Appendix I: Alaska Facts

Appendix II: Alaska Gold Discoveries

Appendix III: Alaska Pioneers Featured in Volumes I, II and IV

Appendix I
Alaska Facts

Alaska Highway: Begins at Dawson Creek, British Columbia (mile 0) and runs 1,520 miles to Fairbanks, Alaska. Prior to its construction in 1942, travel to Alaska was primarily by water.

Arctic Circle: Approximately 66°30' north from the equator. Also is the latitude at which the sun does not set during the summer solstice (June 20 or 21) or rise during the winter solstice (December 21 or 22).

Aurora Borealis: Commonly known as Northern Lights are light displays in the northern hemisphere that occur in response to charged particles entering the Earth's atmosphere. The result of these charged particles striking gas particles is the creation of light displays which are often observed as variably colored movement of serpent type arcs and draperies in the Alaskan skies.

Alaska Bush: areas of wilderness outside the major population areas; includes numerous small towns and villages.

Cabin Fever: A state of discontent produced when a person is snowbound in a small cabin or room.

Cheechako: A newcomer or greenhorn that has recently just arrived in Alaska.

State Capital: Juneau.

Population (1998): 607,800

Size: The largest state; approximately one fifth the size of the conterminous 48 states, with an area of 570,374 square miles (365,000,000 acres).

Coastline: 6,640 miles.

State Bird: Willow Ptarmigan.

State Fish: King Salmon.

State Flower: Forget-Me-Not.

State Fossil: Woolly Mammoth.

State Gem: Jade.

State Insect: Four-Spot Skimmer Dragonfly.

State Marine Mammal: Bowhead Whale.

State Mineral: Gold.

State Motto: North to the Future.

State Sport: Dog Mushing.

State Tree: Sitka Spruce.

Appendix II
Alaska Gold Discoveries

1862-Placer gold discovered on the Stikine River.

1870-Placer gold found at Sumdum Bay, Southeastern Alaska.

1871-Placer gold found near Wrangell, Southeastern Alaska

1872-Gold in quartz found near Sitka (Stewart Mine).

1875-Placer gold found on Shuck River, Windham Bay, Southeastern Alaska.

1880-Joseph Juneau and Richard T. Harris, discover placer and lode gold at Juneau.

1884-Lode gold found at Unga Island in Southwestern Alaska.

1886-Lode gold discovered at Berners Bay, Southeastern Alaska.

1886-Howard Franklin discovers placer gold on Fortymile River and on Franklin Creek.

1887-Placer gold found on beaches of Yakutat and Lituya Bays.

1888-Placer gold found on Resurrection Creek, Kenai Peninsula.

1893-Pitka and Sorresco discover placer gold on Birch Creek (Circle District).

1896-Placer gold found in the Klondike District, Yukon Territory, independently by Robert Henderson and George W. Carmack.

1897-Placer gold found on Ophir Creek, Seward Peninsula.

1898-Klondike Stampede.

1898-Placer gold found in Porcupine District near Haines.

1898-Placer gold found at Nome by Jafet Lindenberg, Jon Bryantson and Eric O. Lindblom.

1899-Placer gold discovered on Upper Koyukuk River.

1899-Nome beach gold discovered.

1902-Placer gold found in the Tanana District (Fairbanks) by Felix Pedro.

1903-Placer gold found in the Bonnifield District.

1903-Placer gold found at Denali (Valdez Creek) on upper Susitna River.

1905-Placer gold found in the Kantishna District.

1906-Placer gold found in Tenderfoot District.

1906-Placer and quartz gold found in Chandalar District by Frank Yasuda and Thomas G. Carter, partners.

1906-Gold in quartz found in Willow District.

1906-Placer gold found on Games Creek, Innoko District.

1907-Placer gold found in Talkeetna (Yentna) District.

1907-Placer gold found in Ruby District.

1907-Gold discovered on Nolan Creek, Upper Koyukuk District.

1909-Placer gold discovered in Iditarod District by John Benton and W.A. Dikeman.

1909-Placer gold discovered on Klery Creek, Kiana, Kobuk District.

1910-Placer gold discovered near Hughes, middle Koyukuk.

1900-1914-Lower Kuskokwim, Arolik River and Wattamus Creek stampeds.

1910-Gold bearing quartz found at Valdez.

1911-Placer gold found on Hammond River, Upper Koyukuk. First copper shipped from Kennicott.

1912-Placer gold discovered at Chisana (Shushana).

1913-Placer gold discovered at Nelchina.

1913-Placer gold discovered at Marshall, lower Yukon.

1914-Placer gold found at Tolavana District (Livengood).

1924-Large scale dredging program at Fairbanks planned.

1926-Placer platinum discovered at Goodnews Bay: small scale mining until 1934 when mining with mechanical equipment began.

1942-Gold mining prohibited by law because of war.

1945-Gold mining again allowed by law.

1970-I.L. Tailleur recognizes potential Red Dog deposit.

1972-Record low gold production of only 8,639 ounces statewide.

1973-O'Dea vein at Grant Mine property discovered by Roger Burggraf and Gilbert Dobbs.

1974-Private ownership of gold permitted.

1974-1983-Rise in gold prices to $850 per ounce stimulates gold rush to Alaska.

1977-Greens Creek silver, lead-zinc prospect near Juneau discovered.

1981-Gold production jumps to 134,200 ounces nearly doubling previous year's total.

1983-Joe Taylor Jr. discovers hardrock gold in the Cleary Summit area near Fairbanks which leads to development of the Fort Knox project.

1985-Underground hardrock ore production begun at the Grant Mine near Fairbanks in October.

1987-"Bima" dredge begins offshore placer mining near Nome June 16.

1987-Surface hardrock ore production begun at the Grant Mine near Fairbanks in October.

1987-Citigold Alaska heap leaches first gold from Ryan lode near Fairbanks.

1989-Greens Creek hard rock silver, lead-zinc mine near Juneau goes into operation.

1990-Red Dog lead-zinc mine near Kotzebue opens.

1991-Cambior Alaska reopens Valdez Creek placer gold mine near Cantwell.

1993-Greens Creek Mine near Juneau closes in April because of low metal prices.

1995-Valdez Creek placer mine near Cantwell closes.

1995-Sumitomo announces gold discovery at Pogo prospect near Delta Junction.

1995-Nixon Fork hard rock gold-copper mine near McGrath goes into production in October.

1996-Greens Creek Mine near Juneau reopens.

1996-Fort Knox hard rock gold mine near Fairbanks goes into production in November.

Life in Alaska's Frontier as Told by the Pioneers who Blazed the Trails

Pioneers Featured in Volume I

Jim Binkley	Don Nelson
Mary Binkley	Jeannette Therriault
Doug Colp	Hector Therriault
Robert Charlie	Rudy Vetter
Tony Gularte	Doris Vogler
Cliff Haydon	Joe Vogler
Orea Haydon	Ernie Wolff
Juanita Helms	William Wood
Duke Kilbury	Shorty Zucchini
Don May	Paul McCarthy

Pioneers Featured in Volume II

Del Ackels	Harold Gillam
Gail Ackles	Mary Hansen
Steve Agbaba	Roy Larson
Paul Barelka	Enid Magill
Bill Boucher	Fred Magill
Frieda Chamberlain	Irene Mead
Emery Chapple	Cy Randell
Don Cook	Hazel Randell
Bettye Fahrenkamp	Stu Rothman
Mack Fenton	Leon Tromley

Pioneers Featured in Volume IV

Felix Pedro	Earl Pilgrim
Johne Binkley	Jim Lounsbury
Terrence Cole	Leah Madonna
Shann Jones	
Massimo Turchi	

Available through A.P Publishing
504 College Rd.
Fairbanks, Alaska 99701
$14.95 each
www.alaskagoldinformationcenter.com

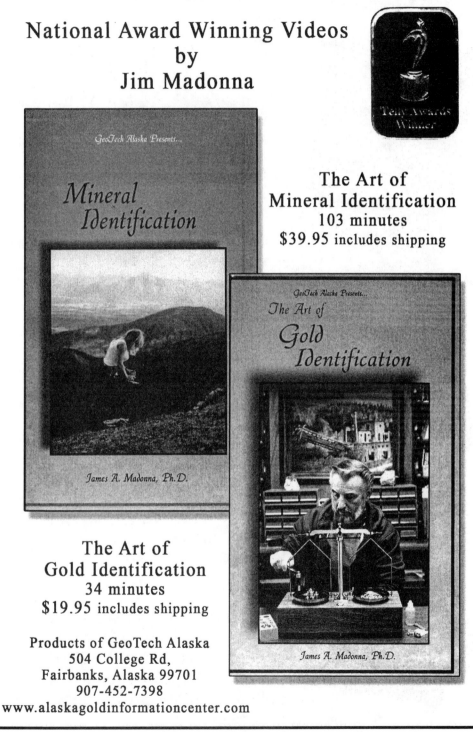